STATES' RIGHTS UNDER FEDERAL CONSTITUTIONS

STATES' RIGHTS UNDER FEDERAL CONSTITUTIONS

CHESTER JAMES ANTIEAU
Emeritus Professor of Constitutional Law
Georgetown University

1984
Oceana Publications, Inc.
London • Rome • New York

Library of Congress Cataloging in Publication Data

Antieau, Chester James.
    States' rights under federal constitutions.

    Includes index.
    1. Federal government—United States.   2. United
States—Constitutional law.   3. State rights.   I. Title.
K F4600.A95   1984   342.73'04   83-13276
ISBN 0-379-20845-8   347.3024

Manufactured in the United States of America

TO
Professor Edward McWhinney
Simon Fraser University, Canada, and
Professor Geoffrey Sawer
The Australian National University
to whom all students of federalism are greatly indebted

SUMMARY TABLE OF CONTENTS

DETAILED
TABLE OF CONTENTS

Chapter Two
STATE POWER TO REGULATE

Chapter Three
STATE REGULATORY POWER OVER TRADE
AND COMMERCE

Chapter Four
STATE POWER TO TAX INTERSTATE AND FOREIGN COMMERCE

Chapter Five
STATE POWER TO TAX

Chapter Six
STATE PROPRIETARY POWERS

Chapter Seven
STATES' RIGHTS AGAINST THE FEDERATION

INTRODUCTION

Prior to nationhood there were many independent governmental entities in what are now the federal societies. The constituent republics of Yugoslavia, such as Serbia, had virtually all the powers of independent sovereigns. This is equally true of the antecedent States that were to become the United States, the cantons of Switzerland, a number of the Laender of the German Federal Republic, and the States of Malaysia. The colonies in what were to become States of modern Australia, as well as the colonies which were to become Provinces of the Dominion of Canada, possessed extensive powers of self-government under the British Empire.

Although there has been a noticeable shift in political power to the center in the past century, the states in federal societies remain the basic unit of government in which the will of the people can be most effectively expressed on a host of matters important in their lives. Here often the initiative allows the electorate to participate directly in the legislative process, and these states should be seen as splendid laboratories for social experimentation in which new laws and new legal institutions can be tested without imperilling the entire nation.

States within federal societies have customarily looked to the other components of the same society for guidance in enacting constitutions and statutes, and in adjudicating controversies. With a growing realization in this generation of the rich dividends that can be easily earned from an examination of the institutions, constitutions, statutes and judicial rulings in comparable law cultures, courts and legislatures in all the federal nations are looking regularly at the materials of the other federal societies. There is here presented for the first time the constitutional provisions and the judicial rulings governing the exercise of governmental powers by the states in the federal societies. Hopefully it will aid the courts and legislatures in all federal societies, in their desire to profit from the experience of the others.

CHAPTER ONE

Chapter One

CONSTITUTIONAL SOURCES OF STATE POWERS AND LIMITATIONS THEREON

§ 1.00 Federal societies with the residuum of power in the states

In some of the federal societies, such as Australia, the United States and Switzerland, the original states at federation had virtually full powers to govern and the federal constitutions have continued them as at least quasi-sovereigns, with all powers of government not denied them by the constitutions.

In these and some other federal societies, the constitutions contain a clause clearly indicating that powers not denied to the states nor assigned exclusively to the federation will all remain within state competence. To illustrate, the Australian Constitution provides: "Every power of the Parliament of a Colony which has become or becomes a State, shall, unless it is by this Constitution exclusively vested in the Parliament of the Commonwealth or withdrawn from the Parliament of the State, continue as at the establishment of the Commonwealth, or as at the admission or establishment of the State, as the case may be."[1] Chief Justice Griffith of Australia has said: "The powers of the Legislature of Queensland extend to making laws for the peace, order and good government of that State in all cases whatsoever."[2]

In the United States Constitution, the Tenth Amendment provides: "The powers not delegated to the United States by the Constitution, nor prohibited by it to the States are reserved to the States respectively, or to the people." Residual state powers, said the great Chief Justice John Marshall, include "an immense mass of legislation which embraces everything within the territory of a State not surrendered to the general government; all of which can be most advantageously exercised by the states themselves."[3]

Residual powers of the Swiss cantons are confirmed in the Constitution, which provides: "The Cantons are sovereign in so far as their sovereignty is not limited by the Federal Constitution, and, as such, they exercise all rights which are not transferred to the Federal power."[4]

In the German Federal Republic, the Constitutional Court has described the Laender as "states with their own sovereign power which, even if limited as to subject matter, is not derived from the Federation, but recognized by it."[5] The Grundgesetz or Basic Law acknowledges that the residuum of power is in the Laender. It provides: "The exercise of governmental powers and the discharge of governmental functions shall be incumbent on the Laender insofar as this Basic Law does not otherwise prescribe or permit,"[6] and adds: "The Laender shall have the right to legislate insofar as this Basic Law does not confer legislative power on the Federation."[7] However, the Federal Parliament has the bulk of legislative powers, either exclusively or concurrently with the Laender, with the latters' exclusive power limited largely to church-state relations, education below the university level, the police, and local government.[8] The Laender take on additional importance in the breadth of powers they exercise in the administration of federal policies.[9]

In a number of additional federal societies, the constitutions indicate that residual powers are in the component entities, and not in the central government. For example, the Constitution of Argentina provides: "The Provinces retain all powers not delegated by the Constitution to the Federal Government and those expressly reserved by special covenants at the time of their incorporation."[10] Comparably, the Constitution of Brazil provides that: "All powers that this Constitution does not explicitly or implictly prohibit the States from exercising are conferred upon the States."[11] In Venezuela, the Constitution confers upon the states power over "anything which, in conformity with this Constitution, does not pertain to national or municipal jurisdiction."[12] The Constitution of Malaysia provides that: "The Legislature of a State shall have power to make laws with respect to any matter not enumerated in any of the Lists set out in the Ninth Schedule, not being a matter in respect of which Parliament has power to make laws."[13] The residuum in Malaysia, however, is not very large, inasmuch as the Federal List and the Concurrent List give to the federation virtually all important powers of government, including powers over the civil and criminal law, public health, education, social welfare, etc. The Mexican Constitution provides: "The powers not expressly granted by this constitution to federal officials are understood to be reserved to the States."[14] By the Constitution of Pakistan, the residuum of power is in the Provinces.[15]

When the Republic of the Cameroon was a federal society, residual powers were reserved to the two states.[16] It has since become a unitary society.

One should not magnify the importance of states being the posses- sors of the residuum of powers under the constitution. Frequently, the central government is the recipient of extensive powers under an exclusive federal list, and can also exercise an abundance of power under a concurrent list, leaving a very small residuum to the states.[17] Justice Brenda, President of the German Constitutional Court, in 1981 noted "a tendency to 'dry up' the Laender in favour of the federal state."[18] It is "the preponderant presence of the federal *executive* branch" that characterizes the federal system in Mexico.[19]

§ 1.01 Federal societies with the residuum of power in the federation

In a number of federal societies, the residuum of power is in the central government, not in the component entities. For example, the residuum of power in India is with the central government, not the states.[1]

In Canada, too, under the British North America Act, the residuum of power is with the Dominion Government.[2]

In Austria, the power is concentrated in the federal government which in effect has the residuum of power in the Constitutional clause giving it power over "the maintenance of the public peace, order and safety."[3] Power is also concentrated in the center in Nigeria where the federal government is granted extensive powers in an exclusive list and can utilize, as well, a concurrent list.[4] Similarly, in Malaysia the important powers of government are assigned to the federation in an impressive exclusive list.[5] Although the Russian constitution in Article 70 says it is a federal state, a capable New Zealand scholar who has studied the system extensively wrote that "the constitutional forms of federalism are a facade," that "union legislative power is unbounded," and added that "the republics have no policy-making authority, either foreign or domestic."[6]

In those federal societies in which the residuum of power is by the constitution in the federation, the component entities must rely upon specific grants of power in the constitution, or in delegations from the central government. In Canada, Section 92 of the British North America Act indicates the Provincial powers, the most important of which are: Section 92(10) giving the Provinces power over "local works and under-takings," Section 92(13) conferring power on the Provinces over "Property and Civil Rights in the Province," and Section 92(16) providing for Provincial legislative competence over "generally all matters of a merely local or private nature in the Province."

The Constitution of India contains a state list in Article 246(3) conferring particular powers upon the state governments, including power to protect "public order,"[7] power to legislate in regard to "public health and sanitation,"[8] and power over "trade and commerce within the State."[9] A leading Indian scholar observes that the States can legislate on "very few matters of general import."[10]

The Constitution of Nigeria provides that: "The House of Assembly of a State shall have power to make laws for the peace, order and good government of the State or any part thereof."[11]

In some of the federal societies where the residuum of power is in the center, such as India, Nigeria and Malaysia, the constitutions contain concurrent lists of powers available to the states as well as the federation, but in virtually all federations, there is no state power in these areas to act inconsistently to federal legislation.

Constitutional grants of power to states should not be construed in a narrow and pedantic sense but should be given a large and liberal construction.[12] In federal systems, where power is concentrated in the center, the role of the component entities is apt to be more administrative than policy-making.[13]

§ 1.02 Constitutional limitations on state powers—grants of power to the federation

In all the federal societies, there is in effect a denial of state power by constitutional clauses granting exclusive powers to the federation, the most frequent of which are powers over external affairs, over defence, over the currency, over bankruptcies, over customs, and over the federal capitol territory.

The Indian Constitution contains an extensive Union List of powers exclusively vested in central government.[1] Under the 1979 Constitution of Nigeria, the federal government has an extensive exclusive legislative list.[2] In Austria, too, the federal list is lengthy and contains most of the important powers of government; the task of legislation being generally for the federal government and administration for the Laender.[3] Comparably, in Switzerland the federal government possesses many exclusive powers.[4] In Malyasia the federal list is lengthy and important, embracing many areas, including civil and criminal law, so that when read together with the concurrent list, virtually all significant powers of government can be exercised by the federation. The state list is rather inconsequential.[5] The orthodox theory in Canada is that Section 91 of the British North America Act, enumerating the Dominion powers, makes such powers exclusive—not to be exercised under any circumstances by the Provinces.[6] Clearly the power of the Privy Council and now the Supreme Court of Canada to characterize a provincial statute affecting the use of property in the province as a matter regarding "aliens," an exclusive Dominion power, effectively limits the competence of the Provincial legislatures.[7] In Canada the Dominion Parliament also has exclusive legislative power over the criminal law,[8] and this inevitably limits greatly the power of the provinces to punish what they deem misbehavior.[9] However, the provinces have been sustained in protecting the public health, safety, morality and general welfare by imposing heavy fines upon those who violate provincial legislation and local government by-laws.[10]

The Grundgesetz of the German Federal Republic in Article 73 lists eleven items of exclusive federal power, including foreign affairs, customs, post and monetary affairs; the Constitutional Amendment of 1956 added defence. Comparably, the Constitution of Austria has in Article 10 an extensive list of federal legislative powers, including power to maintain public peace, order and safety (except for the local police). So, also, the 1973 Constitution of Pakistan in Article 142 has an extensive list of exclusive federal powers and a long list of Union powers is contained in Article 8 of the Constitution of Brazil, as amended.

In many federal societies there is a concurrent list of legislative powers available to both the central government and the component entities. Seemingly a source of state power, this in practice becomes a limitation upon such power; once the central government exercises a power on the concurrent list, the states are unable to legislate in that area, at least in ways inconsistent with the federation's exercise of power.

The Grundgesetz of the German Federal Republic contains a list of concurrent powers, including laws "relating to economic matters," the civil and criminal law, organization of the courts, public welfare, the care of refugees, immigration, labor law, traffic regulation and all forms of transport.[11] These concurrent powers "have provided the basis for most of the extensive legislative activity of the Bund."[12] Even without inconsistency, the Laender are unable to legislate in these areas once the central government has legislated on these matters, since the Basic Law provides: "In matters within concurrent legislative powers the Laender shall have power to legislate as long as the Federation does not exercise its right to legislate."[13]

The 1979 Constitution of Nigeria also includes a concurrent list of powers available to both the central government and the states, adding: "If any law enacted by the House of Assembly of a State is inconsistent with any law made by National Assembly, the law made by the National Assembly shall prevail, and that other law shall to the extent of the inconsistency be void."[14] Similarly, the 1973 Constitution of Pakistan has an extensive concurrent list available to the federal government,[15] with the provision that provincial legislation contra is void to the extent of the inconsistency.[16] The 1969 Constitution of Brazil indicates the specific matters on which the states can supplement Union legislation.[17]

§ 1.03 Constitutional limitations on state powers—territorial limitations on state power

In all federal societies, the judiciary or any other ultimate allocator of legislative power generally confines the legislative powers of the states to their own territorial boundaries, customarily finding something in the Constitution of the federation to authorize such a ruling.

In the United States, the Supreme Court has used the due process clause of the Fourteenth Amendment to the Constitution to confine state legislation in its impact to its own territory under most circumstances. In 1897 the Court ruled that the Louisiana Legislature could not prevent the making of a contract in New York by a resident of Louisiana in regard to cotton located in Louisiana.[1] In 1975 the Court held that Virginia could not prevent abortion ads in Virginia papers when the abortion was to be performed in New York where it was legal. Said the Court:

> A State does not acquire power or supervision over the internal affairs of another State merely because the welfare and health of its own citizen may be affected when they travel to that State. . . . It may not, under the guise of exercising internal police powers, ban a citizen of another State from disseminating information about an activity that is legal in the State.[2]

The fact remains, however, that the United States Supreme Court is willing to allow the states to legislate with considerable extraterritorial effects when it considers the person affected has substantial contacts with the state and the imposed controls are reasonably necessary to protect legitimate interests of the local community. In 1950, for instance, the Court upheld the Virginia Corporation Commission, under a grant of power from the Legislature, in issuing a cease and desist order against a Nebraska company to have it stop soliciting Virginians by mail to purchase health insurance. It was enough, said the Court, that there were "sufficient minimum contacts" by the defendant with Virginia to enable the Court to conclude the control was "consistent with fair play and substantial justice," and thus in accord with substantive due process.[3] Nine years earlier the Supreme Court held that Florida could regulate the taking of sponges within nine nautical miles of the shore and within its territorial waters. "In the absence of conflicting federal legislation," said the Court, such control "is within the police power of the State." The Court further ruled that a state "may exercise its authority over its citizens on the high seas."[4] So long as a state has "substantial interests" involved and a foreign insurance company has reasonable contacts with that state, it can apply its laws to the company—as when it is insuring risks within the state under contracts made outside the state.[5]

In Australia, the acts of the Parliament of Great Britain that conferred constitutions on the constituent states typically conferred upon the state legislature power to act "for the peace, welfare and good government" of that state.[6] From this language the Privy Council and, later, the High Court of Australia have restricted a number of attempts by Australian States to give extraterritorial effect to their legislation. In 1932 a New South Wales act demanding a death duty from a person domiciled in Victoria holding shares in a Victoria company, on the ground the company was engaged in mining in New South Wales, was voided by the High Court. This, said Justice Rich for the Court, is "a connection which is too remote," and accordingly, "the provision goes beyond the legislative powers of the State."[7]

In 1937 Chief Justice Latham of Australia admitted that "the degree of connection which would bring the subject matter within the territorial competence of the state legislature" is "a difficult question,"[8] but the High Court held New South Wales could tax the income earned by a Victoria corporation carrying on business in New South Wales, and could include in the tax base income earned on a loan made outside that state, when the loan was secured by property in New South Wales. The Chief Justice stated: "The fact that money is secured by property in New South Wales constitutes a sufficient territorial connection with New South Wales to entitle the Parliament of New South Wales to legislate so as to impose a tax upon persons who receive the interest. . . ."[9] Latham added generally: "There is no doubt that the Legislature of New South Wales can impose such conditions as it thinks proper by way of taxation or otherwise upon persons who carry on business in New South Wales and therefore bring themselves within the legislative authority of the State."[10]

Writing in the same case, Justice Dixon readily agreed that in Australia there are "territorial limitations upon the legislative power" of the states.[11] He wrote: "The power to make laws for the peace, order and good government of a State does not enable the State Parliament to impose by reference to some act, matter or thing occurring outside the State a liability upon a person unconnected with the State, whether by domicile, residence or otherwise."[12] Nevertheless, Dixon agreed with the decision in the case and added generally:

> It is within the competence of the State legislature to make any fact, circumstance, occurrence or thing in or connected with the territory the occasion of the imposition upon any person concerned therein of a liability to taxation or any other liability. It is also within the competence of the legislature to base the imposition of liability on no more than the relation of the person to the territory. The relation may consist in presence within the territory, residence, domicile, carrying on business there, or even remoter connections. If a connection exists, it is for the legislature to decide how far it should go in the exercise of its powers.[13]

In 1967, a New South Wales court held that State could tax the transfer of shares in a New South Wales corporation, even though the actual transfer occurred outside the state and neither the transferor nor the transferee were residents of New South Wales.[14]

However, the territorial limitation upon the legislative jurisdiction of Australian States continues when the connection between the state and the subject of the law is "too remote," not "relevant," or the person exposed to regulation or taxation has not been (in the earlier language of Dixon) "concerned in" the matter occurring within the territory of the state. In 1956 Privy Council (in agreement with the New South Wales Court) held that state could not impose a tax on a Victoria resident to reach Victoria property passing to him as a remainderman under a will of a New South Wales domiciliary.[15] Finding an insufficient connection, the High Court in 1969 refused to allow New South Wales to impose liability upon a South Australian director of a South Australian corporation because the company had failed to file returns and pay charges for the use of New South Wales roads by it vehicles.[16] Two years later the High Court voided a substantially similar provision in a South Australia statute. Chief Justice Barwick wrote for the Court: "The stretch of the State's legislative power, founded on that territorial extent, does not reach, in my opinion, beyond those who are in a substantial sense participant in that event. . . ."[17] In 1977 the High Court held a state could not control the salvage of wrecks within three miles of its coast. Chief Justice Barwick for the Court indicated that a state law can operate beyond the boundaries of the state but only if "it can properly be said to be a law for the peace, order and good government of that territory" of the state—the facts did not bring the regulation within that test, according to the Courts majority.[18]

In Canada, the Privy Council, and later the Supreme Court of Canada, have fashioned a constitutional doctrine limiting extraterritoriality of the provincial legislative competence. Section 92 of the British North America Act (the principal grant of power to the provinces) begins "In each province. . . ." and this has been a basis for confining provincial legislative authority to matters within the provinces. In 1913 the Privy Council held that Alberta, which had guaranteed the bonds of a railway, could not expropriate the bond proceeds which were in the custody of a bank whose headquarters were in Quebec, although the bank had a branch in Alberta where the funds seem to have been physically present.[19] This has been the precedent controlling later cases, most of which are seen as provincial attempts to extraterritorially interfere with rights created outside the province.[20] The most important modern case is *Interprovincial Cooperatives v. The Queen*[21] decided in 1975. In a four-to-three decision, the Supreme Court held Manitoba could not create a civil cause of action against Ontario and Saskatchewan firms which were operating under licenses from their own provincial governments, but were polluting waters flowing into Manitoba to the injury of fisheries there. Justice Ritchie with the majority indicated that Manitoba was attempting to interfere with rights created outside that province. Justice Pigeon, also with the majority, stated that a province cannot "destroy the effect of legislation passed in adjacent Provinces," and remarked that "the fact that a party is amenable to the jurisdiction of the courts of a Province does not mean that the Legislature of that Province has unlimited authority over the matter to be adjudicated upon."[22] Chief Justice Laskin, with two other Justices, dissented, urging affirmance of the Manitoba Court ruling to the effect that in cases where property interests within a province are damaged by activities originating outside the province, the perpetrators can constitutionally be made subject to the substantive law of the province where the damage was done.[23] Where a province or state has substantial interests at stake, and it is clear that persons or corporations outside the province knew their acts would have effects within the legislating province, it seems undesirable to use a doctrine of extraterritoriality to avoid application of that province's laws. In 1979, the Canadian Supreme Court ruled that where a manufacturer's contractual promise to re-purchase farm implements was breached in Alberta, that province's statute could be applied, even though the manufacturer was never in Alberta and the parties had agreed that the contract was to be governed by New Brunswick law.[24]

The ban upon extraterritoriality of state legislation is explicitly stated in the Mexican Constitution as follows: "The laws of a State shall have effect only within its own territory and consequently are not binding outside of that State."[25]

In India, too, states have customarily been unable to give their legislation extraterritorial effect.[26]

§ 1.04   Constitutional limitations on state powers—bans on discrimination against citizens of other states

Constitutions of federal societies typically contain clauses forbidding discrimination by a state against citizens of other states in the federation. Illustratively, the Australian Constitution provides: "A subject of the

Queen, resident in any State, shall not be subject in any other State to any disability or discrimination which would not be equally applicable to him if he were a subject of the Queen resident in such other State."[1] The High Court has held the *previous* residence in another state does not occasion the protection of the clause; only contemporary residence is protected.[2] The clause has not been of much use in banning discrimination in Australia. A capable scholar has complained of the "very narrow and literalistic interpretations of its language," and added: "It is difficult to resist the general conclusion that the High Court has practically read Section 117 out of the Constitution."[3]

The United States Constitution provides: "The citizens of each State shall be entitled to all Privileges and Immunities of Citizens in the several States."[4] Historical evidence is overwhelming that the Americans responsible for the language desired to protect a citizen of one state in his fundamental rights (such as freedom of religion, speech and movement) when he travelled in the other states, but for some time the Supreme Court has construed the clause so as to permit some discrimination against citizens of other states. When it voided a state statute providing for fishing fees of $25 for residents, but $2,500 for non-residents, the Court acknowledged that "substantial" reasons at times may justify discrimination, and that "the inquiry in each case must be concerned with whether such reasons do exist and whether the degree of discrimination bears a close relation to them." Concluding that "the reasons advanced in support of the statute do not bear a reasonable relationship to the high degree of discrimination practiced upon citizens of other States," the Court found the statute unconstitutional.[5] Although voiding most discriminations by states against persons simply because they are citizens of another state,[6] the Supreme Court has sustained preferences by states to their own citizens in access to the courts,[7] and in such avocational pursuits as hunting.[8]

The constitutions of many other federal societies prohibit discriminations against citizens of the other component entities of the federation. Thus, the Constitution of Argentina provides: "The citizens of each Province enjoy all the rights, privileges and immunities inherent in the status of citizens in the others."[9] Comparably, the Austrian Constitution states that every federal citizen has in every land the equal rights and duties as the citizen of the land itself.[10] By the Constitution of Brazil, the states are forbidden to create distinctions between Brazilians.[11] The Grundgesetz of the German Federal Republic states that: "Every German shall have in every Land the same political rights and duties."[12] The Constitution of Malaysia bans discrimination against residents of other parts of the federation.[13] In Nigeria there is a right to freedom from discrimination due to one's membership in a particular community, or ethnic group, or because of one's place of origin, sex, religion or political opinion.[14]

The British North America Act applicable to Canada does not contain any specific provision prohibiting a province from discriminating against residents of other provinces.[15]

§ 1.05 Constitutional limitations on state powers—bans on unreasonable discrimination generally

Some of the federal societies, such as Australia, have no general constitutional clause prohibiting discrimination by the states. Prior to the Constitution Act 1981, Canadian provinces were not restrained by a constitutional clause requiring equality or equal protection, and a variety of legislative discriminations was sustained.[1] Canadian Provinces were sustained in denying certain religious groups an opportunity to purchase land within the Province,[2] and in denying nonresidents full opportunity to acquire land within a province.[3] The power of the Supreme Court of Canada to characterize legislation is of critical importance, as the latter case indicates. In severely restricting the opportunity of aliens to own land, the statute obviously affected "aliens," an exclusive Dominion concern, yet the Court sustained the provincial statute which it characterized as involving "property within the province," a provincial competence under the British North America Act. Earlier, the Privy Council had voided a Provincial statute limiting the use of aliens in mining within the province, concluding this did not involve "property within the Province," but rather "aliens."[4] Since 1981 the Constitution of Canada provides that: "Every individual is equal before and under the law and has the right to the equal protection and equal benefit of the law without discrimination. . . ."[5] It is too early to forecast accurately the construction of the clause by the Supreme Court, but it seems likely that reasonable provincial differentiated treatment of individuals and groups will survive.

Since 1868, the states of the United States have been limited by the Equal Protection Clause of the Fourteenth Amendment. The clause does not prevent classification, differentiated treatment of individuals or groups, or reasonable discriminations.[6] What is forbidden is unreasonable, arbitrary or invidious discrimination.[7] In general, classifications deemed prudent by state legislatures are presumed to be reasonable and constitutional.[8] However, where the discrimination is based upon what the Supreme Court calls a suspect classification (race, sex, alienage and ethnic origin), there is in effect a presumption of unconstitutionality.[9] Again, where a person is discriminated against in what the Supreme Court calls a fundamental right for equal protection purposes (such as voting, the right of access to the ballot and freedom of domestic travel), there is in effect a presumption of unconstitutionality.[10] In both the exceptional areas, discriminations by the states will be voided unless they can show that they are imperatively necessary to protect a substantial interest of society that could not adequately be safeguarded in ways with less discrimination.[11]

The Constitution of India provides: "The State shall not deny to any person equality before the law or the equal protection of the laws within the territory of India."[12] Reasonable classifications have been sustained,[13] while unreasonable classifications have been invalidated as unconstitutional.[14]

The Constitution of Argentina provides that: "All its inhabitants are equal before the law."[15] The Supreme Court of Argentina invalidates unreasonable classifications by the provinces,[16] but sustains reasonable classifications.[17]

The Grundgesetz or Basic Law of the German Federal Republic states that: "All persons shall be equal before the law,"[18] and the Austrian Constitution similarly provides that: "All Federal citizens are equal before the law."[19] Somewhat comparably, the Constitution of Malaysia provides that: "All persons are equal before the law and entitled to the equal protection of the laws."[20]

By the Constitution of Venezuela, discrimination on the basis of race, sex, creed or social condition is prohibited.[21]

In all the federal societies with equality and equal protection clauses, it can be anticipated that the component entities will be able to include in their legislation differentiated treatments of individuals and groups, so long as the distinction is imperatively necessary to protect or advance an important interest of the society.

§ 1.06 Constitutional limitations on state powers—the "reasonableness" requirement

In some federal societies, the constitution generally limits state powers to affect the lives and liberties of the people by requiring such governmental action to be reasonable. Thus, in the United States, the Due Process Clause of the Fourteenth Amendment requires state legislation affecting private interests to be reasonable, and to have a reasonable relationship to one of the legitimate governmental ends, such as the public health, safety, etc.[1] United States courts customarily accord to laws enacted by the state legislatures a presumption of reasonableness and constitutionality.[2] Such a presumption does not apply, however, where the legislation impacts upon fundamental rights, such as freedom of communication.[3]

Even in the federal societies without substantive due process clauses, the courts note various constitutional clauses specifically protecting private rights, such as freedom of religion, freedom of movement, the property right, freedom of contract, etc., and sustain state and provincial legislation impacting upon these protected rights only when clearly reasonable.[4] Illustratively, where there is a constitutional clause protecting freedom of religion, it can be expected that only a reasonable law impacting upon this interest will be sustained.[5]

Where in federal societies the states can to some extent interfere with interstate and foreign commerce, courts generally determine the validity of state regulation under reasonableness norms.[6]

Where states are subject to an equality or equal protection clause the reasonableness of the differentiated treatment customarily determines if the state discrimination is to survive.[7] Comparably, where states are subject to a constitutional clause prohibiting discrimination against citizens or residents of the other states of the federation, a reasonableness norm will likely be applied to determine whether preferences favoring local citizen or residents is permissible.[8]

Where state or provincial legislation under the constitution requires a precondition, such as emergency or a crisis, it can be anticipated that courts will inquire whether the contested legislation is reasonably related to the required precondition.[9]

§ 1.07 Constitutional limitations on state powers—bans on retroactive legislation

The constitutions of federal countries at times specifically forbid retroactive legislation.[1]

In the United States, retroactive legislation is specifically barred by the state constitutions in Colorado,[2] Georgia,[3] Missouri,[4] New Hampshire,[5] Ohio,[6] Tennessee,[7] and Texas.[8] However, there is in the Constitution of the United States no specific ban upon retroactive legislation of a civil nature.

In the United States there is a constitutional ban upon *ex post facto* laws,[9] that might have been intended by the framers of the Constitution to ban all retroactive legislation,[10] but since 1798 the clause has been interpreted so as to ban only retroactive criminal laws.[11] A constitutional ban upon a specific form of retroactive legislation exists in the United States in the prohibition upon state laws impairing the obligation of contracts.[12] However, this is not an absolute barrier and courts consider the relevance of protecting other societal interests in passing upon laws changing contractual obligations.[13]

Under the due process of law clauses in the Fifth and Fourteenth Amendments to the United States Constitution, police power regulations are not invalid because they are made applicable to structures completed earlier in accordance with the law. "In no case," says the Supreme Court, "does the owner of property acquire immunity against the exercise of the police power because he constructed it in full compliance with existing laws."[14] Retroactive regulations are judged under the customary due process test of reasonableness.[15] Retroactive zoning was traditionally unconstitutional,[16] but increasingly courts are sustaining legislation which reasonably terminates uses which were permissible under zoning when constructed.[17]

In the Commonwealth countries, there is typically a presumption that legislation was not intended to have retrospective application,[18] but there is no constitutional ban upon retrospective legislation as such.[19] Ordinarily, there is no expressed ban upon *ex post facto* laws,[20] although such prohibitions are present in the Constitutions of India,[21] Nigeria[22] and Pakistan.[23]

§ 1.08 Constitutional limitations on state powers—bans on alliances between states of the federation

Frequently in federal systems the constitutions ban alliances between the component states of the federation, at least without consent of the central government.

The Constitution of Switzerland, in Article Seven, provides: "All separate alliances and all treaties of a political character between Cantons are forbidden," but adds that the cantons can enter into conventions "upon matters of legislation, administration and justice" if approved by the federal government.

The Mexican Constitution contains a clause to the effect that: "The states may not in any case make any alliance, treaty, or coalition with another State. . ."[1]

The United States Constitution provides: "No State shall, without the consent of Congress. . .enter into any Agreement or Compact with another State. . . ."[2] The Supreme Court has said: "The articles inhibiting any treaty, confederation, or alliance between the states without the consent of Congress were intended to prevent any union of two or more states, having a tendency to break up or weaken the league between the whole. . . ."[3] On another occasion the Court said:

> Looking at the clause in which the terms "compact" or "agreement" appear, it is evident that the prohibition is directed to the formation of any combination tending to the increase of political power in the states, which may encroach upon or interfere with the just supremacy of the United States.[4]

The Supreme Court has now made it clear that it is only such an agreement that is forbidden, and that "not all agreements between States are subject to the strictures of the Compact Clause."[5] State courts have upheld many interstate agreements for which the consent of Congress was not sought, and they would almost certainly be affirmed today by the United States Supreme Court.[6]

In the German Federal Republic the Laender have entered into hundreds of treaties (Staatsverträge) and administrative agreements with other Laender.[7]

The Constitution of Brazil of 1891, in Article 65, § 1 gave the states the right to conclude agreements and conventions of a nonpolitical character with each other, subject to federal approval.

§ 1.09 Constitutional limitations on state powers—bans on treaties with foreign nations and states

A number of federal constitutions provide that the component entities are forbidden to enter into treaties with foreign countries.

The Constitution of Argentina provides that: "The Provinces. . .may not enter into partial treaties of a political character. . . ."[1] However it also indicates that: "The Provinces may, with the knowledge of the Federal Congress, enter into partial treaties for the purposes of administration of justice, of economic interests, and works of common utility."[2]

The Mexican Constitution provides that: "The states may not in any case make any alliance, treaty or coalition with another State, or with foreign powers."[3]

Although Section 10 of Article One of the United States Constitution provides that: "No State shall enter into any treaty. . .," it later permits states to make an "agreement or compact with another State, or with a foreign Power" with the consent of the federal Congress. There is some belief that not all "agreements or compacts" require Congressional approval, but only those that might diminish the political rights and powers of the federal government. A number of agreements exist between states and neighboring Canadian Provinces. In affirming such an agreement, the North Dakota Supreme Court stated that "not all intercourse is forbidden, or contracts prohibited, but only those agreements or compacts which affect the supremacy of the United States, or its political rights, or which tend in any measure to increase the power of the states as against themselves."[4]

In a number of other countries, including India[5] and Nigeria,[6] there is no explicit ban upon the states making treaties, but it is clearly implicit in constitutional clauses giving the central governments exclusive powers over external affairs or foreign relations. Although there is no exclusive grant of power over external affairs to the Commonwealth in the Australian Constitution, it is as clearly established that the states do not have a treaty-making power.[7]

A later section, concerned generally with state competence in foreign affairs, treats the constitutions of some countries which expressly authorize treaty-making by the component entities, as well as instances where the power is claimed without express constitutional authorization.

§ 1.10 Constitutional limitations on state powers—bans on establishment of religion

The Constitution of Nigeria indicates that the government of a state "shall not adopt any religion as a State Religion."[1]

In the United States the Supreme Court has ruled that the states under the Fourteenth Amendment are bound by the ban upon establishment of religion contained in the First Amendment.[2] However, the Court has held that the ban does not prevent states granting tax exemptions to churches and church-related institutions.[3] The Supreme Court has also ruled that states can if they desire, provide transportation to children attending church-related schools.[4] State authorities can also authorize the release of students at public schools for limited periods for religious instruction away from the public school.[5] State construction grants to church-related colleges and universities have been sustained so long as the structures are to be used solely for secular purposes.[6] The Supreme Court has also sustained a state in giving annual grants to church-related colleges, applying the customary test that determines validity of state aid under the Establishment Clause: (a) it must be for a secular purpose; (b) it must have a primary effect that neither advances nor inhibits religion; and (c) there must be an absence of excessive entanglement between church and state.[7] States can also lend free of charge textbooks on secular subjects to students attending church-related schools.[8]

Under the Establishment Ban, the Supreme Court has held constitutional state re-imbursement to church-related schools for expenses in connection with testing programs required by state law.[9] However, the Court holds unconstitutional state payments to teachers of secular subjects in church-related schools.[10] Permitting religious instruction or prayers in public schools is violative of the Establishment Ban, even when children who do not desire to participate are excused from the exercise.[11] The Supreme Court has also held unconstitutional a statute forbidding public schools to teach the Darwinian theory of evolution, which theory was opposed by some religious groups.[12]

Although the Grundgesetz of the German Federal Republic provides that: "Religious instruction shall form part of the ordinary curriculum in state and municipal school . . . ,"[13] it adds: "The person entitled to bring up a child shall have the right to decide whether it shall receive religious instruction."[14]

The Constitution of Brazil imposes a ban upon states "establishing religious sects or churches."[15] While the Constitution of Australia bars the Commonwealth from establishing a religion,[16] that clause is not binding upon the states.

§ 1.11 Federal paramountcy

In all the federal societies, state, provincial and cantonal laws become void when they clash or conflict with federal legislation enacted by the central government under its constitutional powers.[1]

The Constitution of Switzerland, among its transitional provisions at adoption, provided that: "Cantonal constitutions and laws, which are in contradiction with the new Federal Constitution cease to have effect."[2] Federal paramountcy has become permanent constitutional doctrine in Switzerland, commonly known as "Federal law breaks cantonal law."

The United States Constitution provides that: "This Constitution, and the Laws of the United States which shall be made in Pursuance thereof; and all Treaties made, or which shall be made, under the Authority of the United States, shall be the supreme Law of the Land; and the Judges in every State shall be bound thereby, any Thing in the Constitution or Laws of any State to the Contrary notwithstanding."[3] "It is settled," said the Supreme Court in 1913, "that the state may not . . . under the guise of exercising its police power or otherwise, enact legislation in conflict with the statutes of Congress passed for the regulation of the subject, and, if it does, to the extent that the state law interferes with or frustrates the operations of the acts of Congress, its provisions must yield to the superior Federal power given to Congress by the Constitution."[4]

The Constitution of Australia states: "When a law of a State is inconsistent with a law of the Commonwealth, the latter shall prevail, and the former shall, to the extent of the inconsistency, be invalid."[5] Comparable are the constitutional clauses of Malaysia,[6] Nigeria,[7] Pakistan,[8] and Argentina.[9] In India, state laws become unconstitutional when the federal government has either occupied the field within its constitutional competence or enacted valid inconsistent legislation.[10]

Even without inconsistency the Laender of the German Federal Republic are seemingly unable to legislate in areas where the central government has legislated, under a provision of the Grundgesetz or Basic Law stating: "In matters within concurrent legislative powers the Laender shall have power to legislate as long as the Federation does not exercise its right to legislate."[11]

In Canada, there is no supremacy clause in the British North America Act, but the courts have read into the constitution a supremacy doctrine whereby legislation of the Dominion Parliament authorized by section 91 of the Act prevails over provincial legislation authorized by section 92 or any other section, in event of conflict.[12] Courts in Canada find no inconsistency of provincial with Dominion legislation when the former either duplicates or complements the latter.[13] Courts in Canada refuse to invalidate provincial laws unless there is "operating incompatability" between federal and provincial laws, so that honoring the latter would always breach the former.[14]

Clash or conflict appears most obviously when there is an express contradiction between the texts of federal and state statutes.[15]

By the better view, there is no clash or conflict when the state legislation duplicates[16] or complements[17] federal controls.

Where a federal government has occupied or preempted a field by the exercise of its constitutional powers, the states can no longer legislate in such field, even though there is no clash or conflict.[18]

FOOTNOTES

§ 1.00

1 Constitution of Australia, § 107.
2 Duncan v. Queensland (1916) 22 C.L.R. 556, 576.
3 Gibbons v. Ogden (1824) 9 Wheat. 1, 6 L Ed 23, 72.
4 Constitution of Switzerland, Article 3. The Swiss Cantons have importance in administration of federal policies, Hughes, *The Federal Constitution of Switzerland* (Oxford U. Press 1954).
5 The Southwest Case (1951) 1 BVerGE 14.
6 Grundgesetz of German Federal Republic, Article 30.
7 Grundgesetz of German Federal Republic, Article 80(1).
8 Johnson, *Federalism and Decentralisation in the Federal Republic of Germany* (H.M.S.O.,London 1973) 7, 11; Edinger writes that the power of the Laender "has suffered from a continuous process of erosion with the trend toward a nationalization of political life." Political Change in Germany: The Federal Republic After the 1969 Election, 2 Comparative Politics 571 (1970). Cole notes the increased presence of the central government in areas traditionally deemed for the Laender, such as education, health, police and internal security, and protection of the environment, but recognizes as important the place of the Laender in German federalism. Cole, "West German Federalism Revisited," 23 *Amer. J. Comp. L.* 325, 329 (1975). Brenda (Pres. of Constl. Ct.), "Constitutional Jurisdiction in West Germany," 19 *Col. J. Transn. L.* (1981) 1, 5. Zurcher, *Constitutions and Constitutional Trends since World War II* (2d ed. 1955, New York) 139.
9 Blair, *Federalism and Judicial Review in West Germany* (Oxford U. Press 1981) 5, 72; Johnson, *Federalism and Decentralisation in the Federal Republic of Germany* (H.M.S.O., London 1973) 16. Sawer, "Federalism in West Germany," 1961 *Public Law* 26, 28.
10 Argentina Constitution of 1853, as amended, Article 104.
11 Constitution of Brazil 1969, as amended, Article 13, par. 1.
12 Constitution of Venezuela, Art. 17(7).
13 Constitution of Malaysia, Art. 77.
14 Constitution of Mexico, Title VII, Art. 124.
15 Constitution of Pakistan,1973, Article 142.
16 Enonchong, *Cameroon Constitutional Law* (Yaounde 1967) 23.
17 Sawer, *Modern Federalism* (London 1969) 35. "The vast bulk of the legislative powers in the Federal Republic belong to the 'concurrent' category . . . . " Blair, *Federalism and Judicial Review in West Germany* (Oxford U. Press 1981) 72. Lewis, *The Governments of Argentina, Brazil and Mexico* (New York 1975) 91, 97, 105.
18 Brenda, "Constitutional Jurisdiction in Western Germany," 19 *Col. J. Trans. L.* 1, 5 (1981).
19 Romero, "Mexico's Fedralist Tradition," 42 *Pub. Ad. Rev.* 399, 401 (Sept-Oct 1982) (emphasis supplied).

§ 1.01

1 Constitution of India, List I, Entry 97; Article 248; Durgeshwar v. Secretary of the Bar Council, A.I.R. (1954) All. 728.
2 British North America Act, § 91.
3 Constitution of Austria 1920/1929, Art. 10(7).
4 Constitution of Nigeria 1979, Second Schedule Parts I & II.
5 Constitution of Malaysia 1968, as amended, Ninth Schedule, Federal and Concurrent Lists.
6 Hodge, "Federalism and the Soviet Constitution of 1977, Commonwealth Perspective," 55 *Wash. L. Rev.* 505,525,542 (1980).
7 Constitution of India, Article 246(3), Entry 1.
8 Constitution of India, Article 246(3), Entry 6.

9   Constitution of India, Article 246(3), Entry 26.

10 Sen, *A Comparative Study of the Indian Constitution* (New Delhi 1967) 161.

11 Constitution of Nigeria 1979, First Schedule, Part II(7).

12 Antieau, *Constitutional Construction* (Dobbs Ferry 1982) 40; Sri Ram Ram Narain v. State of Bombay, A.I.R. (1954) S.C. 49.

13 Constitution of Austria 1920/1929, Articles 11 and 12; Sawer, *Modern Federalism* (London 1969) 35; Hodge, "Federalism and the Soviet Constitution of 1977, Commonwealth Perspective," 55 *Wash. L. Rev.* 505, 542 (1980).

§ 1.02

1   Constitution of India, Article 246(1).

2   Constitution of Nigeria, Second Schedule, Part I.

3   Constitution of Austria 1920/1929, Articles 10 through 15.

4   E.g. Constitution of Switzerland, Articles 39 & 41.

5   Constitution of Malaysia 1968, as amended, Ninth Schedule.

6   Tennant v. Union Bank (1894) A.C. 31; Henry Birks & Sons v. Montreal (1955) 5 D.L.R. 321.

7   Union Colliery v. Bryden (1899) A.C. 580.

8   British North America Act, § 91(27).

9   Switzman v. Elbling (1957) S.C.R. 285.

10 E.g., Levkoe v. The Queen (1977) 18 O.R. 2d 265 (fines up to $2,000). When the Cameroon Republic was a federal society, the Constitution vested "the establishment of penalties of any kind" in the Federal Government. Art. 24(3) (c).

11 Grundgesetz of German Federal Republic, Art. 74(11).

12 Johnson, *Federalism and Decentralisation in the Federal Republic of Germany* (H.M.S.O., London 1973) 10.

13 Grundgesetz of German Federal Republic, Art. 72(1).

14 Constitution of Nigeria, 1979, First Schedule, Part II(5).

15 Constitution of Pakistan 1973, Art. 142.

16 Constitution of Pakistan 1973, Art. 143.

17 Constitution of Brazil 1969, as amended, Art. XVII, sole par.

§ 1.03

1   Allgeyer v. Louisiana (1897) 165 US 578, 17 S Ct 427, 41 L Ed 832.

2   Bigelow v. Virginia (1950) 339 US 643, 70 S Ct 927, 94 L Ed 1154.

3   Travelers Health Insurance Co. v. Virginia (1950) 339 US 643, 70 S Ct 927, 94 L Ed 1154.

4   Skiriotes v. Florida (1941) 313 US 69, 77, 61 S Ct 924, 85 L Ed 1193.

5   Hoopeston Canning Co. v. Cullen (1943) 318 US 313, 63 S Ct 602, 87 L Ed 777.

6   E.g., New South Wales Constitution Act 1902, § 5; "In and for Victoria in all cases whatsoever." Victoria Constitution Act 1855 (U.K.) § 1.

7   Millar v. Commissioner for Stamp Duties (1932) 48 C.L.R. 618, 632. Pryles, "The Applicability of Statutes to Multi-State Transactions," 46 *Aust. L.J.* 629 (1972).

8   Broken Hill South Ltd. v. Commissioner of Taxation (NSW) (1937) 56 C.L.R. 337, 356.

9   Ibid. p. 355.

10 Ibid., p. 355.

11 Ibid., p. 375.

12 Ibid., p. 375.

13 Ibid., p. 375.

14 Myer Emporium Ltd. v. Commissioner for Stamp Duties (NSW) (1967) 68 S.R.(NSW) 220.

15 Johnson v. Commissioner for Stamp Duties (NSW) (1956) A.C. 331.

16 Walker v. Hewett (1969) 120 C.L.R. 503.

17 Cox v. Tomat (1971) 126 C.L.R. 105, 110-111.

18 Robinson v. Western Australia Museum (1977) 138 C.L.R. 283, 294. Only two years

earlier Justice Gibbs had stated the rule more liberally. State laws, he wrote, can have extraterritorial application if "a relevant connexion between the persons or circumstances on which the legislation operates and the State" exists, adding that "the test should be liberally applied, and that legislation should be held valid if there is any real connexion between the subject matter of the legislation and the State." Pearce v. Florenca (1975) 135 C.L.R. 507, 518. It is respectfully suggested that the statement of the test and the judicial attitude expressed are preferable to the Court's response in Robinson. Worth noting is: Castles, "Limitations on the Autonomy of the Australian States," 1962 *Pub.L.* 175, 196 ff.

[19] Royal Bank of Canada v. The King (1913) A.C. 283.
[20] Burns Foods v. Attorney-General for Manitoba (1973) 1 S.C.R. 494; Credit Foncier Franco-Canadien v. Ross (1937, Alberta) 3 D.L.R. 365; Beauharnois Light, Heat and Power Co. v. Hydro Electric Power Commission (1937) Ontario Reports 796.
[21] Interprovincial Cooperatives v. The Queen (1975) 53 D.L.R. 3d 321, (1976) 1 S.C.R. 477.
[22] D.L.R. 3d pp. 353, 355.
[23] Interprovincial Cooperatives v. The Queen (Man Ct App 1973) 38 D.L.R. 367.
[24] Regina v. Thomas Equipment Co. Ltd. (1979) 96 D.L.R. 3d 1; Edinger, "Territorial Limitations on Provincial Powers," 14 *Ottawa L. Rev.* 57 (1982).
[25] Constitution of Mexico, Art. 121(I).
[26] State of Bombay v. R.M.D. Chanarbaugwala, A.I.R. (1957) S.C. 699; State of Bombay v. Narayandas, A.I.R. (1958) H. Ct. Bombay, 68.

§ 1.04

[1] Constitution of Australia, § 117.
[2] R. v. Smithers, ex parte Benson (1912) 16 C.L.R. 99.
[3] Pannam, "Discrimination on the Basis of State Residence in Australia and the United States," 6 *Melb. L.R.* 105, 131, 148 (1967).
[4] Constitution of the United States, Article IV, § 2.
[5] Toomer v. Witsell (1948) 334 US 385, 68 S Ct 1156, 1162, 92 L Ed 1460.
[6] Ward v. Maryland (1871) 12 Wall. 418, 20 L Ed 449, 452; Doe v. Bolton (1973) 410 US 179, 93 S Ct 739, 35 L Ed 2d 201; Austin v. New Hampshire (1975) 420 US 656, 95 S Ct 1191, 43 L Ed 2d 530; Hicklin v. Orbeck (1978) 437 US 518, 98 S Ct 2482, 57 L Ed 2d 397.
[7] Douglas v. New York, N.H. & H. Rr. (1929) 279 US 377, 49 S Ct 355, 73 L Ed 747; Canadian Northern Rr. v. Eggen (1920) 252 US 553, 40 S Ct 402, 64 L Ed 713.
[8] Baldwin v. Fish and Game Commission (1978) 435 US 371, 98 S Ct 1852, 56 L Ed 2d 354.
[9] Argentina Constitution of 1853, as amended, Article 8.
[10] Constitution of Austria 1920/1929, Art. 6(3).
[11] Constitution of Brazil 1969, as amended, Art. 9(1).
[12] Grundgesetz of German Federal Republic, Article 33.
[13] Constitution of Malaysia 1968, as amended, Art. 8(4).
[14] Constitution of Nigeria 1979, Chapter IV, § 39.
[15] Walter v. Attorney-General for Alberta (1969) S.C.R. 383, 3 D.L.R. 3d 1; Morgan v. Prince Edward Island (1975) 55 D.L.R. 3d 527, (1975) 2 S.C.R. 349.

§ 1.05

[1] R. v. Marchioness of Donegal (1924) 2 D.L.R. 1191; Hogg, *Constitutional Law of Canada* (Toronto 1977) 423, 441.
[2] Walter v. Attorney-General for Alberta (1969) S.C.R. 383, 3 D.L.R. 3d 1.
[3] Morgan v. Attorney-General for Prince Edward Island (1975) 2 S.C.R. 349, 55 D.L.R. 3d 527.
[4] Union Colliery v. Bryden (1899) A.C. 580.
[5] Constitution Act 1981, Part I, Schedule B, Section 15(1). It should be noted that the Act

also provides that the legislature of a province may expressly declare in an act of the legislature that the Act or a provision thereof shall operate notwithstanding a provision included in Section 15 of the Constitution Act 1981.

6 New Orleans v. Dukes (1976) 427 US 297, 96 S Ct 2513, 49 L Ed 2d 511.

7 Wheeling Steel Corp. v. Glander (1949) 337 US 562, 69 S Ct 1291, 93 L Ed 1544.

8 "The general presumption of constitutionality afforded state statutes and the traditional approval given state classifications if the Court can conceive of a 'rational basis' for the distinction made . . . . " Kramer v. Union Free School Dist. (1969) 395 US 621, 627-8, 89 S Ct 1886, 23 L Ed 2d 583.

9 "A racial classification . . . is presumptively invalid and can be upheld only upon an extraordinary justification." Personnel Administrator of Massachusetts v. Feeney (1979) 442 US 256, 272, 99 S Ct 2282, 60 L Ed 2d 870.

10 Harper v. Virginia Board of Elections (1966) 383 US 663, 86 S Ct 1079, 16 L Ed 2d 169; Kramer v. Union Free School Dist. (1969) 395 US 621, 89 S Ct 1886, 23 L Ed 2d 583.

11 Regents of the University of California v. Bakke (1978) 438 US 265, 305, 98 S Ct 2733, 57 L Ed 2d 750; McLaughlin v. Florida (1964) 379 US 184, 196.

12 Constitution of India, Article 14.

13 Seervai, *Constitutional Law of India* (Bombay 1968) 987.

14 Vajravelu's Case (1965) A.S.C. 1017.

15 Constitution of Argentina, Article 16.

16 Cruz v. Santiago del Estero (1938) 179 S.C.N. 98.

17 Moran v. Entre Rios (1934) 171 S.C.N. 390.

18 Grundgesetz of German Federal Republic, Art. 3(1).

19 Constitution of Austria 1920/1929, as amended, Art. 7(1).

20 Constitution of Malaysia 1968, as amended, Art. 8.

21 Constitution of Venezuela 1961, Article 61.

§ 1.06

1 Nebbia v. New York (1934) 291 US 502, 54 S Ct 505, 78 L Ed 940.

2 Goldblatt v. Hempstead (1962) 369 US 590, 82 S Ct 987, 8 L Ed 2d 130.

3 Cantwell v. Connecticut (1940) 310 US 296, 60 S Ct 900, 84 L Ed 1213.

4 Canale v. Mendoza (1913) 118 S.C.N. 278 (Argentina); Barrera v. San Juan (1930) 168 S.C.N. 305 (Argentina).

5 Cf. Adelaide Company of Jehovah's Witnesses v. Commonwealth (1943) 67 C.L.R. 116.

6 Armstrong v. Victoria (No. 1) (1955) 93 C.L.R. 264, 275, 284, 290; "Our prior cases make clear that a state can regulate so long as no undue burden is imposed on interstate commerce . . . . " Lloyd A. Fry Roofing Co. v. Wood (1952) 344 US 157, 73 S Ct 204, 207, 97 L Ed 168.

7 Lindsley v. Natural Carbonic Gas Co. (1911) 220 US 61, 78-9, 31 S Ct 337, 55 L Ed 369.

8 Toomer v. Witsell (1948) 334 US 385, 68 S Ct 1156, 92 L Ed 1460.

9 Cf. Reference re Anti-Inflation Act (1976) 68 D.L.R. 3d 452, 488; "This Court would be unjustified in concluding . . . that the Parliament of Canada did not have a rational basis for regarding the Anti-Inflation Act as measure . . . temporarily necessary to meet a set of economic crisis imperiling the well-being of the people of Canada." (Laskin, C.J.C.)

§ 1.07

1 E.g., the 1891 Constitution of Brazil, Art. 11(3).

2 Colorado Constitution, Art. II, § 11.

3 Georgia Constitution of 1976, § 2-107.

4 Missouri Constitution of 1945, Art. I, § 13.

5 New Hampshire Constitution of 1784, Part I, Art. 23.

6 Ohio Constitution of 1851, Art. II, § 28.

7 Tennessee Constitution of 1870, Art. I, § 20.

8 Texas Constitution of 1876, Art. I, § 16.

9 Article I, § 9.

[10] Crosskey, "The True Meaning of the Constitutional Prohibition of Ex Post Facto Laws," 14 *U. Chi. L. Rev.* 539 (1947).

[11] Calder v. Bull (1798) 3 U.S. 386, 1 L Ed 648.

[12] United States Constitution, Article I, Section 10.

[13] Home Building & Loan Ass'n v. Blaisdell (1934) 290 US 398, 54 S Ct 231, 78 L Ed 413.

[14] Queenside Hills Co. v. Saxl (1946) 328 US 80, 83, 66 S Ct 850, 90 L Ed 1096.

[15] Chase Securities Corp. v. Donaldson (1945) 325 US 304, 65 S Ct 1137, 89 L Ed 1628; Lyons v. Betts (1969) 184 Neb 746, 171 NW 2d 792.

[16] Adams v. Kalamazoo Ice & Fuel Co. (1928) 245 Mich. 261, 222 NW 86; O'Reilly, "The Nonconforming Use and Due Process of Law," 23 *Geo L J* 218 (1935).

[17] People v. Kesbec Inc. (1939) 281 NY 785, 24 NE 2d 476; People v. Miller (1952) 304 NY 105, 106 NE 2d 34; Suffolk Outdoor Advertising Co. v. Hulse (1977) 43 NY 2d 483, 373 NE 2d 263.

[18] Ward v. British Oak Insurance Co. Ltd. (1932) 1 K.B. 392 (C.A.)

[19] R.v. Kidman (1915) 20 C.L.R. 425; Lane, *The Australian Federal System* (2d ed. 1979 Sydney) 230.

[20] R.v. Kidman (1915) 20 C.L.R. 425.

[21] Constitution of India, Art. 20.

[22] Constitution of Nigeria 1979, Art. 33(8).

[23] Constitution of Pakistan, Art. 12(1) (a).

§ 1.08

[1] Constitution of Mexico, Art. 117(I).

[2] Article I, § 10, United States Constitution.

[3] Wharton v. Wise (1894) 153 US 155, 14 S Ct 783, 38 L Ed 669, 674.

[4] Virginia v. Tennessee (1893) 148 US 502, 13 S Ct 728, 37 L Ed 537, 543.

[5] United States Steel Corp. v. Multistate Tax Commission (1978) 434 US 452, 98 S Ct 799, 54 L Ed 2d 682 (agreement by states to allocate for tax purposes the income of corporations operating in multiple states).

[6] Dover v. Portsmouth Bridge (1845) 17 NH 200 (agreement on bridge over stream between two states); Union Branch Rr. Co. v. Texas & Georgia Rr. Co. (1853) 14 Ga 327 (agreement for two states to operate railroads extraterritorially); Fisher v. Steele (1887) 39 La Ann 447, 1 So 882 (agreement to erect levee along river); Dixie Wholesale Grocery Inc. v. Martin (1939) 278 Ky 705, 129 SW 2d 181, certiorari denied 308 US 609 (agreement to exchange tax information).

[7] Wells, *The States in West German Federalism* (New York 1961) 68.

§ 1.09

[1] Argentine Constitution of 1853, as amended, Art. 108.

[2] Argentine Constitution of 1853, as amended, Art 107.

[3] Constitution of Mexico, Article 117(I).

[4] McHenry County v. Brady (1917) 37 ND 59, 163 NW 540.

[5] Constitution of India, List I, Entries 10 & 14.

[6] Constitution of Nigeria 1979, Second Schedule, Part I(25).

[7] Zines, *The High Court and the Constitution* (Sydney 1981) 220.

§ 1.10

[1] Constitution of Nigeria 1979, Ch. I, Art. 10.

[2] Engel v. Vitale (1962) 370 US 421, 82 S Ct 1261, 8 L Ed 2d 601.

[3] Walz v. Tax Commission of New York (1970) 397 US 664, 90 S Ct 1409, 25 L Ed 2d 697.

[4] Everson v. Board of Education (1947) 330 US 1, 67 S Ct 504, 81 L Ed 711.

[5] Zorach v. Clauson (1952) 343 US 306, 72 S Ct 679, 96 L Ed 954.

[6] Tilton v. Richardson (1971) 403 US 672, 91 S Ct 2091, 29 L Ed 2d 790.

[7] Roemer v. Board of Public Works (1976) 426 US 736, 96 S Ct 2337, 49 L Ed 2d 179.

8 Meek v. Pittinger (1975) 421 US 349, 95 S Ct 1753, 44 L Ed 2d 217.

9 Committee for Public Education and Religious Liberty v. Regan (1980) 444 US 646, 100 S Ct 840, 63 L Ed 2d 94.

10 Lemon v. Kurtzman (1971) 403 US 602, 91 S Ct 2105, 29 L Ed 2d 745.

11 School District of Abington Township v. Schempp (1963) 374 US 203, 83 S Ct 1560, 10 L Ed 2d 844.

12 Epperson v. Arkansas (1968) 393 US 97, 89 S Ct 266, 21 L Ed 2d 228.

13 Grundgesetz of German Federal Republic, Art. 7(3).

14 Grundgesetz of German Federal Republic, Art. 7(2).

15 Constitution of Brazil 1969, as amended, Art. 9(2).

16 Constitution of Australia, § 116.

§ 1.11

1 Wheare, *Federal Government* (4th ed. 1963) 74. Constitution of the U.S.S.R. 1977, Art. 74.

2 Constitution of Switzerland, Transitory Provisions, Article 2; Hughes, *The Federal Constitution of Switzerland* (Westport, Conn. 1970) 6.

3 Constitution of the United States, Article VI, par. 2.

4 McDermott v. Wisconsin (1913) 228 US 115, 132, 33 S Ct 431, 57 L Ed 754.

5 Constitution of Australia, § 109.

6 Constitution of Malaysia, Article 75: "If any State law is inconsistent with a federal law, the federal law shall prevail, and the State law shall, to the extent of the inconsistency, be void."

7 Constitution of Nigeria 1979, First Schedule - Part II(5): "If any law enacted by the House of Assembly of a State is inconsistent with any law validly made by the National Assembly, the law made by the National Assembly shall prevail, and that other Law shall to the extent of the inconsistency be void." Chiroma Giremabe v. Bornu Native Authority (1961) All N.L.R. 469.

8 Constitution of Pakistan 1973, Article 143.

9 Constitution of Argentina, Article 31.

10 Tika Ramji v. State of U.P., A.I.R. (1956) S.C. 698-699.

11 Grundgesetz of German Federal Republic, Art. 72(1).

12 Attorney-General for Canada v. Attorney-General for British Columbia (1930) A.C. 111; Attorney-General for Ontario v. Attorney General for Canada (1931) A.C. 326; Hogg, *Constitutional Law of Canada* (Toronto 1977) Chapter Six.

13 Prince Edward Island v. Egan (1941) S.C.R. 396; Hogg, *Constitutional Law of Canada* (Toronto 1977) 107, 110.

14 Smith v. The Queen (1960) S.C.R. 776, 800, 25 D.L.R. 2d 225, 246; Magnet, "The Presumption of Constitutionality," 18 *Osgoode Hall L.J.* 87, 90 (1980).

15 Smith v. R. (1960) S.C.R. 776; Attorney-General for British Columbia v. Attorney-General for Canada (1924) A.C. 203; McDermott v. Wisconsin (1913) 228 US 115, 33 S Ct 431, 57 L Ed 754; Castle v. Hayes Freight Lines (1954) 348 US 61, 75 S Ct 191, 99 L Ed 68; R. v. Licensing Court of Brisbane; ex parte Daniell (1920) 28 C.L.R. 23; Hume v. Palmer (1926) 38 C.L.R. 441; Mendoza v. San Juan (1865) 3 S.C.N. 131 (Argentina). Tammelo, "Inconsistency between Commonwealth and State Laws," 22 *Australian L.J.* 45 (1948).

16 Smith v. The Queen (1960) S.C.R. 776; California v. Zook (1949) 336 US 725, 69 S Ct 841, 93 L Ed 1005.

17 Mann v. The Queen (1966) S.C.R. 238; Kelly v. Washington (1937) 302 US 1, 58 S Ct 87, 82 L Ed 3; Florida Lime & Avocado Growers v. Paul (1963) 373 US 132, 83 S Ct 1210, 10 L Ed 2d 248; Australian Boot Trade Employees Federation v. Whybrow & Co. (1910) 10 C.L.R. 266.

18 Napier v. Atlantic Coast Line Rr. (1926) 272 US 605, 47 S Ct 207, 71 L Ed 432; International Longshoremen's Association v. Ariadne Shipping Co. (1970) 397 US 195, 90 S Ct 872, 25 L Ed 2d 218; Ex parte McLean (1930) 43 C.L.R. 472, 483 (Dixon, J.); Wenn v. Attorney-General for Victoria (1948) 77 C.L.R. 84; O'Sullivan v. Noarlunga

Meat Ltd. (#1) (1954) 92 C.L.R. 565; Clyde Engineering Co. Ltd. v. Cowburn (1926) 37 C.L.R. 466 (Isaac, J.). Aihe & Oluyede, *Cases and Materials on Constitutional Law in Nigeria* (Oxford U. Press 1979) 80. Murray-Jones, "The Tests for Inconsistency under § 109 of the Constitution," 10 *Fed. L. Rev.* 25 (1979).

CHAPTER TWO

CHAPTER TWO

Chapter Two

STATE POWER TO REGULATE

§ 2.00 State power to regulate—generally

All the states in federal societies have rather adequate "police powers" (as they are known in the United States) to impose such regulations upon persons and corporations as are necessary to protect the public health, safety, morality and general welfare.[1]

In the federal systems having judicial review of state and provincial legislation, courts have generally applied a "reasonableness" norm, sustaining regulations that are reasonable and voiding those that are clearly arbitrary or unreasonable.[2]

There is a good deal of judicial deference to the legislative determination that particular regulations are necessary, not only in British Commonwealth countries with a tradition of parliamentary supremacy, but elsewhere as well.

Where there is judicial review, the task of the courts is to balance prudentially the societal interest, for instance, in public health, supporting the action of the state legislature, against opposed societal interests in particular cases. Dealing with judicial review of legislation in the Federal Republic of Germany, Professor McWhinney has aptly observed that the judicial task often "is one of balancing interests in speech and association against countervailing interests in public order."[3]

At times, some courts have said that power to regulate does not embrace a power to prohibit,[4] but this is wrong. All regulation is prohibition of something and if a line could be drawn between the two terms, it would not ordinarily be acceptable social engineering. The question is not whether the statute prohibits, but whether—under the prevailing circumstances—prohibition is a reasonable exercise of the police power.[5]

Where there is judicial review of state regulations under the "reasonableness" norm, retroactive regulation can be reasonable and constitutional. The United States Supreme Court has said it is clearly settled that "in no case does the owner of property acquire immunity against the exercise of the police power because he constructed it in full compliance with existing laws."[6] However, at times in federal societies, the constitutions specifically forbid the states to enact retroactive legislation.[7]

State regulatory law enacted to safeguard aesthetic interests and values can be reasonable and constitutional.[8]

Generally states having power to regulate cannot give their controls extraterritorial effect.[9]

§ 2.01 State power to protect the public health

Protection of the public health is one of the most important responsibilities of any government, and states in federal societies custom-arily have ample power to legislate in this regard. Many states possess such power because they have the residuum of power in the federal system, as indicated in an earlier section. In other federations where the states do not possess residual powers, they customarily have constitu-tional grants adequate to protect the public health. For example, in India under the Constitution the states are given power to legislate in regard to "Public Health."[1] So too, in Canada under § 92(7) of the British North America Act, the provinces have legislative competence to protect the public health,[2] and measures deemed necessary by provincial legislatures are generally held constitutional.[3] The Constitution of Switzerland confers upon the cantons a specific power to control restaurants and cafes.[4] To protect the public health, states customarily have adequate power to control the traffic in intoxicating liquor.[5] Sustaining such state control, the Supreme Court of India observed that such regulation is "connected with the public health."[6]

In all the federal societies, state attempts to safeguard the public health are judicially voided when they clash with valid legislation enacted by the federation,[7] as well as when the central government has occupied a field within its exclusive or concurrent powers under the constitution.[8]

In the federal societies which were constituents of the British Empire, courts review legislation of the component units under the doctrine of *ultra vires*,[9] but they do not ordinarily void state legislation enacted to protect the public health because the judiciary deems the statute unreasonable.[10] In Canada, under the British North America Act, the entire area of the criminal law is exclusively a dominion jurisdiction[11] and, consequently, provincial controls attempting to protect the public health, are *ultra vires* when they usurp the criminal law powers of the dominion.[12]

In the United States, the power of the states to legislate for the public health is limited by the Due Process Clause of the Fourteenth Amendment which requires state laws to be reasonable and reasonably related to the legitimate end.[13] In Argentina, too, governmental action designed to protect the public health has been voided by the Supreme Court when it concluded the local action was unreasonable.[14] In the United States there is a presumption that state statutes enacted to protect the public health are reasonable and constitutional,[15] and many such statutes have been upheld by the Supreme Court. Illustratively, when a state's political subdivision forbade industrial activity in a neigh-borhood where people resided, because of its air pollution, the Court held constitutional the governmental action, stating:

> It is to be remembered that we are dealing with one of the most essential powers of government, one that is the least limitable. It may, indeed, seem harsh in its exercise, [it] usually is on some individual, but

> the imperative necessity for its existence precludes any limitation upon it when not exerted arbitrarily.[16]

Among the state and local controls designed to safeguard the public health sustained by the United States Supreme Court are laws:

(a) requiring the inspection and labelling of foods;[17]
(b) restricting child labor;[18]
(c) requiring vaccinations;[19]
(d) prescribing a common day of rest;[20]
(e) authorizing destruction of food unfit for human consumption;[21]
(f) providing for inspection and regulation of bakeries;[22]
(g) authorizing inspection and regulation of dairies;[23]
(h) controlling the practice of the healing arts;[24]
(i) imposing quarantines denying entrance into the state of cattle and sheep from infected areas;[25]
(j) authorizing housing inspectors to enter and examine dwellings for health facilities;[26]
(k) requiring garbage and refuse to be placed in watertight containers;[27]
(l) controlling noise;[28]
(m) prohibiting the sale of alcohol;[29] and
(n) banning the sale of cigarettes.[30]

Even the free movement of persons and goods between states can be controlled in the interest of the public health.[31] At times, however, the interstate commerce clauses in the federal constitutions will result in the invalidation of state efforts to protect the public health when they discriminate against persons engaged in interstate commerce. The statute's burden upon such commerce is deemed unreasonable, either because its impact upon the commerce is great, with only a small contribution to protecting the public health, or because reasonable alternatives are available that would adequately protect the public health with less effect upon interstate commerce.[32]

In the United States, and other countries with equality or equal protection clauses, state legislation intended to protect the public health will be invalidated when the statute results in invidious or unreasonable discrimination between citizens.[33]

State statutes protecting the public health may, at times, be voided when they clash with the important societal interest in freedom of conscience and religion, specifically protected in most federal constitutions. The California Supreme Court has held that freedom of religion prevented application to American Indian religious services of the state ban upon the use of peyote, a narcotic root.[34] However, in a number of cases the interest in freedom of religion has bowed before the interest in protecting the public health. The United States Supreme Court sustained the punishment of a Jehovah's Witness for allowing her nine-year-old niece to sell religious literature approximately twenty feet away from the aunt on public sidewalks, outside of school hours. The Court remarked:

"The right to practice religion freely does not include liberty to expose the community or the child to communicable disease or the latter to ill health or death." Justice Murphy dissented since the state had produced no "convincing proof that such a practice constitutes a grave and immediate danger to the state or to the health, morals or welfare of the child."[35] The United States Supreme Court on another occasion held that Sabbatarians and others who worshipped on days other than Sunday would have to pay the price for their religions by closing on Sundays, as well as the other days ordained by their faiths, under compulsory Sunday closing laws enacted to provide a common day of rest.[36]

Other courts have sustained the states in ordering blood transfusions to be given to children and adults, who would otherwise likely perish, over objections based on religious convictions.[37] The use of dangerous instrumentalities (such as snakes) in religious ceremonies can be forbidden.[38] Compulsory physical examinations, as conditions for marriage licenses, have been sustained over an argument allegedly based on freedom of conscience.[39] Chest x-ray requirements have been upheld as conditions for admission to public educational institutions, over protests of persons who found the practice objectionable to their Christian Science faith.[40] Persons claiming religious exemptions have nevertheless been subjected to statutes regulating the healing arts.[41] States have generally been able to expose residents to fluoridation of the water supply, over opposition based upon religious beliefs.[42]

§ 2.02 State power to protect the public safety

Protection of the public safety is an important societal interest everywhere. States in federal societies customarily have adequate power to protect this interest, either as residuaries of power or as recipient of constitutional grants.

Where, as in the United States, there is judicial review of state legislation under the test of reasonableness, state legislation designed to protect the public safety must be reasonable and reasonably related to that end.[1] There is generally a presumption of reasonableness accorded to such legislation,[2] except where the statute impacts upon fundamental freedoms or utilizes invidious discriminations.[3]

Dozens of statutes aimed at protecting public safety have been sustained by the United States Supreme Court under the foregoing rules.[4] Illustratively, in upholding a state law requiring sprinkler systems to be installed in non-fireproof lodging houses, the Court stated: "Little need be said on the due process question. We are not concerned with the wisdom of this legislation or the need for it."[5] Among the other state laws designed to protect public safety, which have been found constitutional by the Supreme Court, are those:

(a) controlling the location of high fire-risk operations;[6]

(b) banning gasoline storage facilities from cities;[7]
(c) regulating peddlers, hawkers and solicitors;[8]
(d) limiting the speed of trains passing through populous areas;[9]
(e) requiring railroads to provide safety precautions at crossings;[10]
(f) requiring railroads to eliminate grade crossings at their expense;[11]
(g) regulating the operation of trams or street cars;[12] and
(h) regulating the operation of trucks.[13]

Where the societal interest in protecting public safety clashes with other important interests of society, the task of courts having judicial review is to identify and balance prudently the competing societal interests.

When state legislation designed to protect the public safety amounts only to a reasonable burden upon interstate commerce, such legislation is not violative of the interstate commerce clauses customarily found in federal societies.[14]

In federal societies, such as the United States, having equality or equal protection clauses, state legislation intended to protect the public safety must avoid invidious or unreasonable discriminations.[15] However, there is generally a presumption that the classification or disparate treatment is reasonable and constitutional,[16] and many such classifications have been judicially sustained.[17]

In federal societies, such as the United States, having constitutional bills of rights protecting freedoms of religion, speech, press, assembly and association, legislation aimed at protecting public safety is voided by the courts when it unnecessarily impacts upon such interests,[18] as well as when the societal interest in these freedoms outweighs, under the circumstances, the interest in safety.[19]

In the federal systems that were once part of the British Empire, the courts do not ordinarily invalidate legislative action of the state legislatures aimed at protecting the public safety on the ground the law is unreasonable.[20] States and provinces in these federal systems generally have adequate powers to protect the public safety, either having the residuum of power under the constitution or grants in the constitution. Thus, in Canada, the provinces under the British North America Act have legislative power over "local works and undertakings."[21] This enables them to protect the public safety in many areas such as the local or intraprovincial operation of railroads,[22] bus lines,[23] and trucking.[24] A provincial ban upon smoking in public places of assembly has also been sustained.[25]

In federal societies sharing the Westminster heritage, the doctrine of *ultra vires* applies. Consequently, when states or provinces act beyond their powers under the constitution, statutes designed to protect the public safety are judicially voided,[26] as they are also when they unreasonably burden the free flow of interstate or interprovincial commerce.[27] Nevertheless, states have successfully defended safety legislation which affected such commerce, when the courts concluded the regulation was necessary and the burden upon the commerce slight.[28] The extent to which the states and provinces can interfere generally with interstate commerce is treated more fully in the following chapter.

In all the federal systems, state attempts to protect the public safety are voided when they conflict with federal regulations,[29] as well as when they fall within fields constitutionally occupied by the central government.[30]

§ 2.03 State power to protect the public morality

Protection of the public morality is deemed an important societal interest in virtually all federal systems. The component entities customarily have extensive powers to protect this interest. The Constitution of India specifically confers upon the states power to legislate in regard to "betting and gambling."[1]

In federal systems that were once part of the British Empire, the courts do not ordinarily pass upon the reasonableness of legislation enacted by the state legislatures to protect the public morality. However, the doctrine of *ultra vires* prevails and state attempts to protect the public morality are voided when they are beyond the power of the component entities in the federation.[2] In Canada, under the British North America Act, power over the criminal law is exclusively in the Dominion Parliament. Provincial efforts to protect the public morality are *ultra vires* when they trespass upon this federal domain.[3] Thus, an Ontario statute regulating betting was held *ultra vires* when the court concluded it, in effect, amended a dominion statute.[4] However, so long as provincial statutes do not enact "criminal laws," they can effectively deal with protecting public morality.[5]

Many state statutes—and by-laws enacted by local governments under state authorization—designed to protect morality have been sustained, including legislation:

(a) outlawing lotteries;[6]
(b) forbidding gambling, generally;[7]
(c) prohibiting machines having a tendency to suggest gambling;[8]
(d) regulating and banning the sale of liquor;[9]
(e) prohibiting prostitution;[10]
(f) controlling massage parlors;[11]
(g) forbidding the commercial use of pool and billiard equipment;[12]
(h) controlling pool and billiard establishments;[13]
(i) prohibiting obscene publications, films, and performances;[14]
(j) prohibiting the establishment of bull-fighting arenas;[15] and
(k) prohibiting horse racing.[16]

In the United States, the Due Process Clause of the Fourteenth Amendment requires that state and local regulations intended to protect public morality be both reasonable and reasonably related to that end.[17]

There is generally a presumption that such legislation is reasonable and constitutional, except where freedom of expression is being limited.[18] Where there is broad judicial review of state legislation under federal constitutions, courts have held that the interest in protecting public morality at times has to be subordinated to other important interests of the society. Illustratively, in honoring the societal interests in privacy and private property, the United States Supreme Court has held that a state can not constitutionally punish a citizen for the mere possession of obscene materials in the privacy of his home.[19]

Clauses in federal constitutions acknowledging important societal interests in freedom of communication and expression will require the invalidation of state legislation designed to protect the public morality when the legislation impacts upon communication or expression and is unduly vague, when it is not reasonably necessary to protect public morality, or when, in general terms, the societal interest in communication and expression outweighs, under the circumstances, the societal interest in protecting the public morality.[20]

In federal systems having constitutional equality or equal protection clauses, states legislating to protect the public morality must avoid invidious or unreasonable discriminations, but the courts have condoned some rather startling discriminations.[21]

§ 2.04 State power to legislate for the general welfare

In all the federal societies where the component states have the residuum of power, they are generally authorized to legislate for the general welfare. In the other federal systems, where the states must rely upon constitutional grants of power, they customarily have been recipients of grants in language broad enough to enable them to legislate for the general welfare.[1]

Power to legislate for the general welfare has permitted states to enact laws protecting the financial safety of the public, by punishing consumer fraud and deception,[2] as well as regulating the sale of securities.[3]

States have been able to control the wholesale and retail prices at which goods are sold in purely intrastate or intraprovincial commerce.[4]

States have generally been sustained in regulating the practice of the professions within their borders.[5]

Under the concurrent power over road traffic, possessed by the Laender as well as the central government of the German Federal Republic,[6] the land of North Rhine Westphalia has been sustained in prohibiting outdoor advertising along roa'.s in developed areas.[7]

The Grundgesetz of the German Federal Republic establishes the

Laender as the exclusive custodians of cultural leadership, giving them control over, *inter alia,* education, broadcasting and television transmissions.[8] However, in India, the Constitution gives the Union Parliament control over any institution of learning declared by it to be of national importance;[9] the Supreme Court has ruled that a state could not compel university instruction to be in the Gujarati language.[10] In Canada, the provinces have control over education.[11]

States and provinces have been sustained in enacting legislation banning discrimination on the basis of race, sex, religion, ethnicity and place of origin in regard to such important areas of life as housing, employment, transportation, dining and recreational facilities.[12]

§ 2.05 State power to regulate private enterprise

States having the residuum of power under federal constitutions generally have full power to regulate private enterprise within their borders, subject only to limitations incorporated in those constitutions. The Australian Constitution provides that: "Every power of the Parliament of a Colony which has become or becomes a State, shall, unless it is by this Constitution exclusively vested in the Parliament of the Commonwealth or withdrawn from the Parliament of the State, continue as at the establishment of the Commonwealth, or as at the admission or establishment of the State, as the case may be."[1] Section 112 of the constitution additionally recognizes the power of the states to impose inspection laws upon goods and animals coming into their territory.

There is no substantive due process of law clause in the Constitution of Australia, so neither the High Court nor the State Supreme Courts ordinarily pass upon the reasonableness of state legislative controls of private enterprise and the economy. The High Court has said: "There is no doubt that the Legislature of New South Wales can impose such conditions as it thinks proper by way of taxation or otherwise upon persons who carry on business in New South Wales and therefore bring themselves within the legislative authority of the State."[2]

In Australia, the principal constitutional limitation upon state regulation of private enterprise is found in the interstate commerce clause (section 92) which topic is treated at length in the following chapter. Section 117 of the constitution forbids states from discriminating against residents of other states.[3] There is some judicial dictum that this can be used to void discrimination against entrepreneurs from other states,[4] but it has never resulted in a High Court ruling to that effect; discrimination in commercial matters is customarily litigated under section 92.

The doctrine of *ultra vires* is available in Australia to protect the interest in freedom of enterprise from unauthorized state and local controls. Chief Justice Griffith of Australia has said: "English jurisprudence has always recognized that the Acts of a legislature of limited jurisdiction (whether the limits be as to territory or subject matter) may be examined by any tribunal before whom the point is properly raised. The term 'unconstitutional' used in this connection, means no more than ultra vires."[5]

The United States recognizes a constitutionally protected societal interest in freedom of private enterprise;[6] but it can be readily outweighed by other important societal interests, such as those in protecting the public health or safety. The Fourteenth Amendment Due Process Clause requires only that state regulations of private enterprise be reasonable and reasonably related to the legitimate legislative end.[7] The Supreme Court said in 1963 that it is now "settled" "that States have power to legislate against what are found to be injurious practices in their internal commercial and business affairs, so long, as their law do not run afoul of some specific federal constitutional prohibition, or of some valid federal law." The Court added: "We refuse to sit as a 'superlegislature to weigh the wisdom of legislation'" in this area, and remarked that it was unable and unwilling "to draw lines by calling a law 'prohibitory' or 'regulatory'."[8] Unless they impact upon fundamental rights or employ invidious discriminations, state laws regulating private enterprise are presumed to be both reasonable and constitutional.[9]

From an early date, the Supreme Court has held reasonable and constitutional state regulation of public utilities,[10] as well as the issuance and sale of securities.[11] Under the norm of reasonableness, dozens of state regulations affecting both the professions and trades have been sustained,[12] including regulations:

(a) of the hours of work;[13]
(b) fixing maximum fees to be charged by employment agencies;[14]
(c) fixing prices for the sale of goods;[15]
(d) fixing minimum wages;[16]
(e) requiring employers to grant employees time off to vote;[17]
(f) forbidding opticians to sell eyeglasses without prescription;[18]
(g) protecting consumers against fraud and deception;[19]
(h) banning the use of trading stamps;[20]
(i) controlling trusts and restraints of trade;[21]
(j) requiring inspection and labeling of foods;[22]
(k) prohibiting racial discrimination;[23]
(l) of the hours operated by business establishments;[24]
(m) setting maximum rates to be charged by grain elevators;[25]
(n) prohibiting the sale of alcohol;[26]
(o) banning the sale of cigarettes;[27]
(p) prohibiting the commercial use of pool and billiard equipment;[28]
(q) controlling the professions;[29]
(r) controlling insurance companies;[30]
(s) prohibiting unfair trade practices;[31]
(t) prohibiting the sale of groceries below cost;[32] and
(u) controlling the business of debt adjustments.[33]

In Argentina, the provinces have been able to reasonably regulate the practice of the professions and trades.[34] However, there is authority indicating that the Supreme Court will invalidate unreasonable restraints upon freedom of contract and enterprise.[35]

States that do not possess the residuum of power must look to particular grants of power in the constitution to enable them to regulate private enterprise and the economy. In Canada, for example, the provinces have to rely principally upon three subsections in section 92 of the British North America Act. Subsection 13 gives them power over "property and civil rights in the province"; subsection 9 gives them power to impose "shop, saloon, tavern, auctioneer, and other licenses in order to the raising of a revenue for provincial, local or municipal purposes"; and subsection 16 gives the provinces power over "generally all matters of a merely local or private nature in the province." The House of Lords, in an appeal involving subsection 9, indicated this was a source of power to raise revenue, but not to regulate. Said that tribunal: "With regard to . . . No. 9, it is to be observed that the power of granting licenses is not assigned to the Provincial Legislatures for the purposes of regulating trade. . . ."[36] The House of Lords in 1881 held the provinces could regulate the business of insurance,[37] and extensive provincial regulation of the professions and trades has been judicially sustained.[38] The Supreme Court of Canada holds that the provinces have power to regulate the labor relations of firms operating within the provinces.[39] The Court also recognizes provincial power to control the prices at which commodities are sold within the province in intraprovincial trade.[40] Provincial trade and marketing acts limited to practices within the provinces are upheld.[41] Canadian provinces can fix the closing of hours of business establishments.[42] Regulation of the sale of securities by the provinces has been sustained by the Supreme Court.[43] The Supreme Court has also upheld the Ontario Unconscionable Transactions Relief Act, under which provincial courts can readjust the terms of contracts that are unconscionable.[44] Courts concerned with judicial review of provincial legislation customarily indicate they do not pass upon the reasonableness of the statutes, and the record generally supports such language.

The doctrine of *ultra vires* is available in Canada to protect the interest in freedom of enterprise from unauthorized provincial regulations.[45] The Privy Council in 1899 protected mine owners who desired to employ Chinese as workers, by voiding a provincial act restricting such employment, characterizing the statute as one involving aliens, an exclusive Dominion competence.[46] Provinces act *ultra vires* when they legislate in regard to the criminal law, which is an exclusive Dominion power, and consequently provincial and local regulations of business have been voided when the courts saw them as criminal law matters.[47] By the British North America Act, the matter "interest" is an exclusive power of the Dominion Parliament, beyond the legislative control of the provinces.[48]

In India, a citizen has the constitutional right "to practice any profession, or to carry on any occupation, trade or business,"[49] but the Constitution adds that this does not "prevent the State from making any law imposing reasonable restrictions on the exercise of the right."[50]

The Constitution of Venezuela recognizes and protects freedom of enterprise, but adds that it is subject to limitations "for reasons of safety, health or others of social interest."[51]

§ 2.06 State power to regulate private property

In most federal systems there is a societal interest in the protection of individual ownership, use and disposition of private property, safeguarded in the United States by the Fourteenth Amendment due process clause.[1] This demands only that the state and local regulations of private property be reasonable and reasonably adapted to protecting the public health, safety, morality or general welfare.[2] Aesthetic considerations today generally justify controls of the use of private property, under the foregoing test.[3] State and local regulations upon private property uses are presumed to be reasonable and constitutional.[4]

Many state and local regulations of private property have been sustained by the United States Supreme Court under the norm of reasonableness, including laws:

(a) prohibiting the use of property near residences for brickyards;[5]
(b) prohibiting use of property as a livery stable;[6]
(c) restricting land use by zoning ordinances;[7]
(d) limiting land use as a sand and gravel pit;[8]
(e) permitting a state official to order the destruction of cedar trees to protect nearby apple trees from cedar rust;[9]
(f) controlling the size, location, and construction of signs and billboards;[10]
(g) requiring buildings to be set back a designated distance from the street;[11]
(h) requiring fire protection devices and fire-resistant materials in buildings;[12]
(i) requiring properties to be connected to sewer systems;[13] and
(j) limiting the destruction of, and changes in, landmarks.[14]

State power to regulate the ownership and use of land and other properties is subject, in the United States, to the Equal Protection Clause of the Fourteenth Amendment which forbids invidious or unreasonable discriminations.[15] The United States Supreme Court at one time sustained states that desired to ban ownership of agricultural lands by aliens;[16] but resident aliens are entitled to Equal Protection of the Laws and currently the Supreme Court would probably rule otherwise. However, nonresident aliens are generally thought not to be entitled to the benefits of that clause since they are not "within the jurisdiction," as required by its language, and there are state decisions holding valid statutes disqualifying nonresident aliens from owning land within the state.[17] There is always the possiblity that such statutes may be void as violative of federal treaties or as impermissible interferences with foreign affairs.[18]

Argentine provinces have been able to destroy private property when necessary for the common good, without having to make compensation to the owners.[19] However, the Supreme Court of Argentina has voided as an unreasonable interference with the property right, a provincial statute requiring the removal of all private hospitals to sites on the edge of a city within thirty days.[20]

The Grundgesetz of the German Federal Republic provides that "property and the right of inheritance are guaranteed,"[21] but it is not anticipated that regulation of the use of private property by the Laender will readily be judicially voided.

In the federal societies that were once part of the British Empire, the states can generally regulate the ownership, use, and disposition of private property free from substantive due process clauses. Courts are not inclined to hold unreasonable and unconstitutional state controls, so long as they are not *ultra vires* under the federal constitutional allocation of powers.

In Canada, § 92(13) of the British North America Act giving the provinces power to legislate in regard to "property and civil rights in the province," has been the basis for considerable provincial regulation of the ownership, use, and disposition of property.[22] Under this section, Canadian provinces can destroy and confiscate private property without having to make compensation.[23] Provincial laws based upon this section have also been supported at times by § 92(16), giving the provinces power to make laws affecting "generally all matters of a merely local or private nature in the province."

In sustaining Ontario's Prohibition Act, the Privy Council remarked: "A law which prohibits retail transactions and restricts the consumption of liquor within the ambit of the province, and does not affect transactions in liquor between persons in the province and persons in other provinces or in foreign countries, concerns property in the province."[24] In regulating the ownership or use of private property, Canadian provinces have not traditionally been subject to a rule of reasonableness nor to an equal protection clause limiting discrimination.[25] However, the Constitution Act of 1981 has, in § 15(1), an equal protection clause[26] and, henceforth, the provinces' statutes affecting private property may be judicially voided if they contain unreasonable classifications.

In Canada, as well as in other federal systems, characterization powers of the courts may result in the invalidation of provincial controls of the use of private property. Thus, the Privy Council concluded British Columbia's regulation of the operation of mines to exclude Chinese workers was more a matter of "aliens" than of "property" and, the former being an exclusive Dominion concern, the law was voided.[27] Under the British North America Act, § 91(19) gives the Dominion sole power over "interest," and this has at times resulted in voiding attempts by the provinces to reduce interest on obligations.[28] By § 91(21) of the Act, all matters involving "bankruptcy and insolvency" are also exclusive dominion competences.

In India, a citizen has the constitutional right "to acquire, hold and dispose of property,"[29] but the Constitution also adds that this does not "prevent the State from making any law imposing reasonable restrictions on the exercise of the right."[30]

In Australia, the Constitutional clause requiring "just terms" when property is taken is binding only upon the Commonwealth, and not upon the states.[31]

§ 2.07 State power to acquire property

States in federal societies have often been characterized as "sovereigns" or at least "quasi-sovereigns" and they customarily possess the sovereign power to acquire property, without the consent of the owner. This is, says the High Court of Australia, "a power inherent in sovereignty." The Court added: "The only condition of its exercise is that the property, real or personal, shall at the moment of the exercising of the power of expropriation be within the territorial limits of the State."[1]

In Australia, the compulsory acquisition of property by the states may run afoul of § 92 of the Constitution—the interstate commerce clause. Thus, the High Court has set aside, as an impermissible interference with freedom of interstate commerce, a Queensland peanut marketing scheme under which all of the crop of peanuts automatically vested in the state, so that growers could not negotiate or consummate sales into interstate commerce. "Compulsory acquisition," said Justice Rich, "may directly operate to interfere with the freedom of interstate commerce."[2] Six years later, Justice Evatt explained the effect of the commerce clause upon state power of expropriation. He said: "If the object is to prohibit or limit trade, including trade among the States, section 92 forbids it. If the object is otherwise, section 92 has nothing to say about the matter."[3]

The Australian constitutional clause requiring "just terms" when the Commonwealth takes property, is inapplicable to the states.[4]

Generally, states in federal societies which were formerly part of the British Empire are not under constitutional obligations to make compensation when private property is expropriated for the common weal.[5]

In the United States, the Fourteenth Amendment compels the states to make just compensation when they take private property.[6] Under the Due Process Clause of that Amendment it has traditionally been said that states can take private property only for "public uses";[7] but the Supreme Court today virtually accepts every determination of a state legislature that the acquisition with compensation of private property is for a public use.[8]

In the United States, the exercise of all state powers affecting private rights must be reasonable, and such a limitation exists in theory when states are exercising their power to take private property;[9] but courts today can be expected to defer greatly to the decision of a state legislature that a particular taking is reasonable under the circumstances prevailing locally.[10]

By the Argentine Constitution, previous payment of compensation must be made by the provinces before they take private property,[11] and the compensation must be just.[12] So, too, in Brazil, prior and just compensation must be paid.[13] In both countries expropriation can only be for public purposes.[14]

In the German Federal Republic, expropriation is permitted, but only "in the public weal" with compensation required and judicial review of the adequacy of the compensation offered.[15]

In states not having the residuum of power under the federal constitutions, they must rely upon constitutional grants to enable them to acquire property, but such grants are present in virtually all federal systems. For example, in Canada, the British North America Act in section 92(13) confers upon the provinces power to expropriate private property.[16] Although not generally accepted, the idea persists that the provinces, in expropriating private property, are limited to the legislative areas authorized to them by the BNA Act.[17] In Canada, the provinces are not under any federal constitutional compulsion to make compensation for private property expropriated.[18] It is uncertain whether the granted power to expropriate property enables the provinces to reach property owned by the Dominion.[19]

In India, the adequacy of compensation to be paid when property is expropriated by the states has been made nonjusticiable by constitutional amendment, but the law authorizing the taking must fix the compensation or specify the principles to determine the amount of compensation.[20] By Article 31(2) of the Constitution of India, property can only be taken "for a public purpose," but courts have deferred to legislative determinations that particular takings were for a public purpose.[21] Article 18 of the Constitution (the equality clause) is violated by statutes authorizing the taking of private property when they employ unreasonable classifications.[22]

In virtually all the federal societies, property found at the death of the owner without known heirs escheats to the state in which it is situated.[23] Bank deposits can be escheated by the state in which the bank is located.[24] The United States Supreme Court, in 1951, allowed the state of corporate domicile to escheat unclaimed stock in the corporation.[25] Ten years later, the same Court refused to allow Pennsylvania, the state where unclaimed and unpaid telegraphic money orders originated, to escheat the funds which were being held by a New York corporation.[26] In 1965, the Court ruled generally that escheat can be effectuated by the state of each creditor's last known address on the books of the company owing the funds; if there is no such address, the funds can escheat to the state of the debtor company's domicile, at least until an address of the creditor is discovered and that state provides for escheat.[27]

§ 2.08 State fiscal powers

States having the residuum of power in federal societies have plenary power to spend, being confined only by constitutional clauses such as those banning establishment of a state religion[1] or religion generally.[2] The due process clause of the Fourteenth Amendment to the United States Constitution was once generally thought to restrict state spending to "public purposes,"[3] but currently the United States Supreme Court seems willing to accept the determination of state legislatures that particular expenditures are for public purposes.[4]

In federal societies where the component entities do not have the residuum of power, their spending power may be limited in areas over which they have been granted legislative power in the federal constitution. However, Canadian Provinces seem to feel that their spending powers are not so restricted,[5] and this broad view of state spending powers will likely prevail not only in Canada,[6] but also in other federal societies where the states operate under specific grants of legislative power in federal constitutions.

In federal societies where the states possess only powers granted to them in the constitution, their power to borrow may be somewhat restricted. In India, the states cannot float foreign loans, being limited to (a) borrowing money from the Government of India; or (b) securing from that Government guarantees of bond issues.[7]

§ 2.09 State power to regulate the federal government, and those associated with it

States in federal societies cannot generally impose regulatory controls upon the federal government so as to prevent, or seriously impede, the accomplishment of federal responsibilities or the execution of valid federal powers.[1] "The United States," said the Supreme Court in 1931, "may perform its functions without conforming to the police regulations of a state."[2] The denial of the power of the Australian States to bind the Commonwealth has generally been accepted.[3] In ruling that New South Wales could not deny the Commonwealth's priority over other creditors when a company was being dissolved, the High Court probably established the broader proposition that states cannot deny Commonwealth rights, nor bind the Commonwealth when it is dealing—within its admitted powers—with the rights and duties of Commonwealth citizens.[4]

A 1918 decision held that the Dominion of Canada was not bound by Ontario's arbitration act,[5] but a 1933 ruling held that another Ontario statute could bind the Dominion.[6] The Supreme Court has held, in 1948, that a provincial minimum wage act is inapplicable to the Dominion in its relation to its postal workers,[7] and it would be surprising if that Court allowed any province to seriously interfere with the Dominion in exercising its powers assigned to it by the British North America Act. In such assigned areas, it is agreed that the Dominion Parliament can prevent provincial interference.[8]

To some extent, states in federal societies have been able to regulate federal personnel while performing their duties. The High Court of Australia held, in 1925, that Victoria could punish a member of the Royal Australian Air Force for driving an RAAF vehicle in that state on RAAF business, without having a valid Victorian driver's license.[9] Five years earlier, the United States Supreme Court had held that a state could not compel drivers of mail trucks using the Maryland roads to procure state driver's licenses.[10] It is suggested this ruling is undesirable. The functioning of the federal government would not be seriously burdened if in hiring drivers for mail trucks, it required applicants to produce local driver's licenses. There are many instances where it is sound federalism to allow the states to apply their laws to federal personnel. In the Johnson Case, the Supreme Court remarked:

> Of course, an employee of the United States does not secure a general immunity from state law while acting in the course of his employ-ment. . . . It very well may be that, when the United States has not spoken, the subjection to local law would extend to general rules that might affect incidentally the mode of carrying out the employment—as, for instance, a statute or ordinance regulating the mode of turning at the corner of streets.[11]

There is some Canadian authority indicating that Provincial laws can apply to Dominion personnel driving cars in careless or unsafe manners, at least in the absence of superior orders requiring breach of the statute.[12]

Federal instrumentalities often are private entities (e.g., the national banks in the United States) performing some functions deemed by federal authorities to be necessary to the functioning of that government. It is clear in the United States that Congress can prevent their regulation by the states when they are aiding in the performance of federal functions.[13] Generally, however, it is suggested that privately owned for-profit organi-zations, only remotely of help to the federal government, should be amenable to the laws of the state in which they operate, in common with all other citizens and entities. The High Court of Australia has held that a company chartered by the Commonwealth Government in Victoria was not a federal instrumentality, and was subject to Victorian price controls.[14] Persons and corporations simply dealing with the United States federal government are not thereby immunized from applicable state laws.[15] Thus, the United States Supreme Court has ruled that a state could impose its safety regulations governing construction upon a contractor erecting a post office for the federal government.[16]

In the language of Canadian jurisprudence, provinces cannot "steri-lize" federally incorporated companies, in the sense that it was once held that the provinces could not prevent the accomplishment of the powers authorized by the Dominion.[17] More recently, however, it is being recognized that such federally incorporated companies can be subjected to many provincial statutes.[18] Chief Justice Laskin in 1975 said that federally incorporated companies have a constitutional right in any province "to establish themselves as viable corporate entities (beyond the mere fact of their incorporation) as by raising capital through issue of shares and debentures. . . ," and then he added with great significance: "Beyond this, they are subject to competent provincial regulations in respect of business or actions which fall within provincial legislative power."[19] This language has been accepted as authoritative on later occasions.[20]

Canadian courts have also applied the doctrine that any companies subject to federal regulation cannot be subjected to provincial laws which affect vital aspects of the management and operation of the company.[21] Said the Supreme Court in 1966: "All matters which are a vital part of the operation of an interprovincial undertaking as a going concern are matters which are subject to the exclusive legislative control of the federal Parliament."[22]

Federal governments frequently have exclusive jurisdiction over certain areas, and the states, accordingly, are unable to impose their regulatory controls in those areas, without the consent of federal authorities. The Australian Constitution, for example, provides that the Commonwealth Parliament "shall . . . have exclusive power to make laws . . . with respect to the seat of government of the Commonwealth, and all places acquired by the Commonwealth for public purposes."[23] The High Court has held that New South Wales legislation governing safety provisions for workers could not be applied at an R.A.A.F. base in that State.[24] Commonwealth legislation provides generally that state law will now apply in such areas, unless inconsistent with Commonwealth law.[25] In the United States, there are "exclusive" and "non-exclusive" federal enclaves. In the former, State law cannot apply without the consent of Congress.[26] In the latter, if the state has reserved powers when the federal government acquired the area, it can apply those of its police power regulations which do not clash with federal law, or do not interfere with the performance of the federal function.[27]

§ 2.10 State power to regulate national concerns—generally

In federal societies, even where the constitution does not explicitly confer upon the federal government exclusive legislative authority over a particular matter, courts will deny power over such a matter to the states and provinces when the matter requires uniformity of control throughout the society or, for any other reason, it is clear to the courts that it is of such overwhelming national interest that it must be dealt with, if at all, by the central government.

At times, control of aviation and airports is assigned by the constitution to the federal government,[1] but even in the absence of such explicit grant of exclusive power, courts have seen the need to restrain state and provincial power in this matter. When, for example, a city in Manitoba, under provincial authority, enacted a by-law forbidding construction of an airport, the Supreme Court of Canada voided the legislation, explaining that this is a "matter of national interest and importance" and hence, *ipso facto,* beyond provincial legislation.[2] The Canadian Supreme Court recalled the language of Viscount Simon, who had said that where a matter "is such that it goes beyond local or provincial concern or interests and must from its inherent nature be the concern of the Dominion as a whole," it would be an exclusive Dominion concern.[3] In the Manitoba case, Justice Kerwin stated: "If, therefore, the subject of aeronautics goes beyond local or provincial concern because it has attained such dimensions as to affect the body politic of Canada," the matter fell within the "Peace, Order and Good Government" Clause conferring power on the Dominion Parliament, and removing it from provincial jurisdiction.[4] Later Canadian cases have held that federally licensed airports are not subject to local government by-laws.[5]

Although the Constitution of Australia does not specifically confer legislative power over aeronautics upon the Commonwealth Parliament, it is generally conceded that there, too, this matter is one of primary federal concern.[6]

Matters are apt to be of national concern and hence beyond state regulation where uniformity of control is required by the nature of the subject matter. At a time prior to the adoption of the Twenty-first Amendment to the United States Constitution, Iowa's attempt to cope with the liquor traffic was set aside by the United States Supreme Court on the ground that the problem was national. Said the Court: "Where the subject matter requires a uniform system as between the States, the power controlling it is vested exclusively in Congress, and cannot be encroached upon by the States. . . ."[7] Radio broadcasting and telecasting, by their very nature, require a single control and it is everywhere for the central government even when the constitution is silent on point.[8] There is Canadian authority to the effect that a provincial public utilities commission cannot control "land stations" operated by cable television firms to pick up broadcast signals for relay to their customers.[9]

Matters are also apt to be national, and beyond state competence, when the problem is so large and so universal that a single state simply could not effectively deal with the problem. The Grundgesetz of the German Federal Republic provides for concurrent jurisdiction to the federation whenever "a need for regulation by federal legislation exists," and adds that a matter is one of national concern, for instance, when "a matter cannot be effectively regulated by the legislatures of individual Laender."[10] When, during the most severe depression in American history, California attempted to keep out indigents from other states, the Supreme Court voided the legislation as an impermissible effort to cope with a national problem. The Constitution, implicitly, said the Court, contains "the prohibition against attempts on the part of any single State to isolate itself from difficulties common to all of them by restraining the transportation of persons and property across its borders."[11]

To the federal government belongs "any matter . . . which pertains to it by its nature or kind," states the Constitution of Venezuela.[12]

§ 2.11 State power to regulate national concerns—foreign affairs

Section 1.08 has indicated the constitutional provisions frequently found in federal systems banning states from entering into treaties with foreign powers.

However, there are a number of federal countries wherein the component entities have some power to make treaties and other formal agreements with foreign powers. In Germany, under the 1871 Constitution, the member states could enter into agreements with foreign countries, except on matters exclusively reserved for the Empire.[1] The present German Federal Republic in its Grundgesetz or Basic Law presently provides: "Insofar as legislation falls within the competence of the Laender, these may, with the approval of the Federal Government, conclude treaties with foreign States."[2] The Laender of Bavaria, Baden-Würtemberg and Rhineland-Palatinate had by 1967 concluded a number of agreements with foreign countries.[3]

The Constitution of Switzerland provides that: "In special cases, the Cantons retain the right of concluding treaties with foreign Powers upon the subjects of public economic regulation, cross-frontier intercourse, and police relations; but such treaties shall contain nothing repugnant to the Confederation, or to the rights of the other Cantons."[4] A "great number of treaties" between cantons and foreign states are reported to exist.[5]

In Canada, the British North America Act does not specifically ban treaties by the provinces, the likely assumption at the time of the Act being that the British Parliament would make any necessary treaties for Canada. The provinces can make agreements, other than treaties binding in international law, with states in the United States and even foreign countries,[6] and many are said to exist.[7] All of the provinces maintain Agents-General abroad.[8] Quebec has from time to time claimed a treaty-making power,[9] but its authority in this regard has generally been contested.[10] Although in Canada matters involving aliens are, by the BNA Act, within the exclusive jurisdiction of the Dominion Parliament, the Supreme Court of Canada has sustained a provincial law limiting significantly the right of aliens to own land in the province.[11]

Australian states cannot conclude treaties with foreign countries, but have separate representation in both England and the United States, with State Agents-General and permanent representatives in many foreign cities to promote tourism, immigration, etc. On occasion they have had direct contact with the British Secretary for Commonwealth Relations.[12]

The Constitution of the Union of Soviet Socialist Republics provides: "A Union Republic has the right to enter into relations with other states, conclude treaties with them, exchange diplomatic and consular representatives, and take part in the work of international organizations."[13]

As indicated in section 1.08, both the Constitution of Argentina[14] and that of the United States[15] specifically authorize the constituent political entities to enter into agreements of a limited nature with foreign states, with the consent of the federal congress.

The power of states in the United States to operate in the area of foreign affairs is minimal. In 1968, the Supreme Court voided as unconstitutional a state statute providing generally that foreigners could take lands in the state by inheritance only if, generally, his nation accorded reciprocal rights to Americans. The statute had to fail, said the Court, because it was "an intrusion by the State into the field of foreign affairs which the Constitution entrusts to the President and the Congress."[16] Furthermore, there is state court authority for the proposition that local "Buy American" acts are unconstitutional interferences with the federal foreign relations power.[17]

§ 2.12 State power to regulate national concerns—defence

In federal systems, legislative power to deal with national defence is customarily committed exclusively to the central government.[1] In the German Federal Republic, the Grundgesetz or Basic Law confers the defence power upon the federation,[2] and the Constitutional Court has characterized this as "exclusive," holding that the Laender cannot authorize referenda to pressure the federal authorities on how to, or not to defend the nation.[3]

In Canada, defence is a Dominion concern exclusively.[4] The provinces have also had legislation concerned with internal security voided when such laws invaded the field of "criminal law," exclusively a Dominion concern under the British North America Act.[5]

In Australia, the Commonwealth Parliament is given legislative power over "the naval and military defence of the Commonwealth and of the several States."[6] All important responsibilities in this area will inevitably be those of the central government, but it has at times been suggested that the states may have some powers involving defence, such as participating in the rehabilitation of servicemen[7] and controlling prices in wartime.[8]

In the United States, the individual states have been permitted to participate to a limited extent in the matter of national defence. In 1920, with dissents from Chief Justice White, and Justices Holmes and Brandeis, the Supreme Court allowed a state to punish a person who advocated that others refrain from joining the armed forces.[9] In 1956, federal preemption resulted in voiding a state sedition statute, intended to protect national security;[10] but three years later, the Supreme Court held that "a State could proceed with prosecutions for sedition against the State itself."[11]

The Mexican Constitution provides that without the consent of the Federal Congress, the states shall not "make war themselves on any foreign power, except in cases of invasion and of danger so imminent that it does not admit of delay."[12]

The Constitution of Argentina indicates that: "No Province may declare or wage war against another Province."[13]

§ 2.13 State power to regulate national concerns—aborigines

Canadian law is probably not yet settled on the extent of provincial power over Indians and Indian lands. The British North America Act, in section 91(24), assigns to the Dominion Parliament exclusive authority over "Indians and lands reserved to Indians." Professor Abel, in the fourth edition of Laskin's *Canadian Constitutional Law,* stated in 1975 that "provincial laws are applicable on a reservation";[1] but Professor Hogg, writing two years later, said Abel's statement was "incorrect."[2] With Chief Justice Laskin and two other Justices dissenting, the Supreme Court had held in 1974 that a province could punish an Indian who had sold to a non-Indian at the Indian's home on an Indian reserve, moose-meat, the sale of which was banned by provincial law.[3] British Columbia courts had earlier held that non-Indians could be punished under provincial laws for shooting game birds on an Indian reserve out of season,[4] but a Manitoba court ruled in 1923 that the province had no power to regulate trapping and hunting by Indians on their own reservation.[5] It is likely that Laskin's views will prevail in time, and that the Dominion government's power to regulate Indian affairs will be seen as a power to insulate them from provincial controls, at least when they are acting on their own reserves.

In the United States, nontribal Indians living off of reservations are subject to the general laws of the state where they reside, unless Congress, as the guardian of the Indian wards, has provided otherwise.[6]

Reservation Indians can be subjected to state controls when they act off the reservation, so long as there is no Congressional preemption or conflict, and so long as the reservation does not discriminate against Indians and is necessary to protect an important interest of the state.[7]

States generally do not have power to regulate the activities of Indians on their own reservations.[8] The right of Indian tribes to make their own laws and be governed by them has often resulted in courts voiding attempts by states to impose their laws on activities occurring on reservations. Thus, Arizona was unable to apply its motor carrier license and use fuel taxes to an enterprise conducted on an Indian reservation by non-Indians.[9] Washington could not impose an excise tax for using motor vehicles, mobile homes, campers, and travel trailers on a reservation.[10]

Some activity on Indian reservations can be regulated by the states, absent Congressional law to the contrary or federal occupation of the field, so long as the state law does not impermissibly interfere with rights of self-government belonging to the tribe.[11] Illustratively, the United States Supreme Court has held a state could impose sales and cigarette taxes on sales at Indian reservations to non-Indians, and compel the Indian vendors to keep required records.[12] Crimes committed by non-Indians against other non-Indians on reservations can be tried in the state courts, unless Congress provides otherwise.[13] However, crimes committed on reservations by or against Indians cannot be tried in the state courts, without consent of the federal Congress.[14] Congress has allowed states to try civil causes involving Indians which have arisen on Indian reservations, but only after a majority of the tribe has given approval.[15] In 1980, the United States Supreme Court stated: "There is no rigid rule by which to resolve whether a particular state law may be applied to an Indian reservation or to tribal members."[16]

State authority over non-Indians acting on tribal reservations has at times been voided because of Congressional preemption.[17]

§ 2.14 State power to regulate national concerns—miscellaneous

Although control of admiralty and maritime matters is generally of federal rather than state concern, states in the United States have been able to apply their pilotage laws to vessels coming into their ports from other states and foreign countries.[1] They have been able to inspect vessels for dangers to health and impose quarantines,[2] and they have been able to impose their employers' liability laws when an injury within their territorial jurisdiction was not covered by federal laws.[3]

In federal societies, matters involving bankruptcy and insolvency are customarily assigned to the federation.[4] However, in the United States, where the grant of power to the federal government is over "bankruptcies," the states have power to enact legislation governing insolvency of municipal corporations,[5] appointing receivers for insolvents,[6] and controlling voluntary assignments by insolvents for benefit of creditors,[7] all so long as they do not discharge debtors from obligations to creditors or otherwise violate the Contract Clause, and do not conflict with legislation enacted by the federal Congress under its bankruptcy powers.

By the constitutions of both Malaysia[8] and the U.S.S.R.,[9] the component entities have legal authority to secede from the federation, although Ozakwe states with reference to the latter that "the right of secession . . . is tantamount to a constitutional farce."[10]

FOOTNOTES

§ 2.00

[1] "There is no doubt that the Legislature of New South Wales can impose such conditions as it thinks proper by way of taxation or otherwise upon persons who carry on business in New South Wales and therefore bring themselves within the legislative authority of the State." Broken Hill South Ltd. v. Commissioner of Taxation (NSW) (1937) 56 C.L.R. 337, 355 (Latham, C.J.).

[2] Nebbia v. New York (1934) 291 US 502, 54 S Ct 505, 78 L Ed 940; Canale v. Mendoza (1913) 118 S.C.N. 278 (Argentina).

[3] McWhinney, *Constitutionalism in Germany and the Federal Constitutional Court* (Leyden 1962) 44.

[4] Vermont Salvage Co. v. St. Johnsbury (1943) 113 Vt. 341, 34 A 2d 188, 194.

[5] The United States Supreme Court states that it is both unable and unwilling "to draw lines by calling a law 'prohibitory' or 'regulatory.'" Ferguson v. Skrupa (1963) 372 US 726, 83 S Ct 1028, 10 L Ed 2d 93; "A municipal ordinance enacted pursuant to the police power . . . cannot be considered invalid merely because it prohibits instead of regulates." Benjamin v. Columbus (1957) 167 Ohio St 103, 146 NE 2d 854, 856. "The right to regulate under proper circumstances has been held to include the right to prohibit . . . . The real question is not whether, under the power to regulate, a municipality can prohibit, but . . . whether the measure is a reasonable exercise of the police power." Chicago National Bank v. Chicago Heights (1958) 14 Ill 2d 135, 150 NE 2d 827, 830.

[6] Queenside Hills Co. v. Saxl (1946) 328 US 80, 83, 66 S Ct 850, 90 L Ed 1096.

[7] Constitution of Brazil 1891, Art. 11(3).

[8] It has "long been accepted that a government may reasonably restrict an owner in the use of his property for the cultural and aesthetic benefit of the community." Society for Ethical Culture v. Spatt (1980) 51 NY 2d 449, 415 NE 2d 922, 925.

[9] State of Bombay v. R.M.D. Chanarbaugwala, A.I.R. (1957) S.C. 699. Section 1.03 treats of this topic generally.

§ 2.01

[1] Constitution of India, State List, Number 6.

[2] Hogg, *Constitutional Law of Canada* (Toronto 1977) 60.

[3] St. Louis du Mile-End v. Montreal (1885) 2 S.C. 218 (quarantine); Levkoe v. The Queen (1977) 18 O.R. 2d 265 (regulation of pharmacy).

[4] Constitution of Switzerland, Article 31(3).

[5] Constitution of India, State List, Number 8; Constitution of Switzerland, Art. 32(4).

[6] Balsora's Case (1951) S.C.R. 682.

[7] McDermott v. Wisconsin (1913) 228 US 115, 33 S Ct 431, 57 L Ed 754.

[8] Cloverleaf Butter Co. v. Patterson (1942) 315 US 148, 62 S Ct 491, 86 L Ed 754 (renovated butter).

[9] "English jurisprudence has always recognized that the Acts of a legislature of limited jurisdiction (whether the limits be as to territory or subject matter) may be examined by any tribunal before whom the point is properly raised. The term 'unconstitutional' used in this connection, means no more than ultra vires." Baxter v. Commissioners of Taxation (1907) 4 C.L.R. 1087, 1125 (Griffith, C.J.).

[10] Pearce, *Delegated Legislation* (Sydney 1977) 199.

[11] British North America Act, § 91(27).

[12] Birks v. Montreal (1955) S.C.R. 799 (ultra vires was Quebec statute in effect allowing the City of Montreal to impose criminal penalties upon persons violating a Sunday closing ordinance).

[13] Nebbia v. New York (1934) 291 US 502, 54 S Ct 505, 78 L Ed 940.

14 Canale v. Mendoza (1913) 118 S.C.N. 278.
15 Huron Portland Cement Co. v. Detroit (1960) 362 US 440, 80 S Ct 813, 4 L Ed 2d 852 (air pollution controls); Head v. New Mexico Board of Examiners in Optometry (1963) 374 US 424, 83 S Ct 1759, 10 L Ed 2d 983 (regulation of sale of eyeglasses); Breard v. Alexandria (1951) 341 US 622, 71 S Ct 920, 95 L Ed 1233 (controls upon house-to-house peddlers and solicitors).
16 Hadacheck v. Sebastian (1915) 239 US 394, 410, 36 S Ct 143, 60 L Ed 348.
17 Savage v. Jones (1912) 225 US 501, 32 S Ct 715, 56 L Ed 1182.
18 Prince v. Massachusetts (1944) 321 US 158, 64 S Ct 438, 88 L Ed 645.
19 Jacobson v. Massachusetts (1905) 197 US 11, 25 S Ct 358, 49 L Ed 643.
20 Braunfeld v. Brown (1961) 366 US 599, 81 S Ct 1144, 6 L Ed 2d 563.
21 North American Cold Storage Co. v. Chicago (1908) 211 US 306, 29 S Ct 101, 53 L Ed 195.
22 Jay Burns Baking Co. v. Bryan (1924) 264 US 504, 44 S Ct 412, 68 L Ed 813.
23 Fischer v. St. Louis (1904) 194 US 361, 24 S Ct 673, 48 L Ed 1018.
24 Head v. New Mexico Board of Examiners in Optometry (1963) 374 US 424, 83 S Ct 1759, 10 L Ed 2d 983.
25 Rasmussen v. Idaho (1901) 181 US 198, 21 S Ct 594, 45 L Ed 820.
26 Ohio ex rel. Eaton v. Price (1960) 364 US 263, 80 S Ct 1463, 4 L Ed 2d 1708.
27 Gardner v. Michigan (1905) 199 US 325, 26 S Ct 106, 50 L Ed 212.
28 Grayned v. Rockford (1972) 408 US 104, 92 S Ct 2294, 33 L Ed 2d 222.
29 Mugler v. Kansas (1887) 123 US 623, 8 S Ct 273, 31 L Ed 205.
30 Austin v. Tennessee (1900) 179 US 343, 21 S Ct 132, 45 L Ed 224.
31 Compagnie Francaise de Navigation a Vapeur v. Louisiana State Board of Health (1902) 186 US 380, 22 S Ct 811, 46 L Ed 1209; Smith v. St. Louis & S.W. Rr. Co. (1901) 181 US 248, 255-6, 21 S Ct 603, 45 L Ed 847.
32 Dean Milk v. Madison (1951) 340 US 349, 71 S Ct 295, 95 L Ed 329.
33 Cf. Allied Stores v. Bowers (1959) 358 US 522, 79 S Ct 437, 441, 3 L Ed 2d 480.
34 People v. Woody (1964) 61 Cal 2d 716, 394 P 2d 813. Contra: Oliver v. Udall (DC Cir 1962) 306 F 2d 819, certiorari denied 372 US 908.
35 Prince v. Massachusetts (1944) 321 US 158, 64 S Ct 438, 88 L Ed 645, 653, 656.
36 Braunfeld v. Brown (1961) 366 US 599, 81 S Ct 1144, 6 L Ed 2d 563 (but note dissents of Brennan and Stewart, Jj.).
37 Application of the President and Directors of Georgetown College (DC Cir 1964) 331 F 2d 1000, 1010, certiorari denied 377 US 978.
38 Harden v. State (1948) 188 Tenn 17, 216 SW 2d 708.
39 Peterson v. Widule (1914) 157 Wis 641, 147 NW 966.
40 State ex rel. Holcomb v. Armstrong (1952) 39 Wash 2d 860, 239 P 2d 545.
41 State v. Harrison (1951) 260 Wis 89, 50 NW 38.
42 Baer v. Bend (1956) 206 Or. 221, 292 P 2d 134.

§ 2.02

1 Pennsylvania Coal Co. v. Mahon (1922) 260 US 393, 43 S Ct 158, 67 L Ed 322; Nebbia v. New York (1934) 291 US 502, 54 S Ct 505, 78 L Ed 940.
2 Goldblatt v. Hempstead (1962) 369 US 590, 82 S Ct 987, 8 L Ed 2d 130.
3 Yick Wo v. Hopkins (1886) 118 US 356, 6 S Ct 1064, 30 L Ed 220; Schware v. Board of Bar Examiners (1957) 353 US 232, 77 S Ct 752, 1 L Ed 2d 796, 802.
4 Atlantic Coast Line Rr. v. Goldsboro (1914) 232 US 548, 34 S Ct 364, 58 L Ed 721.
5 Queenside Hills Realty Co. v. Saxl (1946) 328 US 80, 66 S Ct 850, 90 L Ed 1096.
6 Soon Hing v. Crowley (1885) 113 US 703, 5 S Ct 730, 28 L Ed 1145.
7 Standard Oil Co. v. Marysville (1929) 279 US 582, 49 S Ct 430, 73 L Ed 856.
8 Breard v. Alexandria (1951) 341 US 622, 61 S Ct 920, 95 L Ed 1233.
9 Erb v. Morasch (1900) 177 US 584, 20 S Ct 819, 44 L Ed 897.
10 Nashville Railway v. White (1929) 278 US 456, 49 S Ct 189, 73 L Ed 452.
11 Atchison, Topeka & Santa Fe Rr. v. Public Utilities Commission (1953) 346 US 346, 74 S Ct 92, 98 L Ed 51.

[12] Sullivan v. Shreveport (1919) 251 US 169, 40 S Ct 102, 64 L Ed 205.
[13] Railway Express Co. v. New York (1949) 336 US 106, 69 S Ct 463, 93 L Ed 533.
[14] South Carolina State Highway Department v. Barnwell Bros. (1938) 303 US 177, 58 S Ct 510, 82 L Ed 734; Kerr v. Pelly (1957) 97 C.L.R. 310.
[15] Lindsley v. Natural Carbonic Gas Co. (1911) 220 US 61, 31 S Ct 337, 55 L Ed 369.
[16] Railway Express Co. v. New York (1949) 336 US 106, 69 S Ct 463, 93 L Ed 533.
[17] Kotch v. Board of River Pilot Commissioners (1947) 330 US 552, 67 S Ct 910, 91 L Ed 1093.
[18] Thornhill v. Alabama (1940) 310 US 88, 60 S Ct 736, 84 L Ed 1093.
[19] "Courts must balance the various community interests in passing on the constitutionality of local regulations of the character involved here. But in that process they should be mindful to keep the freedoms of the First Amendment in a preferred position." Saia v. New York (1948) 334 US 558, 68 S Ct 1148, 92 L Ed 1574, 1578.
[20] Lane, *The Australian Federal System* (2d ed. 1979, Sydney) 1135-1174.
[21] British North America Act, § 92(10).
[22] Montreal v. Montreal Street Ry. (1912) A.C. 333; British Columbia Electric Ry. v. C.N.R. (1932) S.C.R. 161.
[23] Attorney-General for Ontario v. Winner (1954) A.C. 541 (dictum).
[24] Re Tank Truck Transport (1960) O.R. 497 (Ont. H. Ct.) affirmed (Ont. S. Ct.); R. v. Cooksville Magistrate Court; ex parte Liquid Cargo Lines Ltd. (1963) 1 O.R. 272, (1965) 1 O.R. 84 (Ont. H. Ct.).
[25] R. v. Barry (N.B. 1950) 1 D.L.R. 284.
[26] Attorney-General for Ontario v. Winner (1954) 4 D.L.R. 657; Regina v. Letco Bulk Carriers Inc. (Ont. H. Ct. 1979) 105 D.L.R. 3d 725, 729.
[27] Hughes & Vale Pty. Ltd. v. New South Wales (#1) (1953) 80 C.L.R. 432.
[28] Kerr v. Pelly (1957) 97 C.L.R. 310 (requirement trucks detour slightly and stop at a state weighing station); Boardman v. Duddington (1959) 104 C.L.R. 456 (reasonable road charges); Armstrong v. Victoria (#2) (1957) 99 C.L.R. 28 (same).
[29] Castle v. Hayes Freight Lines (1954) 348 US 61, 75 S Ct 191, 99 L Ed 68; New York Central Rr. v. Winfield (1917) 244 US 147, 37 S Ct 546, 61 L Ed 1045; Southern Rr. v. Indiana Railroad Commission (1915) 236 US 439, 35 S Ct 304, 59 L Ed 661.
[30] Napier v. Atlantic Coast Line Rr. (1926) 272 US 605, 47 S Ct 207, 71 L Ed 432.

§ 2.03

[1] Constitution of India, State List, Number 34; State of Bombay v. R.M.D. Chanarbaugwala, A.I.R. (1957) S.C. 699.
[2] R. v. Lichtman (1923) 54 O.L.R. 502.
[3] Switzman v. Elbling (1957) S.C.R. 285.
[4] R. v. Lichtman (1923) 54 O.L.R. 502.
[5] R. v. Fink (1967) 2 O.R. 132.
[6] Stone v. Mississippi (1880) 101 US 814, 25 L Ed 1079.
[7] People v. Lim (1941) 18 Cal 2d 872, 118 P 2d 472; Buenos Aires v. Diaz (1905) 101 S.C.N. 126.
[8] Dallman v. Luchesky (1938) 229 Wis 169, 282 NW 9.
[9] California v. LaRue (1972) 409 US 109, 93 S Ct 390, 34 L Ed 2d 342.
[10] Bedard v. Dawson (1923) S.C.R. 681 (prohibiting use of property as a disorderly house); Carpenter v. Boyles (1938) 213 NC 432, 196 SE 850.
[11] Smith v. Keater (1974) 419 US 1043, 95 S Ct 613, 42 L Ed 2d 636.
[12] Murphy v. California (1912) 225 US 623, 32 S Ct 697, 56 L Ed 1229.
[13] Clarke v. Deckebach (1927) 274 US 392, 47 S Ct 630, 71 L Ed 1115.
[14] Miller v. California (1973) 413 US 15, 93 S Ct 2607, 37 L Ed 2d 419.
[15] Empresa de Toras v. Buenos Aires (1869) 7 S.C.N. 450.
[16] Morley v. Oak Bay Corporation (B.C. 1923) 1 D.L.R. 869.
[17] Cf. Nebbia v. New York (1934) 291 US 502, 54 S Ct 505, 78 L Ed 940.

18   California v. LaRue (1972) 409 US 109, 93 S Ct 390, 34 L Ed 2d 342; Miller v. California (1973) 413 US 15, 93 S Ct 2607, 37 L Ed 2d 419; State v. Renendsland (1955) 160 Neb 206, 69 NW 2d 860 (prohibiting lewd and indecent acts in public).
19   Stanley v. Georgia (1969) 394 US 557, 89 S Ct 1243, 22 L Ed 2d 542.
20   Winters v. New York (1947) 333 US 507, 68 S Ct 665, 92 L Ed 840; Butler v. Michigan (1957) 352 US 380, 77 S Ct 524, 1 L Ed 2d 412; Near v. Minnesota (1931) 283 US 697, 51 S Ct 625, 75 L Ed 1357; Joseph Burstyn Inc. v. Wilson (1952) 343 US 495, 72 S Ct 777, 96 L Ed 1098; Gelling v. Texas (1952) 343 US 960, 72 S Ct 1002, 96 L Ed 1359; Superior Films v. Department of Education (1954) 346 US 587, 74 S Ct 286, 98 L Ed 329.
21   Clarke v. Deckebach (1927) 274 US 392, 47 S Ct 630, 71 L Ed 1115.

§ 2.04

1   Constitution of Nigeria, First Schedule, Part II(7); Constitution of India, State List, Entry 1; Constitution of Canada, § 92(13); Constitution of Malaysia, State List, Number 9.
2   Plumley v. Massachusetts (1894) 155 US 461, 15 S Ct 154, 39 L Ed 223; Florida Lime & Avocado Growers v. Paul (1963) 373 US 132, 83 S Ct 1210, 10 L Ed 2d 248.
3   Smith v. The Queen (1960) S.C.R. 776; R. v. McKenzie Securities Ltd. (1966) 56 D.L.R. 2d 56.
4   Highland Farms Dairy v. Agnew (1937) 300 US 608, 57 S Ct 549, 81 L Ed 835; Home Oil Distributors Ltd. v. Attorney-General for British Columbia (1940) 2 D.L.R. 609; Carnation Co. Ltd. v. Quebec Agricultural Marketing Board (1968) 67 D.L.R. 2d 1; Indian Constitution, Concurrent List #34.
5   "Professional regulation is within the competence of the provincial Legislature." Levkoe v. The Queen (1977) 18 O.R. 2d 265 (pharmacy); Dent v. West Virginia (1889) 129 US 114, 9 S Ct 231, 32 L Ed 623.
6   Grundgesetz, Art. 74, Number 22.
7   BVerfGE 32, 319.
8   Television Judgment of 1961, BVerfGE 12, 205. "Broadcasting is one of the few fields of importance remaining almost exclusively in hands of the Laender." Blair, *Federalism and Judicial Review in West Germany* (Oxford 1981) 253. Braunthal, "Federalism in Germany: the Broadcasting Controversy," 24 *J of Pols.* 545 (1962); Concordat Case (1957) BVerfGE 6, 309.
9   Constitution of India, List I, Entry 63.
10   Gujarat University, Ahmedabad v. Krishna Ranganath Modholkar (1963) 1 S.C.R. 112.
11   Constitution of Canada (British North America Act) 93.
12   Bob-lo Excursion Co. v. Michigan (1948) 333 US 28, 68 S Ct 358, 92 L Ed 455; Pittsburgh Press Co. v. Pittsburgh Commission on Human Relations (1973) 413 US 376, 93 S Ct 2553, 37 L Ed 2d 669; Colorado Anti-Discrimination Commission v. Continental Air Lines (1963) 372 US 714, 83 S Ct 1022, 10 L Ed 2d 84; R. v. McKay (1956) 5 D.L.R. 2d 403 (Ontario Fair Accommodation Provision Act).

§ 2.05

1   Constitution of Australia, § 107.
2   Broken Hill South Ltd. v. Commissioner of Taxation (NSW) (1937) 56 C.L.R. 337, 355 (Latham, C.J.).
3   "A subject of the Queen, resident in any State, shall not be subject in any other State to any disability or discrimination which would not be equally applicable to him if he were a subject of the Queen resident in such other State." Constitution of Australia, § 117.
4   Davies and Jones v. Western Australia (1904) 2 C.L.R. 29, 38 (Griffith, C.J.); Chapman v. Suttle (1963) 110 C.L.R. 321, 346 (Windeyer, J.).
5   Baxter v. Commissioners of Taxation (1907) 4 C.L.R. 1087, 1125.
6   Allgeyer v. Louisiana (1897) 165 US 578, 17 S Ct 427, 41 L Ed 832.
7   Nebbia v. New York (1934) 291 US 502, 54 S Ct 505, 78 L Ed 940.
8   Ferguson v. Skrupa (1963) 372 US 726, 731, 83 S Ct 1028, 10 L Ed 2d 93.

9 Williamson v. Lee Optical Co. (1955) 348 US 483, 75 S Ct 461, 464, 99 L Ed 563; and cf.
   Carolene Products Co. v. United States (1944) 323 US 18, 65 S Ct 1, 89 L Ed 15.
10 Railroad Commission Cases (1886) 116 US 307, 6 S Ct 334, 29 L Ed 636.
11 Hall v. Geiger Jones Co. (1917) 242 US 539, 37 S Ct 217, 61 L Ed 480.
12 Dent v. West Virginia (1889) 129 US 114, 9 S Ct 231, 32 L Ed 623; Smith v. Texas (1914)
   233 US 630, 34 S Ct 681, 58 L Ed 1129.
13 Muller v. Oregon (1908) 208 US 412, 28 S Ct 324, 52 L Ed 551.
14 Olsen v. Nebraska (1941) 313 US 236, 61 S Ct 862, 85 L Ed 1305.
15 Nebbia v. New York (1934) 291 US 502, 54 S Ct 505, 78 L Ed 940.
16 West Coast Hotel Co. v. Parrish (1937) 300 US 379, 57 S Ct 578, 81 L Ed 703.
17 Day-Brite Lighting Co. v. Missouri (1952) 342 US 421, 72 S Ct 405, 96 L Ed 469.
18 Williamson v. Lee Optical Co. (1955) 348 US 483, 75 S Ct 461, 99 L Ed 563.
19 Plumley v. Massachusetts (1894) 155 US 461, 15 S Ct 154, 39 L Ed 223; Hutchinson Ice
   Cream Co. v. Iowa (1916) 242 US 153, 37 S Ct 28, 61 L. Ed 217.
20 Rast v. Van Deman & L. Co. (1916) 240 US 342, 36 S Ct 370, 60 L Ed 679.
21 Standard Oil Co. v. Tennessee (1910) 217 US 413, 30 S Ct 543, 54 L Ed 817.
22 Savage v. Jones (1912) 225 US 501, 32 S Ct 715, 56 L Ed 1182.
23 Bob-lo Excursion Co. v. Michigan (1948) 333 US 28, 68 S Ct 358, 92 L Ed 455.
24 Barbier v. Connolly (1885) 113 US 27, 5 S Ct 357, 28 L Ed 923.
25 Munn v. Illinois (1877) 94 US 113, 24 L Ed 77.
26 Mugler v. Kansas (1887) 123 US 623, 8 S Ct 273, 31 L Ed 205.
27 Austin v. Tennessee (1900) 179 US 343, 21 S Ct 132, 45 L Ed 224.
28 Murphy v. California (1912) 225 US 623, 32 S Ct 697, 56 L Ed 1229.
29 Dent v. West Virginia (1889) 129 US 114, 9 S Ct 231, 32 L Ed 623.
30 Daniel v. Family Life Insurance Co. (1949) 336 US 220, 69 S Ct 550, 93 L Ed 632.
31 Old Dominion Distributing Co. v. Seagram Distillers Corp. (1936) 299 US 183, 57 S Ct
   139, 81 L Ed 109.
32 Safeway Stores v. Oklahoma Retail Grocers Association (1959) 360 US 334, 79 S Ct
   1196, 3 L Ed 2d 1280.
33 Ferguson v. Skrupa (1963) 372 US 726, 83 S Ct 1028, 10 L Ed 2d 93.
34 Ex parte Ivanissevich (1913) 117 S.C.N. 432.
35 Barreda v. San Juan, XLII J.A. 593 (1933).
36 Russell v. The Queen (1882) 7 A.C. 829, 837.
37 Citizens Insurance Co. v. Parsons (1881) 7 A.C. 96.
38 Re Imrie (1972) 3 O.R. 275; R. v. Buzunis (1972) 4 W.W.R. 337.
39 Oil, Chemical and Atomic Workers v. Imperial Oil (1963) S.C.R. 584, 33 D.L.R. 2d 732.
40 Home Oil Distributors Ltd. v. Attorney-General for British Columbia (1940) 2 D.L.R.
   609; Carnation Co. Ltd. v.Quebec Agricultural Marketing Board (1968) 67 D.L.R. 2d 1.
41 Shannon v. Lower Mainland Dairy Prod. Bd. (B.C.) (1938) 4 D.L.R. 81 (A.C.); Prince
   Edward Island Marketing Bd. v. Willis (1952) 4 D.L.R. 146, 166 (Rand, J.).
42 Montreal v. Beauvais (1909) 42 S.C.R. 211.
43 Smith v. The Queen (1960) S.C.R. 776.
44 Attorney-General for Ontario v. Barfried Enterprises (1963) S.C.R. 570.
45 Dalaire v. Quebec (1907) 32 Q.S.C. 118; Ouimet v. Bazin (1912) 3 D.L.R. 593;
   Attorney-General for Ontario v. Hamilton Street Railway (1903) A.C. 524; In re Grain
   Marketing Act (1931) 25 Sask. L.R. 273; Wilder v. Montreal (1905) 14 Quebec K.B. 139
   (ban on trading stamps).
46 Union Colliery Case (1899) A.C. 580.
47 Henry Birks and Sons v. Montreal (1955) (1958) S.C.R. 799; Attorney-General for
   Ontario v. Hamilton Street Railway (1903) A.C. 524 (Ontario Lord's Day Act); Ouimet
   v. Bazin (1912) 3 D.L.R. 593 (Quebec Sunday Observance Act).
48 British North America Act, § 91(19).
49 Constitution of India, Art. 19(g).
50 Constitution of India, Art. 19(5).
51 Constitution of Venezuela 1961, Article 96.

§ 2.06

1 Pennsylvania Coal Co. v. Mahon (1922) 260 US 393, 43 S Ct 158, 67 L Ed 322.
2 Goldblatt v. Hempstead (1962) 369 US 590, 82 S Ct 987, 8 L Ed 2d 130.
3 People v. Stover (1963) 12 NY 2d 462, 240 NYS 2d 734, 191 NE 2d 272; and cf. Berman v. Parker (1954) 348 US 26, 75 S Ct 98, 99 L Ed 27.
4 Goldblatt v. Hempstead (1962) 369 US 590, 82 S Ct 987, 8 L Ed 2d 130.
5 Hadacheck v. Sebastian (1915) 239 US 394, 36 S Ct 143, 60 L Ed 348.
6 Reinman v. Little Rock (1915) 237 US 171, 35 S Ct 511, 59 L Ed 900.
7 Euclid v. Ambler Realty Co. (1926) 272 US 365, 47 S Ct 114, 71 L Ed 303.
8 Goldblatt v. Hempstead (1962) 369 US 590, 82 S Ct 987, 8 L Ed 2d 130.
9 Miller v. Schoene (1928) 276 US 272, 48 S Ct 246, 72 L Ed 568.
10 Thomas Cusack Co. v. Chicago (1917) 242 US 526, 37 S Ct 190, 61 L Ed 472.
11 Gorieb v. Fox (1927) 274 US 603, 47 S Ct 675, 71 L Ed 1228.
12 Queenside Hills Realty Co. v. Saxl (1946) 328 US 80, 66 S Ct 850, 90 L Ed 1096.
13 Hutchinson v. Valdosta (1913) 227 US 303, 33 S Ct 290, 57 L Ed 520.
14 Penn Central Transportation Co. v. New York City (1978) 438 US 104, 98 S Ct 2646, 57 L Ed 2d 631.
15 Yick Wo v. Hopkins (1886) 118 US 356, 6 S Ct 1064, 30 L Ed 220.
16 Terrace v. Thompson (1923) 263 US 197, 44 S Ct 15, 68 L Ed 255. But compare: Fujii v. State (1952) 38 Cal 2d 718, 242 P 2d 617; Namba v. McCourt (1948) 185 Or 579, 204 P 2d 569.
17 Lehndorf Geneva Inc. v. Warren (1976) 74 Wis 2d 369, 247 NW 2d 815.
18 Fisch, State Regulation of Alein Land Ownership, 43 Mo. L. Rev. 407 (1978).
19 Podesta v. Buenos Aires (1887) 31 S.C.N. 273.
20 Canale v. Mendoza (1913) 118 S.C.N. 278.
21 Grundgesetz of German Federal Republic, Art. 14.
22 Bedard v. Dawon (1923) S.C.R. 681 (could prohibit use of property as a disorderly house); Morgan v. Prince Edward Island (1976) 55 D.L.R. 3d 527, 533 (dictum).
23 Florence Mining Co. v. Cobalt Lake Mining Co. (1909) 18 O.L.R. 275, affirmed 43 O.L.R. 474 (P.C.).
24 Attorney-General for Ontario v. Attorney-General for Canada (1896) A.C. 348, 364; Semble: Regina v. Gautreau (N.B.S.Ct. 1978) 88 D.L.R. 3d 718.
25 Morgan v. Prince Edward Island (1976) 55 D.L.R. 3d 527 (restricting the ownership of land by nonresidents); Walter v. Attorney-General for Alberta (1969) S.C.R. 383 (restricting ownership of land by communal religious groups).
26 "Every individual is equal before and under the law and has the right to the equal protection and equal benefit of the law without discrimination . . . ." Constitution Act 1981, § 15(1).
27 Union Colliery v. Bryden (1899) A.C. 580.
28 Saskatchewan Farm Security Reference; Attorney-General for Saskatchewan v. Attorney-General for Canada (1949) A.C. 110.
29 Constitution of India, Art. 19(f).
30 Constitution of India, Art. 19(5).
31 Constitution of Australia, Part V, § 51, placitum xxxi: "The acquisition of property on just terms from any State or person for any purpose in respect of which the Parliament has power to make laws."

§ 2.07

1 New South Wales v. Commonwealth (The Wheat Case) (1915) 20 C.L.R. 54, 66 (Griffith, C.J.)
2 Peanut Board v. Rockhampton Harbour Board (1933) 48 C.L.R. 266, 275.
3 Milk Board (NSW) v. Metropolitan Cream Pty. Ltd. (1939) 62 C.L.R. 116, 151.
4 Part V, Section 51, placitum xxxi.
5 New South Wales v. Commonwealth (The Wheat Case) (1915) 20 C.L.R. 54; Florence

Mining Co. v. Cobalt Lake Mining Co. (1909) 18 C.L.R. 275, 279 (Riddell, J.), affirmed 43 O.L.R. 474 (P.C.).

6 Chicago Rr. v. Chicago (1897) 166 US 226, 17 S Ct 581, 41 L Ed 979.

7 Cincinnati v. Vester (1930) 281 US 439, 50 S Ct 360, 74 L Ed 950.

8 Fallbrook Irrigation Dist. v. Bradley (1896) 164 US 112, 17 S Ct 56, 63, 41 L Ed 369; And cf. Berman v. Parker (1954) 348 US 26, 75 S Ct 98, 99 L Ed 27.

9 Opinion of the Justices (1957) 152 Me 440, 131 A 2d 904; David Jeffrey Co. v. Milwaukee (1954) 267 Wis 559, 66 NW 2d 362, 370-1; San Francisco v. Ross (1955) 44 Cal 2d 52, 279 P 2d 529, 532-3.

10 Board of Education v. Park District (ND 1955) 70 NW 2d 899; Adams v. Housing Authority (Fla 1952) 60 So 2d 663, 669; Phoenix v. McCullough (Ariz App 1975) 536 P 2d 230, 235.

11 Constitution of Argentina, Article 17.

12 Provincia de Santa Fe v. Nicchi, 127 La Ley 164 (1967).

13 Constitution of Brazil (1967) as amended, Article 153(22).

14 Rosenn, "Expropriation in Argentina and Brazil," 15 *Va. J. Intl. L.* 277, 281 (1974).

15 Grundgesetz of German Federal Republic, Art. 14(3).

16 McAfee v. Irving Refining Co. (1970) 17 D.L.R. 3d 729; Canadian Gas & Oil Co. v. Saskatchewan (1976) 2 W.W.R. 356.

17 Lajoie, *Expropriation et fédéralisme au Canada* (Montreal 1972) 72-3.

18 Florence Mining Co. v. Cobalt Lake Mining Co. (1909) 18 O.L.R. 275, 279 (Riddell, J.) affirmed 43 O.L.R. 474 (P.C.); Rex v. Stanley (Alberta Ct. App. 1935) (1936) 1 D.L.R. 100.

19 Hogg, *Constitutional Law of Canada* (Toronto 1977) 397.

20 Constitution of India, Articles 31A & 32.

21 State of Bombay v. R.S. Nanji (1956) S.C.R. 18, 26.

22 Vajravelu's Case (1965) A.S.C. 1017.

23 Constitution of India, Article 296; Connecticut Mutual Life Insurance Co. v. Moore (1947) 333 US 541, 68 S Ct 682, 92 L Ed 2d 863.

24 Security Savings Bank v. California (1923) 263 US 282, 44 S Ct 108, 68 L Ed 301.

25 Standard Oil Co. v. New Jersey (1951) 341 US 428, 71 S Ct 822, 95 L Ed 1078.

26 Western Union v. Pennsylvania (1961) 368 US 71, 82 S Ct 199, 7 L Ed 2d 139.

27 Texas v. New Jersey (1965) 379 US 674, 85 S Ct 626, 13 L Ed 2d 596.

§ 2.08

1 Constitution of Nigeria 1979, Ch. I, Art. 10.

2 Constitution of the United States, Amendment I (made binding upon the states by judicial construction of Amendment XIV).

3 Citizens Savings & Loan Ass'n v. Topeka (1874) 20 Wall. 655, 22 L Ed 455; Arens v. Rogers (1953) 240 Minn 386, 61 NW 2d 508, 519, appeal dismissed 347 US 949.

4 Jones v. Portland (1915) 245 US 217, 38 S Ct 112, 62 L Ed 252; Green v. Frazier (1920) 253 US 233, 40 S Ct 499, 64 L Ed 878; Standard Oil Co. v. Lincoln (1927) 275 US 504, 48 S Ct 155, 72 L Ed 395.

5 Re Pacific Western Air Lines (1977) 2 Alta L.R. 272. "Certainly the Provinces have acted as if they had a legally unlimited spending power." LaForest, *The Allocation of Taxing Power under the Canadian Constitution* (Toronto 1981) 75.

6 Hogg, *Constitutional Law of Canada* (Toronto 1977) 72.

7 Seervai, *Constitutional Law of India* (Bombay 1968) 801.

§ 2.09

1 McCulloch v. Maryland (1819) 4 Wheat. 316, 4 L Ed 579; Public Utilities Commission v. United States (1958) 355 US 534, 78 S Ct 446, 2 L Ed 2d 470. But note Commonwealth v. Bogle (1953) 89 C.L.R. 229; "The Commonwealth may, of course, become affected by State laws." (Taylor, J.).

2 Arizona v. California (1931) 283 US 423, 51 S Ct 522, 75 L Ed 1154, 1164.

3   "The reason for the inability of a State to make a law binding on the Commonwealth
    . . . derives from the fact that the Crown has not by the Constitution submitted itself to
    the legislatures of the States." Payroll Tax Case (1969) 122 C.L.R. 353, 373 (Barwick,
    C.J.); Howard, *Australian Federal Constitutional Law* (2d ed. 1972) 102-134; Ex parte
    Goldring (1903) 3 S.R. (NSW) 260 (state courts cannot mandamus federal officers).
4   Commonwealth v. Cigamatic Pty. Ltd. (1962) 108 C.L.R. 372.
5   Gauthier v. The King (1918) 56 S.C.R. 176.
6   Dominion Building Corp. v. The King (1933) A.C. 533.
7   Minimum Wage Act (Sask.) Reference (1948) S.C.R. 248.
8   Hogg, *Constitutional Law in Canada* (Toronto 1977) 94.
9   Pirrie v. McFarlane (1925) 36 C.L.R. 170.
10 Johnson v. Maryland (1920) 254 US 51, 41 S Ct 16, 65 L Ed 126.
11 Ibid., L Ed pp. 128-9.
12 R. v. McLeod (1930) 4 D.L.R. 226; R. v. Stadiotto (1973) 2 O.R. 375. But contra: R. v.
    Rhodes (1934) 1 D.L.R. 251.
13 Franklin National Bank v. New York (1954) 347 US 373, 74 S Ct 550, 98 L Ed 767.
14 Commonwealth v. Bogle (1953) 89 C.L.R. 229.
15 Polar Ice Cream & Creamery Co. v. Andrews (1964) 375 US 361, 84 S Ct 378, 11 L Ed
    2d 389.
16 James Stewart & Co. v. Sadrakula (1940) 309 US 94, 60 S Ct 431, 84 L Ed 596.
17 John Deere Plow Co. v. Wharton (1915) A.C. 300.
18 Canadian Indemnity Co. v. Attorney-General for British Columbia (1976) 73 D.L.R. 3d
    111.
19 Morgan v. Attorney-General for Prince Edward Island (1975) 55 D.L.R. 3d 527, 539.
20 Canadian Indemnity Co. v. Attorney-General for British Columbia (1976) 73 D.L.R. 3d
    111.
21 Campbell-Bennett Ltd. v. Comstock Midwestern Ltd. (1954) 3 D.L.R. 481. and cf.
    dissent of Laskin, J. in Cardinal v. Attorney-General for Alberta (1974) S.C.R. 695.
22 Commission du Salaire Minimum v. Bell Telephone Co. (1966) S.C.R. 767, 59 D.L.R. 2d
    145, 148-9 (Martland, J.).
23 Constitution of Australia, § 52(i).
24 Worthing v. Rowell and Muston Pty. Ltd. (1970) 123 C.L.R. 89.
25 Rose, "The Commonwealth Places Act 1970," 4 *Fed. L. Rev.* 263 (1971).
26 Paul v. United States (1963) 371 US 245, 83 S Ct 426, 9 L Ed 2d 292.
27 Omaechevarria v. Idaho (1918) 246 US 343, 38 S Ct 323, 62 L Ed 763.

§ 2.10

1   E.g., Constitution of Nigeria 1979, Second Schedule, Part I (3).
2   Johannesson v. West St. Paul (1952) 1 S.C.R. 292, 4 D.L.R. 609, 615.
3   Attorney-General for Ontario v. Canada Temperance Federation (1946) A.C. 193.
4   Johannesson v. West St. Paul (1952) 1 S.C.R. 292, 4 D.L.R. 609, 615.
5   Re Orangeville Airport (1976) 11 O.R. 2d 546. Cf. Northern Helicopters Ltd v.
    Vancouver Soaring Association (B.C.S.Ct. 1972) 6 W.W.R. 342 (holding a province
    could apply its law apportioning liability after an air crash until the Dominion Parliament
    legislated such rules).
6   Victoria v. Commonwealth (1937) 58 C.L.R. 618; Airlines of New South Wales Pty. Ltd.
    v. New South Wales (#2) (1965) 113 C.L.R. 54.
7   In re Rahrer (1891) 140 US 545, 11 S Ct 865, 35 L Ed 572.
8   R. v. Brislan, ex parte Williams (1935) 54 C.L.R. 262 (radio); Jones v. Commonwealth
    (#2) (1965) 112 C.L.R. 206 (television).
9   Re Public Utilities Commission v. Victoria Cablevision Ltd. (B.C. Ct. App 1965) 51
    D.L.R. 2d 716.
10 Grundgesetz, Article 72.
11 Edwards v. California (1941) 314 US 160, 176, 62 S Ct 164, 86 L Ed 119.
12 Constitution of Venezuela 1961, Article 136(25).

§ 2.11

[1] *Studies in Federalism* (Bowie & Friedrich eds., 1954 Boston) 256.
[2] German Federal Republic Grundgesetz, Art. 32(3).
[3] Morin, "Treaty-Making Power," 45 *Can. B. Rev.* 160, 168 (1967).
[4] Constitution of Switzerland, Article 9.
[5] Morin, "Treaty-Making Power," 45 *Can. B. Rev.* 160, 167 (1967).
[6] Attorney-General for Ontario v. Scott (1956) S.C.R. 137.
[7] Hogg, *Constitutional Law of Canada* (Toronto 1977) 194.
[8] *Studies in Federalism* (Bowie & Friedrich eds., 1954 Boston) 246, 277; LaForest, *The Allocation of Taxing Power under the Canadian Constitution* (Toronto 1981) 75. "All the Provinces maintain Agents-General abroad."
[9] Morin, "Treaty-Making Power," 45 *Can. B. Rev.* 160 (1967).
[10] Morris, "The Treaty-Making Power, a Canadian Dilemma," 45 *Can. B. Rev.* 478 (1967).
[11] Morgan v. Attorney-General for Prince Edward Island (1975) 53 D.L.R. 3d 527.
[12] Doeker, *The Treaty-Making Power in the Commonwealth of Australia* (The Hague 1966), esp. Chapter VIII, "Competence of the States in 'External Affairs'," pp. 211-242; *Studies in Federalism* (Bowie & Friedrich eds., 1954 Boston) 246. Burmester, "The Australian States and Participation in the Foreign Policy Process," 9 *Fed. L. Rev.* 257 (1978).
[13] Constitution of the U.S.S.R., Article 80.
[14] Constitution of Argentina 1853, as amended, Art. 108.
[15] Constitution of the United States, Article I, § 10.
[16] Zschernig v. Miller (1968) 389 US 429, 88 S Ct 664, 19 L Ed 2d 683, 687.
[17] Bethlehem Steel Corp. v. Board of Commissioner (Cal App 1969) 80 Cal Rptr 800, noted in 6 Tex Intl. L. Forum (1970) 134.

§ 2.12

[1] Constitution of India, List I, Entry 1; Constitution of Australia, § 51, placitum (vi); Constitution of Nigeria 1979, Second Schedule, Part I (16).
[2] Grundgesetz of German Federal Republic, Article 73(1).
[3] Atomic Weapons Referenda Case (1958) 8 BVerfGE 105, 122.
[4] British North America Act, § 91(7).
[5] Switzman v. Elbling (1957) 7 D.L.R. 2d 337.
[6] Constitution of Australia, § 51, placitum (vi).
[7] Cf. Wenn v. Attorney General (Vict.) (1948) 77 C.L.R. 84.
[8] Cf. Farey v. Burvett (1916) 21 C.L.R. 433, 468.
[9] Gilbert v. Minnesota (1920) 254 US 325, 41 S Ct 125, 65 L Ed 287.
[10] Pennsylvania v. Nelson (1956) 350 US 497, 76 S Ct 477, 100 L Ed 640.
[11] Uphaus v. Wyman (1959) 360 US 72, 79 S Ct 1040, 3 L Ed 2d 1090.
[12] Constitution of Mexico, Article 118 (III).
[13] Constitution of Argentina, Article 109.

§ 2.13

[1] Laskin, *Canadian Constitutional Law* (4th Ed., Abel, 1975) 523.
[2] Hogg, *Constitutional Law of Canada* (Toronto 1977) 387.
[3] Cardinal v. Attorney-General for Alberta (1974) S.C.R. 695.
[4] R. v. McLeod (B.C. Co. Ct. 1938) 2 W.W.R. 37; R. v. Morley (B.C. Ct. App. 1931) 46 B.C.R. 28.
[5] R. v. Rodgers (Man. Ct. App. 1923) 2 W.W.R. 353.
[6] Eastern Band of Cherokee Indians v. United States (1886) 177 US 288, 6 S Ct 718, 29 L Ed 880, 886.
[7] Antoine v. Washington (1975) 420 US 194, 95 S Ct 944, 43 L Ed 2d 129 (conservation of fish and game); Mescalero Apache Tribe v. Jones (1973) 411 US 145, 93 S Ct 1267, 36 L Ed 2d 114 (tax on gross receipts from ski resort operated off the reservation).

8 "Where on-reservation conduct involving only Indians is at issue, state law is generally inapplicable." Mountain Apache Tribe v. Bracker (1980) 448 US 136, 144, 100 S Ct 2578, 65 L Ed 2d 665; Moe v. Confederated Salish & Kootenai Tribes of Flathead Reservation (1976) 425 US 463, 96 S Ct 1634, 48 L Ed 2d 96; Williams v. Lee (1959) 358 US 217, 79 S Ct 269, 3 L Ed 2d 251, 254; Worcester v. Georgia (1832) 6 Pet. 515, 561, 8 L Ed 483, 501; Fisher v. District Court (1976) 424 US 382, 96 S Ct 943, 47 L Ed 2d 106.

9 White Mountain Apache Tribe v. Bracker (1980) 448 US 136, 100 S Ct 2578, 65 L Ed 2d 665.

10 Washington v. Confederated Tribes of Colville Indian Reservation (1980) 447 US 134, 100 S Ct 2069, 65 L Ed 2d 10.

11 Kake v. Egan (1962) 369 US 60, 82 S Ct 562, 7 L Ed 2d 573; Utah & N.R. Co. v. Fisher (1885) 116 US 28, 6 S Ct 246, 29 L Ed 542.

12 Washington v. Confederated Tribes of Colville Indian Reservation (1980) 447 US 134, 100 S Ct 2069, 65 L Ed 2d 10. Semble: Moe v. Confederated Salish & Kootenai Tribes of Flathead Reservation (1976) 425 US 463, 96 S Ct 1634, 48 L Ed 2d 96.

13 Seymour v. Superintendent of Washington State Penitentiary (1962) 368 US 351, 82 S Ct 424, 7 L Ed 2d 346.

14 Williams v. Lee (1959) 358 US 217, 79 S Ct 269, 3 L Ed 2d 251; Washington v. Confederated Bands (1979) 439 US 463, 99 S Ct 740, 58 L Ed 2d 740.

15 Kennerly v. District Court (1971) 400 US 423, 91 S Ct 480, 27 L Ed 2d 507.

16 Mountain Apache Tribe v. Bracker (1980) 448 US 136, 142, 100 S Ct 2578, 65 L Ed 2d 665.

17 Mountain Apache Tribe v. Bracker (1980) 448 US 136, 100 S Ct 2578, 65 L Ed 2d 665; Warren Trading Post v. Arizona Tax Commission (1965) 380 US 685, 85 S Ct 1242, 14 L Ed 2d 165.

§ 2.14

1 Cooley v. Board of Port Wardens of Philadelphia (1851) 12 How. 299, 13 L Ed 996.

2 Morgan Steamship Co. v. Louisiana Board of Health (1886) 118 US 455.

3 Hess v. United States (1960) 361 US 314.

4 Constitution of Australia, § 51(xvii); United States Constitution, Art. I, § 8, clause 4: "on the subject of Bankruptcies." British North America Act, § 91(21) ("bankruptcy and insolvency").

5 Faitoute Iron and Steel Co. v. Asbury Park (1942) 316 US 502, 62 S Ct 1129, 86 L Ed 1629.

6 Re Watts (1903) 190 US 1, 23 S Ct 718, 47 L Ed 933.

7 Johnson v. Star (1933) 287 US 527, 53 S Ct 265, 77 L Ed 473.

8 Constitution of Malaysia.

9 Constitution of the U.S.S.R. 1977, Art. 72.

10 Ozakwe, "The Theories and Realities of Modern Soviet Constitutional Law: An Analysis of the 1977 Soviet Constitution," 127 *U Pa L Rev* 1350, 1410 (1979).

CHAPTER THREE

Chapter Three

STATE REGULATORY POWER OVER TRADE AND COMMERCE

§ 3.00 State power over local or intrastate commerce

States having the residuum of power under federal constitutions have what can be described as plenary power over local and intrastate trade and commerce—that is, they have all power not restricted by specific constitutional amendments.

In the United States, Chief Justice Stone has said that "there has thus been left to the states wide scope for the regulation of matters of local state concerns,"[1] and the record fully bears out this statement.[2] In Australia,[3] and in Argentina,[4] too, the states and provinces have broad powers to control local trade and commerce.

Even where the residuum of power is not in the states, but in the central government, the states, generally by constitutional grant, possess adequate power to regulate state and local trade and commerce. In India, for instance, the Constitution specifically confers upon the states power to regulate "Trade and Commerce within the State."[5] In Canada, where the provinces do not have the residuum of power, Section 92(16) of the British North America Act gives them power to control "generally all matters of a merely local or private nature in the Province." Section 92(13) additionally confers power over "Property and Civil Rights in the Province." Justice Rand of the Supreme Court of Canada has said: "Although not specifically mentioned in Section 92 of the British North America Act, there is admittedly a field of trade within provincial power. . . ."[6]

In some federal societies with substantive due process clauses, such as the United States, the states in regulating trade and commerce even within their borders are held to restraints that are reasonable and reasonably related to permissible legislative ends,[7] although the United States Supreme Court currently defers greatly to the judgment of state legislatures in this area.[8]

Where federal societies include equality or equal protection clauses in their constitutions, states, in regulating intrastate or local commerce, must avoid invidious or unreasonable classifications,[9] although courts can be expected to defer greatly to the legislative judgment that disparate treatment is necessary and proper.[10]

In federal societies, the central government customarily has some power over local or intrastate commerce. The effect of federal supremacy clauses in the constitutions,[11] or comparable constitutional doctrine,[12] will result in the invalidation of state controls even of intrastate commerce when they clash or conflict with valid federal legislation, or the federal government has constitutionally occupied a field that includes some state or local commerce.[13]

§ 3.01 Interstateness

Interstate commerce is found, of course, whenever persons, goods, or communications actually cross state lines.[1]

Interstateness is also found, at times, from events occurring within a single state when they are integral and inseverable parts of a larger movement in interstate (or for that matter, foreign) commerce. In 1871, the United States Supreme Court held that the owner of a vessel operating only in Michigan was part of interstate commerce, because the persons or goods he carried frequently began their journeys in other states or terminated them in other states.[2] On another occasion, the same Court held a transportation agency operating only in Illinois was part of interstate commerce because it was engaged largely in transporting passengers from one terminal in Chicago to another terminal in that city, passengers who were frequently moving through the city on interstate journeys. The Supreme Court announced:

> When persons or goods move from a point of origin in one state to a point of destination in another, the fact that a part of that journey consists of transportation by an independent agency solely within the boundaries of one state does not make that portion of the trip any less interstate in character. That portion must be viewed in its relation to the entire journey rather than in isolation. So viewed, it is an integral step in the interstate movement.[3]

Although both the foregoing cases decided only that federal power could reach the persons and companies involved, it follows that federal power could, under paramountcy, void any attempt to interfere with such movements, and even suggests that attempted state burdens upon such commerce would be voided because of their "interstateness" unless clearly needed to protect larger societal interests.

Interstateness can additionally be found in the state of origin, when events there are integrally part of the movement in interstate commerce. In 1957, the High Court of Australia held a party in Tasmania carrying his own goods in that state was immune from Tasmanian controls, since the goods were already moving in the stream of interstate commerce.[4] Four years later, the High Court held Queensland could not subject to its licensing controls a company carrying in its own vehicles timber to a port within that state, as part of a larger shipment on to New South Wales, for which the company was contractually obligated.[5] The United States Supreme Court has held that the sale and purchase of goods for shipment into interstate commerce are themselves part of that commerce.[6]

Interstateness can also be found in the state of destination, even though the physical movement in interstate commerce has ended, when the event regulated is required under the contract calling for interstate movement of goods, such as installation or anything else, in the language of the United States Supreme Court, "inherently relating to and intrinsically dealing with the thing sold."[7]

A transaction calling for the sale of goods, with the delivery of the goods to the buyer in the same state, does not find protection from the commerce clause because the buyer will shortly thereafter deliver some of the goods into other states. Speaking of sales in South Australia of products produced in that state, some of which were later delivered by the plaintiff-buyer to other states, the High Court of Australia said: "That, however, is not enough to convert the sale to the Plaintiff into an interstate transaction. For that result to ensue, it would be necessary that the agreement for sale to the Plaintiff should contain a stipulation that the petroleum products should be dispatched from the refinery in South Australia and delivered by the seller to the Plaintiff in a State other than South Australia."[8]

§ 3.02 State power over interstate commerce—as limited by constitutional clauses

In federal societies, it is everywhere accepted that there is an important societal interest in freedom of movement of both persons and goods throughout the entire nation. Chief Justice Barwick of Australia wrote in 1969: "The advantages of the freedom of national trade is . . . of peculiar advantage to all Australians wherever they may chance to reside."[1] In the language of the United States Supreme Court, there is "a national interest in keeping interstate commerce free from interferences which seriously impede it."[2]

Constitutions in federal societies either explicitly or implicitly impose limits upon the component entities attempting to interfere with interstate commerce. The Constitution of Argentina states: "The circulation of goods of national production or manufacture is free from duties in the interior of the Republic, as is also that of goods and merchandise of all kinds dispatched through the national custom houses."[3] That Constitution adds: "The Provinces . . . may not . . . enact laws dealing with commerce."[4]

The Constitution of Australia provides that "trade, commerce, and intercourse among the States . . . shall be absolutely free."[5]

In Brazil, assignment to the central government of power over "foreign and interstate trade"[6] effectuates an implied limitation upon state powers of interference.

In Canada, the free movement of goods nationally is protected from provincial restraints both by the provision in the British North America

Act giving the Dominion Parliament power over "trade and commerce,"[7] and the provision stating that: "All articles of the growth, produce, or manufacture of any one of the Provinces shall . . . be admitted free into each of the other Provinces."[8] The Supreme Court of Canada has held that a province cannot deny the use of its roads to entrepreneurs in interprovincial commerce.[9] However, some provincial regulations are permissible under Section 121, Justice Rand of the Supreme Court stating in 1958: "What is forbidden is a trade regulation that in its essence and purpose is related to a provincial boundary."[10]

The Grundgesetz of the German Federal Republic assigns to the federation exclusive legislative power over "the unity of the territory as regards customs and commerce . . . and the exchanges of goods and payments with foreign countries."[11] In regulating inter-Laender trade and the national economy, the powers of the Laender are not very extensive, being limited largely to those powers which the federation chooses to allot to them.[12]

In this regard, the Constitution of India was patterned after that of Australia and provides: "Subject to the other provisions of this Part, trade, commerce and intercourse throughout the Territory of India shall be free."[13] Chief Justice Sinha has written that the words of section 301 of the Constitution include

> not only free buying and selling, but also the freedom of bargain and contracts as also transport of goods and commodities for the purpose of production, distribution and consumption in all their aspects, that is to say, transportation by land, air or water. They must also include commerce not only in goods and commodities, but also transportation of men and animals, by all means of transportation. Commerce would thus include dealings over the telegraph, telephone or wireless, and every kind of contract relating to sale, purchase, exchange etc. of goods and commodities.[14]

By the Mexican Constitution, the federal government has power "to prevent the establishment of restrictions on interstate commerce,"[15] and it is further provided that the states may not: "Prohibit or levy duty directly or indirectly, upon the entrance into or exit from their territory of any domestic or foreign goods."[16]

The Constitution of Nigeria assigns to the federal government exclusive legislative authority over "trade and Commerce."[17]

The United States Constitution gives to the federal government power "to regulate Commerce with foreign Nations, and among the several States, and with the Indian Tribes,"[18] and from an early date this has been understood to be not only a grant of power to the federation, but also a limitation upon the states.

The Constitution of Switzerland provides: "Freedom of Trade and Industry is guaranteed throughout the Confederation except in so far as it is restricted by the Constitution itself or by laws made under it."[19] The power to interfere with trade and commerce is thus largely federal, and the "cantons have very small powers to interfere with trade and commerce."[20]

The Constitution of Venezuela indicates that the states may not "prohibit consumption of goods produced outside their territory, or tax them differently from those produced within their jurisdiction."[21] It is further provided that the states may not "create custom houses or taxes on imports, export taxes, or taxes on transit of foreign or domestic goods,"[22] and another Article denies power to the States to "tax consumer goods before they enter into circulation within their territory."[23]

In addition to the foregoing commerce clauses, states are limited at times in regulating interstate commerce by constitutional clauses guaranteeing citizens the right to move freely throughout the land. Every citizen of India by the Constitution has the right "to move freely throughout the territory of India,"[24] and this restricts state power. The Grundgesetz of the German Federal Republic provides also that "all Germans shall enjoy freedom of movement throughout the federal territory."[25] Although there is no such specific constitutional clause in the United States, freedom of movement throughout the country is a constitutional right protected not only under the commerce clause, but also under the privileges and immunities clause of the Fourth Article of the Constitution.[26]

Constitutional freedom of enterprise, generally recognized in federal societies, also serves to limit the states in regulating interstate trade and commerce. In the United States, the due process clause of the Fourteenth Amendment requires state controls upon this freedom to be reasonable and not arbitrary.[27] In India, the Constitution guarantees citizens the right "to practice any profession, or to carry on any occupation, trade or business,"[28] and this, too, serves to limit the power of the states in regulating trade and commerce.

§ 3.03 State power over interstate commerce—permissible regulations generally

Notwithstanding the rather extreme and absolute language of some of the federal constitutions, suggesting that there is no room for state controls, it is the general rule that some state interference with interstate commerce is permissible.

While the Australian Constitution provides that "trade, commerce and intercourse among the States . . . shall be absolutely free,"[1] it is firmly established that "absolutely free" does not mean the interest in interstate trade and commerce cannot be subordinated, in proper cases, to other important interests of that society. Chief Justice Griffith of the High Court stated in 1916 that "free" is not to mean "extra legem,"[2] and established for all time that reasonable state controls necessary to protect legitimate societal interests will be constitutional. Chief Justice Barwick, who believed strongly in a national economy, nevertheless admitted that section 92 must permit "laws regulating the relationships of free men to each other and to their institutions within a society."[3] Justice Lionel Murphy of the High Court urges that tribunal to sustain state regulatory controls of interstate commerce so long as "the Act does not impose, directly or indirectly, any customs duty or any discriminatory fiscal impost."[4] What will likely emerge in Australia, as well as everywhere else, is a judicial balancing of the opposed societal interests in each case, weighing the societal interest in free movement of commerce throughout the land against other important societal interests, such as those in safeguarding the public health, safety, etc. Chief Justice Barwick wrote: "There is thus a need in each case closely to observe a nicety of balance between freedom of trade and commerce and the permissible restrictive legislation of a free and civilized society which is compatible with that freedom."[5]

The commerce clause in the Indian Constitution is patterned on that of Australia and provides: "Subject to the other provisions of this Part, trade, commerce and intercourse throughout the Territory of India shall be free."[6] However, another Constitutional provision allows the states, with the assent of the President of the Union, to impose "such reasonable restrictions on the flow of trade, commerce or intercourse with or within that State as may be required in the public interest."[7] Furthermore, Indian jurisprudence uses the term "regulatory controls" to describe such things as traffic regulations that help the movement of commerce, and these are not violative of Article 301.[8]

Although the British North America Act gives the Dominion Parliament power over "the regulation of trade and commerce,"[9] provincial controls are sustained unless an act "aims at regulation of trade in matters of interprovincial concern."[10] In the other federal societies, too, there has been an inclination on the part of the courts to sustain "indirect" state laws affecting interstate trade, and to void such laws "directly" affecting interstate trade and commerce.[11] In Australia, Chief Justice Barwick once stated that the High Court will invalidate a law "if by its operation directly and not remotely it inhibits or burdens trade and commerce amongst the States in any respect."[12] The High Court on another occasion indicated that "prior restraints" are unconstitutional.[13] "Regulation" has been found acceptable, but "prohibition" condemned.[14] Such indulgence in labeling is frequently but ratiocination to justify a result the judge cannot defend on rational and pragmatic grounds. In any event, such jurisprudence of labels masks the very nature of the judicial task and utterly fails to acquaint the bar and the larger community with the true reasons for the rulings.[15] Courts must identify openly the opposed societal interests being advanced by states in federal societies and provide clear explanations why the judiciary believes on the facts of particular cases such an interest should, or should not, prudentially be deemed to outweigh the admitted societal interest in the free movement of goods.

§ 3.04 State power over interstate commerce—discriminatory regulations affecting interstate commerce

Regardless of the legitimacy of the societal interest advanced by states, and the relevance of their legislation to such important interests, state regulations affecting interstate commerce are everywhere invalidated when they discriminate against the persons or products of such commerce. The Constitution of India specifically forbids the states to give a preference or to impose discriminations against other states "relating to trade and commerce."[1] However, under another article of the Constitution "reasonable restrictions" (seemingly including discriminatory ones) can be imposed by states with the approval of the President of the Union.[2]

The Australian High Court has readily invalidated state interferences with interstate trade and commerce when they discriminated against merchants or products from other Australian States. To illustrate, when a Western Australia statute imposed a license fee of two pounds on the sale of wine from locally grown fruit, but a fee of fifty pounds on wine imported from sister states, it was voided.[3] The High Court has indicated generally that interstate transactions may not be placed at a "greater disadvantage than that borne by transactions confined to the State."[4] Even the broad state powers over liquor acknowledged by Section 113 of the Constitution do not authorize discrimination against the products of other states.[5] This, it is suggested, is far preferable to the rulings of the United States Supreme Court under the Twenty-first Amendment, which have condoned discrimination regarding liquor against beverages coming in from sister states.[6]

The United States Supreme Court has set aside many state regulations affecting interstate commerce because they discriminated against entrepreneurs or products from other states. Thus, it has voided a state statute requiring licenses for vendors of domestically produced goods.[7] Again the Supreme Court invalidated a discriminatory wharfage charge as applied to potatoes coming in from another state.[8] On another occasion, the Court set aside a state statute that had the effect of eliminating from the local market meat processed in other states.[9] Later, the Court annulled a municipal ordinance, authorized by state law, which in effect limited milk sold in the community to locally pasteurized milk.[10]

The Supreme Court of Canada is comparably unsympathetic to interprovincial discriminations, voiding in 1971 a Manitoba egg marketing scheme "the purpose of which is to obtain for Manitoba producers the most advantageous marketing conditions for eggs."[11]

§ 3.05 State power over interstate commerce—attempts by states to restrict the entrance of persons and goods

States have generally been reversed when they attempted to exclude from their midst citizens from other states in the commonwealth. The

Australian High Court has held that New South Wales could not make it a crime for someone to enter from another state, if he had previously been convicted of a crime carrying a punishment of at least one year and had served his sentence.[1] The United States Supreme Court has ruled that the Commerce Clause in the Constitution forbade California from excluding indigents from sister states.[2] The Supreme Court of Canada has said: "A Province cannot prevent a Canadian from entering it except, conceivably, in temporary circumstances, for some local reason as, for example, health.[3] As intimated, quarantine laws clearly necessary to protect the public health would likely be sustained in all federal societies.[4]

States cannot, solely to protect their own producers or merchants, exclude goods from other states or surround the entrance of such products with conditions that would effectively discourage the importation of the goods. When the United States Supreme Court held that New York could not prohibit the sale in the state of milk purchased from farmers outside of New York at prices lower than that set by the state for purchases from New York farmers, Justice Benjamin Cardozo stated well the governing rule. He said: "Neither the power to tax nor the police power may be used by the State of destination with the aim and effect of establishing an economic barrier against competition with the products of another State."[5] In 1964 the Supreme Court reaffirmed that a state could not, except for reasons of health, restrict the importation of milk into the state by out-of-state producers.[6]

Reaffirming that one state cannot "isolate itself in the stream of interstate commerce from a problem shared by all," the United States Supreme Court in 1978 held that New Jersey could not prohibit the introduction into that state of solid or liquid waste matter for disposal there.[7]

In Canada, the provinces cannot control the import into the provinces of goods coming from other provinces and foreign countries.[8] "It is common ground that the prohibition of importation is beyond the legislative jurisdiction of the Province."[9] Then Justice (now Chief Justice) Laskin has written: "The general limitation upon provincial authority to exercise of its powers within or in the Province precludes it from intercepting either goods moving into the Province or goods moving out, subject to possible exceptions, as in the case of danger to life or health." He added: "To permit each Province to seek its own advantage, so to speak, through a figurative sealing of its borders to entry of goods from others would be to deny one of the objects of Confederation."[10] In voiding a British Columbia limitation upon the import of broiler chickens, Justice Legg for the British Columbia Supreme Court stated: "The import order is designed to restrict or limit the free flow of trade between the Province and other Provinces and between the Province and the United States. For that reason it constitutes an invasion of the exclusive legislative authority of the Parliament of Canada over a matter of the regulation of trade and commerce."[11] Manitoba was unable to prevent packers from buying hogs from producers in other provinces, nor could it by banning slaughter in Manitoba require their acquisition from producers in other Provinces to be in accordance with Manitoba law regulating price and other conditions of sale.[12] At an early date the Judicial Committee of the Privy Council had held that a province had no power to prohibit the importation of liquor into the province.[13]

In ruling that Queensland could not fix the price of goods coming into that state from New South Wales on orders solicited in the former by traveling salesmen and accepted in the latter state, the High Court of Australia has said: "The prohibition by a State Legislature of inter-State sales of commodities either absolutely or subject to conditions imposed by State law is in our opinion, a direct contravention of section 92 (the commerce clause) of the Constitution.[14]

By the Grundgesetz or Basic Law of the German Federal Republic, the federal government has exclusive legislative power over "the unity of the territory as regards customs and commerce . . . and the exchanges of goods and payments with foreign countries."[15]

In Argentina, the Supreme Court has denied the power of a province to ban the import of plants.[16]

§ 3.06 State power over interstate commerce—limiting the export of goods

States have traditionally been acknowledged to have a legitimate interest in conserving natural resources and, at times, this interest has been held adequate to support prohibitions upon the export of the state of such resources as oil, coal, water, fish, and game.[1] However, in 1979, the United States Supreme Court voided as violative of the Commerce Clause a state statute forbidding the shipment out of state of minnows procured from waters within the state. Finding the statute discriminated against interstate commerce, the Court announced:

> The burden to show discrimination rests on the party challenging the validity of the statute, but when discrimination against commerce is demonstrated the burden falls on the State to justify it both in terms of the local benefits flowing from the statute and the unavailability of nondiscriminatory alternatives adequate to preserve the local interests at stake.[2]

States have been sustained in imposing inspections upon goods leaving the state to protect the health of subsequent buyers, as well as the reputation of the state's fruits and produce.[3]

Generally, American states cannot prevent the export of articles to sister states purely to protect and advance local economic interests.[4] In ruling that New York could not prevent a Massachusetts dairy from acquiring New York milk, Justice Robert Jackson (a New Yorker) wisely stated:

> Our system, fostered by the Commerce Clause, is that every farmer and every craftsman shall be encouraged to produce by the certainty that he will have full access to every market in the nation, that no home embargoes will withhold his exports and no foreign state will by custom duties or regulations exclude them. Likewise, every consumer may look to the free competition from every producing area in the Nation to protect him from exploitation by any.[5]

Although the Supreme Court in 1908 held a state could restrict the export of its water,[6] the same Court fifteen years later voided the attempt of another state which had encouraged transmission of its natural gas out-of-state to thereafter limit its export.[7] The Supreme Court once upheld a state in which milk was produced in requiring a license and bond of dealers picking up milk in that state, and setting minimum prices to be paid to producers, in application to a dealer from another state wishing to introduce the milk into his state. The Court noted that only about ten percent of the milk produced in the former state moved into interstate commerce, and the Court refused to characterize the control as a serious barrier to the export of milk.[8] In what was an unfortunate decision, the Court once ruled that California, which produced most of the nation's raisin crop, could structure a marketing scheme "in the interests of safety, health and well-being" to raise prices on this product at the expense of all purchasers in sister states, where 95% of the raisins were sold.[9] Over the better-reasoned dissents of Justices Brennan, Powell, White and Stevens, the majority of the Court held in 1980 that a state could limit the sale of cement produced at a state-owned plant to residents of the state.[10]

In Canada, the provinces can impose production controls and conservation measures with respect to natural resources.[11] For example, British Columbia was upheld in an early ruling in prohibiting the export of game animals and birds.[12] However, provincial authority does not extend to controlling the marketing of provincial products, whether minerals or natural resources, in interprovincial or foreign trade.[13] Justice Maitland stated in 1977: "Provincial legislative authority does not extend to fixing the price to be charged or received in respect of the sale of goods in the export market."[14]

Then Justice (now Chief Justice) Laskin wrote in 1971: "Regulation of the marketing of provincial produce intended for export or sought to be purchased for export is beyond that competence." He added that a "Province may not, as a general rule, prohibit an owner of goods from sending them outside the Province." However, recalling the Carnation decision,[15] and the language of the Court in that case, Laskin was compelled to remark: "It cannot be categorically stated that extraprovincial destination will foreclose provincial regulation of intermediate steps in the marketing process."[16] A Quebec court has held that the province could expropriate asbestos, remarking that it was "irrelevant that the natural resource . . . . is almost one hundred per cent an exported product."[17]

In Canada, provincial marketing acts limited to purely provincial or local transactions are valid,[18] but many provincial acts attempting to prohibit or control the marketing of goods going into interprovincial or foreign trade have been invalidated as *ultra vires*.[19]

The High Court of Australia has ruled that South Australia could not prevent growers of dried fruit in that state from marketing their product elsewhere, by imposing upon them quotas for the amount they might sell in interstate trade.[20] Six years later, the High Court held that Queensland could not, in effect, prohibit growers of peanuts from selling them in interstate trade, by a statute which provided for the automatic expropriation by the state of all peanuts grown there. "Compulsory acquisition," said Justice Rich, "may directly operate to interfere with the freedom of interstate commerce."[21] In 1939, Justice Evatt of the High Court indicated when compulsory acquisition would violate the commerce clause. He said: "If the object is to prohibit or limit trade, including trade among the States, section 92 forbids it. If the object is otherwise, section 92 has nothing to say about the matter."[22]

The Supreme Court of Argentina has held that a province could not limit the amount of sugar to be produced in the province and offered for sale, since this would in effect obstruct the movement of goods in interprovincial commerce.[23]

§ 3.07 State power over interstate commerce—state regulation before interstate movement begins

Even though interstate movement of the goods would, in all probability, have begun shortly, states on a number of occasions have been upheld in their regulations when the courts reasoned that the state action affected goods at a point of time before the physical movement had begun, and the earlier occasion was not an essential aspect of the larger interstate transaction.

Some plans for marketing control by state compulsory expropriation have been held valid. In the wartime Wheat Case, New South Wales was sustained in compulsorily acquiring all the wheat in the state to advance the war effort, even such wheat that was under contract for interstate shipment at the time, the High Court explaining that the state was not affecting "trade" but earlier "ownership."[1] The next year the High Court held valid the Queensland Meat Act, under which the owner of meat could not dispose of it without government permission, Chief Justice Griffith pointing out that the word "free" in section 92 (the commerce clause) does not mean "extra legem," and holding that even interstate trade is subject to certain restrictions.[2] The High Court in Duncan overruled a decision earlier that year under the New South Wales Act of 1915 which provided that all meat shall be kept for the disposal of the government. In the earlier case the High Court had held unconstitutional in its application to Queensland bacon manufacturers whose hogs were in New South Wales, a statute of the latter state under which officials would not consent to their export.[3] Four years later, a three-to-two majority of the Court said that *Foggitt, Jones and Company v. New South Wales* had been rightly decided, and that *Duncan* was in error.[4] Justice Dixon wrote in 1952:

> It is pressing section 92 far beyond its meaning and purpose if the immunity it confers is extended to the preservation of movable property against compulsory acquisition, although no overt act has been done with reference to such property which will, or upon a contingency may, result in a dealing or movement interstate.[5]

When, to advantage the local dairy industry, New South Wales enacted legislation that no person in the state could manufacture or prepare table margarine without a license, the High Court found no section 92 protection for the margarine manufacturers even though some, if produced, surely would later move into interstate commerce. Said Justice Dixon: "It is no reason for extending the freedom which section 92 confers upon trade and commerce among the States to something which precedes it and is outside the freedom conferred."[6] Eleven years later, the High Court comparably ruled New South Wales could apply its margarine legislation even to a company receiving orders from out-of-state to provide the buyer with margarine.[7] The same year, in another margarine case, Chief Justice Barwick observed generally that "a quota upon manufacture set by the State in which the manufacture is to take place does not deal with interstate trade or commerce."[8] In 1978 the High Court held that New South Wales could constitutionally limit the number of hens owned, even by a firm later selling its eggs into interstate commerce, ruling generally that any state can prevent the production of articles the producer later intends to dispose of in interstate commerce.[9]

In Canada, the provinces can exert most controls over goods that would ordinarily later move into interprovincial or foreign commerce. Chief Justice Bora Laskin has said: "It is, of course, true that production controls and conservation measures with respect to natural resources in a Province are, ordinarily, matters within provincial legislative authority."[10] The Supreme Court of Canada has held that Ontario could control the price of milk paid by a processor to a producer in that province, even though some of the milk would certainly be sent out of the province in interprovincial trade.[11] The Quebec Court of Appeals in 1981 held that province could expropriate all asbestos in the province, even though virtually all of it otherwise would have been exported.[12] The same year, the Ontario High Court held that province could regulate a firm engaged in arranging and coordinating later interprovincial transfers of goods.[13]

The United States Supreme Court has acknowledged broad power in the states to protect legitimate societal interests by imposing controls upon goods and articles in the state, even though they would undoubtedly soon move into the channels of interstate and foreign commerce. Illustratively, to ensure that milk producers would not be defrauded and that they would be paid a reasonable price for their milk, the United States Supreme Court sustained a Pennsylvania statute requiring dealers purchasing such milk to secure a license and post a bond, as well as pay minimum prescribed prices for the milk, even though the milk was shortly destined for interstate commerce.[14]

At times what would seem to be a local act is so closely interwoven with a larger interstate transaction, and so essential to the movement of goods in interstate commerce, that a court will hold the act is protected by the constitutional commerce clause and immune from state regulation or prohibition. The United States Supreme Court has said: "Where goods are purchased in a first State for transportation to another, the commerce includes the purchase as much as it does the transportation."[15]

§ 3.08 State power over interstate commerce—state regulation after interstate movement has ended

On many occasions states have been able to control goods which have come in earlier from interstate or foreign commerce, as well as dealings with such goods, where the local event was not an inseparable part of the import process. Chief Justice Barwick of the High Court of Australia has said:

> There are transactions occurring within the State with commodities which have come from or are going to another State which, in relation to the terms of a particular law, are so far removed from inter-State movement as not relevantly to form part of that movement.[1]

In 1953 the High Court held that, except as to the first sale by the importer who had brought in the goods, a state could set the prices even on goods that had come in from interstate commerce.[2] Thirteen years later, the Court ruled that a state can regulate the grading of eggs that had come in from interstate commerce, seemingly withdrawing the earlier exception granted to the importer in his first sale.[3]

In 1939 the High Court held New South Wales could apply its milk marketing scheme to milk which had just come in from Victoria, so that title to the milk immediately vested in the State Board.[4] Where agents did their selling in New South Wales, that state could regulate their activities, including charges, even when they were handling goods brought in from other states.[5] In 1953 the High Court held that South Australia could require and deny a permit to an agent for a Victoria manufacturer of meat, when the agent desired to sell in South Australia meat that came in from Victoria.[6] The High Court in 1966 sustained a South Australian regulation requiring the word "Margarine" to be conspicuously displayed on packets of the same, even though the product had come in through the channels of interstate commerce. It was not "a relevant burden" said the Court.[7] Three years later, the High Court found constitutional a Western Australia Stamp Tax requiring payment to the state of a duty of one cent per ten dollars of which receipt was acknowledged by business firms, in application to a company carrying on business in Western

Australia, but receiving the sums as payment for carrying interstate goods. The smallness of the charge seemingly convinced the justices that this was not a forbidden "burden."[8]

Even though the Privy Council ruled that a Canadian province could not prohibit the import of liquor,[9] there is respectable authority for the proposition that a province can, after the liquor has come in, punish the unauthorized possession of it.[10] Where there was no attempt to control the entry into British Columbia of coal or oil, it was held that this province could fix both wholesale and retail prices on these commodities sold in the province, even though the coal and oil came in from other provinces and from California.[11]

The United States Supreme Court generally recognizes a power in the states to impose nondiscriminatory regulations affecting goods that have come into the state from interstate or foreign commerce, once the physical movement has completely terminated. For example, Virginia was able to impose its licensing and price controls upon those who within the state handled milk for consumption there, even though all the milk had just come in from out-of-state.[12] States can protect consumers against deception and fraud, even as to articles brought in from other states.[13]

There have been instances where the state of destination of goods that had moved in interstate or foreign commerce could not control the goods or persons dealing with them, where the event regulated was an essential and inseverable part of the entire import process.

Once, Queensland, which produced no petrol, provided that no petrol could be sold in Queensland except by licensed persons, and licenses were denied unless the Queensland dealer also purchased power alcohol, a product whose manufacture in Queensland that state desired to promote. The scheme was held to violate § 92 (the interstate commerce clause), Justice Dixon stating that the real incidence of the controls fell upon the person seeking to import petrol into Queensland.[14] On another occasion the High Court held Queensland could not punish a retail distributor of fish for selling the same without acquiring the same through the State Fish Marketing Board, where the fish had come in from interstate commerce. Freedom to import goods would be illusory, said the Court, if the importer could not sell the goods.[15]

The High Court has also given indications that expropriations as part of marketing controls by the states may be unconstitutional even after the interstate movement is over. Said the Court: "If the object is to prohibit or limit trade, including trade among the States, section 92 forbids it." The Court added: "If the object is otherwise, section 92 has nothing to say about the matter."[16]

The United States Supreme Court, in an occasional case, has held that the state of destination could not control activities, such as the installation of goods or machinery, which had just come in from interstate commerce, under contracts obligating the seller or his agent to perform the act. The Court indicated that such acts will be immune from control by the state of destination when they are "inherently relating to and intrinsically dealing with the thing sold."[17]

§ 3.09 State power over interstate commerce—fees and charges for services and facilities provided

Federal constitutions at times specifically authorize the states to impose fees in connection with their authorized powers affecting the movement of interstate trade and commerce. Illustratively, the Australian Constitution in section 112 provides: "After uniform duties of customs have been imposed, a State may levy on imports or exports, or on goods passing into or out of the State, such charges as may be necessary for executing the inspection laws of the State. . . ." That section adds: "But the net produce of all charges so levied shall be for the use of the Commonwealth; and any such inspection laws may be annulled by the Parliament of the Commonwealth."

Although not expressed in the organic laws of some other federal societies, the power of states to impose reasonable inspection charges, as a concomitant of their inspection power, is readily implied by the courts.[1]

Where states and their political subdivisions provide unusual facilities for the benefit of entrepreneurs in interstate and foreign commerce, they can impose upon the beneficiaries reasonable charges. The Privy Council, in a case from Australia in 1954, seemingly went out of its way to announce by dictum that states can make charges for trading facilities they provide.[2]

Although the United States Constitution in Article I, § 10, cl. 2 prescribes that "no State shall, without the consent of Congress, lay any duty of tonnage . . . ," the United States Supreme Court has ruled reasonable charges for services provided to owners of vessels are constitutional. The foregoing prohibition, according to the Court, "does not extend to charges made by state authority, even though graduated according to tonnage, for services rendered to and enjoyed by the vessel, such as pilotage, or wharfage, or charges for the use of locks on a navigable river, or fees for medical inspection."[3]

In federal societies, states and their political subdivisions have generally been able to impose reasonable charges upon users of the highways and roads, even when the users were engaged exclusively in interstate or foreign commerce. Justice Dixon for the High Court of Australia, in sustaining such charges, noted that "very many countries . . . place a large part of the cost of highways upon the traffic that uses them." He added that such charges were to be "fair recompense for the actual use made of the highway." By way of dictum, he indicated the same principle would be applicable when states and their subdivisions provided toll-bridges and airports.[4] The United States Supreme Court many times has found consistent with the Commerce Clause, service charges for the use of highways and streets when imposed by the states or their political subdivisions, even upon firms using them solely in interstate commerce.[5] Once the charges become excessive, however, they become unconstitutional.[6]

States and their political subdivisions operating and maintaining airports can impose reasonable charges upon users, without violating federal constitutional commerce clauses.[7]

§ 3.10 State power over interstate commerce—the interest in the free movement of interstate trade and commerce versus the interest in safeguarding the public health

The important societal interest in safeguarding the public health will likely in all federal societies be deemed greater than the interest in the free movement of interstate trade and commerce and, accordingly, many state laws imperatively necessary to protect the public health will prevail, even when interstate trade and commerce is seriously affected, or even stopped. Justice Jackson of the United States Supreme Court, who was probably committed to a free national market more than any of his colleagues, was nevertheless ready to acknowledge "the power of the State to shelter its people from menaces to their health or safety and from fraud, even when those dangers emanate from interstate commerce."[1]

To protect the health of the community, states in federal societies can generally impose quarantine laws, the effect of which is to totally obstruct the movement of interstate and foreign commerce at their borders. The United States Supreme Court has sustained quarantines applicable to persons when introduction of additional people into an infected area would severely increase public health hazards.[2] The Supreme Court of Canada, too, recognizes that the societal interest in preserving the public health may justify limiting the entrance of persons into a province.[3]

"The prevention of disease is the essence of a quarantine law," explains the United States Supreme Court,[4] which has sustained many state quarantine laws applicable to animals.[5] The High Court of Australia has similarly upheld a New South Wales statute prohibiting the entry of cattle from tick-infested areas until they were dipped.[6] In a case arising under the Constitution of Australia, the Privy Council announced by way of dictum that it was "unnecessary to add, that regulation of trade may clearly take the form of . . . excluding from passage across the frontier of a State creatures or things calculated to injure its citizens."[7] In the United States, quarantines imposed by the states are void when in conflict with federal laws and regulations, but the Supreme Court indicates that in this area, conflict will not be found "unless the repugnance or conflict is so direct and positive that the two acts cannot be reconciled or stand together."[8] Quarantine laws are within the legislative power of the federal governments, under the constitutions of Nigeria and Canada.[9]

States in federal societies can generally impose inspection laws on goods coming into, as well as leaving, the state, and can customarily impose inspection fees reasonably necessary to carry out the inspections.[10] In Australia, the Constitution provides that "a State may levy . . . on goods passing into or out of the State, such charges as may be necessary for executing the inspection laws of the State," but adds that "the net produce of all charges so levied shall be for the use of the Commonwealth; and any such inspection laws may be annulled by the Parliament of the Commonwealth."[11] So-called "inspection laws" are invalidated when they are, in reality, discriminatory laws aimed against goods and products of other states.[12] Inspection fees are voided in the United States when they largely or regularly exceed the cost of inspection.[13] Furthermore, state inspection fees are set aside when in conflict with federal laws or regulations or when they intrude into fields occupied by the federal government.[14]

To safeguard the public health, states in federal societies have been sustained even when their statutes are applicable to entrepreneurs in interstate and commerce, so long as the legislation is generally reasonable.[15] Illustratively, the United States Supreme Court has sustained a local ordinance (authorized by state law) controlling smoke pollution by vessels operating in both interstate and foreign commerce.[16]

To protect the public health, states in many federal societies have been accorded extraordinary powers over the manufacture, distribution and sale of alcoholic beverages. The United States Constitution was amended to provide: "The transportation or importation into any State, Territory or possession of the United States for delivery or use therein of intoxicating liquors, in violation of the laws thereof, is hereby prohibited."[17] At one time, the Supreme Court talked as though Twenty-First Amendment controls were beyond the limitations of the Commerce Clause. In 1939 the Court said: "Since that Amendment, the right of a State to prohibit or regulate the importation of intoxicating liquor is not limited by the commerce clause."[18] More recently, however, the Court has characterized as "an absurd oversimplification" the suggestion that the Amendment "somehow operated to 'repeal' the commerce clause whenever regulation of intoxicating liquors is concerned." Today both interests will be considered by the Court.[19]

The Privy Council held in 1896 that a provincial legislature had no power to prohibit the importation of liquor into the province,[20] but a Dominion statute forbids importation of liquor into any province unless for the government.[21] There is good authority that a province can punish the possession in the province of liquor not procured from government stores.[22]

The Indian Constitution, while placing control over "Interstate trade and Commerce" in the Union Government,[23] has given control over "intoxicating liquors" to the individual states.[24]

The Constitution of Australia provides that: "All fermented, distilled, or other intoxicating liquids passing into any State or remaining therein for use, consumption, sale, or storage, shall be subject to the laws of the State as if such liquids had been produced in the State."[25] Persons who make beer and ale can be required to secure licenses, subject to conditions and inspections.[26] The High Court has described the business of selling liquor as "a trade which, traditionally, has been thought to require regulation and supervision in the public interest," and sustained license requirements and fees of those dispensing liquor on the premises.[27]

State controls, interfering with the free movement of interstate and foreign commerce, will be invalidated as unconstitutional under commerce clauses even though allegedly enacted to protect the public health, when evidence clearly shows the measure makes no contribution to the public health, or at most a very insignificant one.[28]

§ 3.11 State power over interstate commerce—the interest in the free movement of interstate trade and commerce versus the interest in protecting the public safety

The societal interest in protecting the public safety is a very important group concern, and when it has clashed with the societal interest in the free movement of interstate trade and commerce, state laws reasonably protective of the former interest have often been sustained. For example, the United States Supreme Court has reported that "the States have usually been allowed to impose burdens on interstate railroads in the interest of local safety."[1]

A state was sustained in prohibiting the employment of trainmen who were colorblind, even where interstate commerce was involved.[2] Reasonable speed controls on interstate trains going through a community have been sustained.[3] Signals and watchmen at train crossings have been successfully required by the states,[4] as have orders compelling railroads to eliminate grade crossings.[5] States have been upheld in requiring full train crews.[6]

Where interstate vehicles use roads within a state, the United States Supreme Court has upheld many local controls that were reasonably necessary to protect the public safety.[7] In one such case, the Court ruled that a state may impose nondiscriminatory restrictions with regard to the character of motor vehicles moving in interstate commerce as a safety measure.[8] Elsewhere the Supreme Court has said:

> Few subjects of state regulation are so peculiarly of local concern as is the use of state highways. . . . Where traffic control and the use of highways are involved and where there is no conflicting federal regulation, great leeway is allowed local authorities, even though the local regulation materially interferes with interstate commerce."[9]

Where the evidence is strong that a state regulation will be very costly to those who move interstate commerce, and proof shows that the regulation will provide no significant increase in safety to the local community, the United States Supreme Court can be expected to void the state regulation.[10]

Even though the Australian Constitution in section 92 provides that interstate trade and commerce shall be "absolutely free," the courts have acknowledged that society has an important interest in protecting the public safety which justifies restraints upon those operating in interstate commerce. Both High Court justices and the Privy Council have admitted that it would be constitutional "on grounds of public safety, to limit the number of vehicles or the number of vehicles of certain types in certain localities" or over certain roads within the states, as well as for the states to limit speeds of all vehicles, and require specified lights and warning devices.[11] However, the Privy Council held in 1954 (following strong dissents at the High Court by Dixon and Fullagar, Jj.) that section 92 is violated when a state gives an official virtually unbridled power to deny licenses for interstate trucking firms seeking to use the roads of a state.[12]

The Privy Council acknowledged that the Canadian provinces can, even as to interprovincial vehicles, prescribe traffic regulations, including the weight of vehicles using the roads and their speeds, but ruled that a province cannot "sterilize" a company doing interstate transportation or "impair its status and capacities in an essential degree."[13] "A Province is competent to legislate with respect to the use of roads within the Province," writes Justice Trainor, adding however: "Such legislation by itself is inapplicable to an undertaking that extends beyond the geographic limits of the Province, if it sterilizes the functions and activities of the extra-provincial undertaking."[14] To protect the public safety, it is generally accepted that the provinces can regulate the local or intraprovincial aspects of railways,[15] bus lines,[16] and trucking[17] under their power to legislate for "local works and undertakings" conferred by § 92(10) of the British North America Act.

§ 3.12 State power over interstate commerce—the interest in the free movement of interstate trade and commerce versus the interest in protecting the public morality

Specific constitutional provisions often acknowledge state power to control the production, sale and consumption of liquor,[1] and these were motivated in part, at least, out of concern for protecting public morality. Under these constitutional authorizations, the states have, in general, been able to adopt all measures necessary to effectuate their policies regarding liquor, even in application to liquor coming in from other states and abroad.[2]

Lotteries have at times been thought to have a demoralizing effect, and the High Court of Australia has sustained action of New South Wales in (a) punishing the sale there of tickets on lotteries conducted in other states, and (b) banning the exhibition of advertising there for such lotteries.[3] Such lotteries were described by Dixon as "pernicious,"[4] and by Williams as "evil things,"[5] but Kilto seems to have sustained the legislation because applicable to "an act preliminary and preparatory to" interstate intercourse.[6]

In the United States, the power of the states over obscene publications and films is very great and, in practice, is made applicable to such items coming in through the channels of interstate commerce.[7] Regardless of the out-of-state source of beverages sold in bars and taverns, the Supreme Court presently permits very extensive state regulation of such establishments, even where freedom of expression is claimed by the proprietors or artists.[8]

§ 3.13 State power over interstate commerce—the interest in the free movement of interstate trade and commerce versus the interest in protecting the public purse

States have a very legitimate interest in protecting consumers from fraudulent and deceptive trade practices and such legislation can be applied even to firms from out-of-state seeking to persuade local residents to part with their funds.

The High Court of Australia has sustained South Australia legislation prohibiting the gift of a trading stamp in connection with the sale of goods in that state, even in application to the Readers Digest which was a New South Wales company that had sent the invitation to deal into South Australia. Justice Taylor wrote:

> There can be no doubt that a law of general application penalizing or prohibiting some classes of conduct, whether it occurs in the course of interstate trade or not, will be valid. For instance, such a law may validly penalize or prohibit false or fraudulent or misleading advertising.[1]

Justice McTiernan for the majority added that the law was valid even though "prohibitory."[2] Though dissenting on the facts, Chief Justice Barwick readily agreed that a state can "outlaw fraudulent or deceitful practices."[3]

Even where travel agents were closely involved with interstate commerce, the United States Supreme Court held that a state could regulate them by licensing and bonds to protect against "fraudulent and unconscionable conduct."[4] Elsewhere, the Court has said that the states have adequate power "to prevent the deception of consumers," even though interstate commerce is affected.[5] For almost a hundred years the Court has sustained state laws aimed at punishing those who "cheat the general public into purchasing that which they did not intend to buy." The Constitution, said the Court, never "took from the states the power of preventing deception and fraud in the sale, within their respective limits, of articles in whatever state manufactured."[6] Many other state and local laws, aimed at protecting the public purse, have been sustained even when they directly impacted upon interstate commerce. These include laws: banning trading stamps,[7] regulating solicitors for out-of-state concerns,[8] and requiring inspection and proper labeling of foods sold within the community.[9]

§ 3.14 State power over interstate commerce—the interest in the free movement of interstate trade and commerce versus the interest in the general welfare

In all federal societies, the states have a broadly stated interest in the general welfare that at times prevails over the interest in the free flow of commerce.

The states are entitled to sufficient revenues to finance the basic operations and responsibilities assigned to them by federal constitutions, and courts have sustained taxes by states upon firms doing therein even purely interstate or foreign commerce, on the reasonable understanding that such commerce, too, "must pay its way."[1] When charges are small, courts have expressed a ready willingness to sustain levies upon firms doing within a state interstate commerce. Western Australia, for example, was sustained in levying a duty upon receipts by a local firm from carrying goods in interstate commerce when the High Court noted that the charge was but one cent upon every ten dollars received by the local merchant in this manner.[2]

The High Court of Australia has, in effect, held that the societal interest in security justifies states in taking ownership of scarce goods in wartime, as a means of advancing the war effort, even when such legislation is applied to goods which the owner was already under contract to ship out of the state.[3] Although in the Wheat Case, the High Court explained the legislation affected not "trade," but "ownership," it would be better to describe the decision, as Professor Howard ably has,[4] as showing the legitimate subordination of the interest in free trade and commerce to the overriding societal interest in protecting security.[5]

Embraced within the general welfare is a strong societal interest in protecting the public peace and quiet, and this prevails at times over the interest in the free movement of interstate commerce. In holding that a state and its political subdivisions can stringently control, almost to elimination, door-to-door solicitors, even for firms doing interstate commerce, Justice Reed for the United States Supreme Court aptly observed: "Unwanted knocks on the door by day or night are a nuisance, or worse to peace and quiet."[6]

The societal interest in the general welfare embraces concern for ending racial and other forms of invidious discrimination, and this justifies states in enacting legislation to that end, even when carriers in interstate and foreign commerce are brought within the controls.[7]

§ 3.15 State power to regulate foreign commerce

In the United States, the power of the states to regulate foreign commerce is very comparable to their power to regulate interstate commerce, that is to say, states are upheld in protecting their legitimate societal interests even when foreign commerce is affected, so long as: (a) there is no conflict with federal laws or regulations; (b) there is no occupation of the field by the federal government; (c) the problem is not a national one; (d) there is no discrimination against entrepreneurs in foreign commerce or goods coming from such commerce; (e) there is not available to the state reasonable alternatives that would protect their interest adequately with less interference to foreign commerce; and (f) the burden upon foreign commerce is a reasonable one.[1]

To protect the public health, a state has been able to impose a quarantine upon passengers coming in from abroad on board a vessel.[2] States can impose air pollution controls upon vessels operating in their waters in foreign commerce.[3] The Constitution impliedly recognizes a right in the states to apply inspection laws to produce and other articles being imported.[4] State power to control the introduction of liquor under the Twenty-first Amendment is very broad,[5] although the Supreme Court recognizes that this Amendment must be considered together with the Commerce Clause.[6]

To protect the public safety, states have been sustained in requiring pilots for vessels entering their ports from abroad.[7]

In 1875 the Supreme Court voided a state fee of $1.50 from every alien passenger arriving at one of its ports from abroad, concluding the matter was a national one. Said the Court: "A regulation which imposes onerous, perhaps impossible conditions on those engaged in active commerce with foreign nations, must of necessity be national in its character."[8]

In Australia, even though the Constitution gives to the Commonwealth Parliament power over "Trade and Commerce with other countries, and among the States,"[9] the states, which possess the residuum of power, are deemed to share with the Commonwealth a concurrent power over foreign commerce.[10] Indeed, under the Constitution the states may have greater powers over foreign commerce than over interstate commerce, since the principal constitutional limitation found in Section 92 only provides that "trade among the States . . . shall be absolutely free"— there being no reference to foreign trade and commerce.

In Canada, Justice Rand of the Supreme Court said in 1957 that "inter-provincial and foreign trade are correspondingly the exclusive concern of Parliament,"[11] and earlier authority generally supported the proposition that control over foreign trade and commerce is exclusively in the Dominion Parliament. The Saskatchewan Supreme Court had held that the province could not prevent the delivery of liquor sold for export to persons outside the province. Said Chief Justice Haultain: "It directly interferes with inter-provincial and foreign trade . . . and directly infringes on the exclusive jurisdiction of Parliament in respect of the regulation of trade in a matter of inter-provincial or international concern."[12] The principal source of power to the provinces (which are not the residuaries of power) under the British North America Act gives them power over "property and civil rights *in the province,*"[13] may well be used to deny provinces power over matters primarily of foreign trade,[14] although it can be expected that legislation having its principal impact within a province will be sustained when there is only a slight, incidental affect upon the foreign commerce.

FOOTNOTES

§ 3.00

[1] Southern Pacific Rr. v. Arizona (1945) 325 US 761, 65 S Ct 1515, 89 L Ed 1915, 1925.
[2] Parker v. Brown (1943) 317 US 341, 73 S Ct 307, 87 L Ed 315; Highland Farms Dairy v. Agnew (1937) 300 US 608, 57 S Ct 549, 81 L Ed 835.
[3] Nygh, "The Police Power of the States in the United States and Australia," 2 *Fed. L. Rev.* 183 (1967).
[4] Oriente v. Costa (1866) 3 S.C.N. 468.
[5] Constitution of India, State List, Entry 26. However, this is subject to Entry 33 on the Concurrent List, in effect enabling the Union Parliament to legislate in this area.
[6] Reference Farm Products Marketing Act (1957) 7 D.L.R. 2d 257, 268.
[7] Nebbia v. New York (1934) 291 US 502, 54 S Ct 505, 78 L Ed 940.
[8] Parker v. Brown (1943) 317 US 341, 63 S Ct 307, 87 L Ed 315.
[9] Allied Stores of Ohio v. Bowers (1959) 358 US 522, 79 S Ct 437, 441, 3 L Ed 2d 480.
[10] McGowan v. Maryland (1961) 366 US 420, 81 S Ct 1101, 6 L Ed 2d 393, 399.
[11] Constitution of the United States, Article VI, par. 2; McDermott v. Wisconsin (1913) 228 US 115, 33 S Ct 431, 57 L Ed 754.
[12] Attorney-General for Canada v. Attorney-General for British Columbia (1930) A.C. 111.
[13] O'Sullivan v. Noarlunga Meat Ltd. (#1) (1954) 92 C.L.R. 565; Napier v. Atlantic Coast Line Rr. (1926) 272 US 605, 47 S Ct 207, 71 L Ed 432.

§ 3.01

[1] Associated Press v. National Labor Relations Board (1937) 301 US 103, 57 S Ct 650, 81 L Ed 953.
[2] The Daniel Ball (1871) 10 Wall. 557, 19 L Ed 999.
[3] United States v. Yellow Cab Co. (1947) 332 US 218, 67 S Ct 1560, 1566, 91 L Ed 2010.
[4] Russell v. Walters (1957) 96 C.L.R. 177.
[5] Simms v. West (1961) 107 C.L.R. 157.
[6] Dahnke-Walker Milling Co. v. Bondurant (1921) 257 US 282, 42 S Ct 106, 66 L Ed 239.
[7] York Manufacturing Co. v. Colley (1918) 247 US 21, 38 S Ct 430, 62 L Ed 963, 11 ALR 611.
[8] Sleigh Ltd. v. South Australia (1977) 136 C.L.R. 475, 495.

§ 3.02

[1] Samuels v. Readers Digest Association Pty. Ltd. (1969) 120 C.L.R. 1, 14 (dissenting).
[2] Southern Pacific Co. v. Arizona (1945) 325 US 761, 65 S Ct 1515, 89 L Ed 1915.
[3] Constitution of Argentina, Article 10.
[4] Constitution of Argentina, Article 108.
[5] Constitution of Australia, section 92.
[6] Constitution of Brazil, Article XVII(L).
[7] Constitution of Canada (British North America Act) § 91(2).
[8] Constitution of Canada (British North America Act) § 121.
[9] Winner v. S.M.T. Ltd. (1951) S.C.R. 887, 918.
[10] Murphy v. C.P.R. Co. (1958) 15 D.L.R. 2d 145, 153.
[11] Grundgesetz of German Federal Republic, Article 72.
[12] *Studies in Federalism* (Bowie & Friedrich eds., Boston 1954) 347.
[13] Constitution of India, Part XIII, § 301.
[14] Atiabari Tea Co. v. State of Assam, A.I.R. 1961 S.C. 232, 240 (dissenting).
[15] Constitution of Mexico, Article 73, § IX(4).
[16] Constitution of Mexico, Article 117(V).

[17] Constitution of Nigeria 1979, Second Schedule, Part I(61).

[18] Constitution of the United States, Article I, § 8.

[19] Constitution of Switzerland, Article 31.

[20] Studies in Federalism (Bowie & Friedrich eds., Boston 1954) ^ '^.

[21] Constitution of Venezuela, Article 18(3).

[22] Constitution of Venezuela, Article 18(1).

[23] Constitution of Venezuela, Article 18(2).

[24] Constitution of India, Article 19(1) (d).

[25] Grundgesetz of German Federal Republic, Article 11(1).

[26] Shapiro v. Thompson (1969) 394 US 618, 89 S Ct 1322, 22 L Ed 2d 600; United States v. Guest (1966) 383 US 745, 86 S Ct 1170, 16 L Ed 2d 239.

[27] Nebbia v. New York (1934) 291 US 502, 54 S Ct 505, 78 L Ed 940.

[28] Constitution of India, Art. 19(1) (g).

§ 3.03

[1] Constitution of Australia, § 92.

[2] Duncan v. Queensland (1916) 22 C.L.R. 556, 575.

[3] Samuels v. Readers Digest Association Pty. Ltd. (1969) 120 C.L.R. 1, 15 (dissenting).

[4] Smith v. Capewell (1979) 142 C.L.R. 509, 529 (dissenting); Bartter's Farm Pty. Ltd. v. Todd and Others (1978) 139 C.L.R. 499, 525.

[5] Samuels v. Readers Digest Association Pty. Ltd. (1969) 120 C.L.R. 1, 15 (dissenting).

[6] Constitution of India, Part XIII, § 301.

[7] Constitution of India, Part XIII, § 304(b).

[8] Automobile Transport Co. v. State of Rajasthan, A.I.R. 1962 S.C. 1406.

[9] Constitution of Canada (British North America Act) § 91(2).

[10] Reference re Farm Products Marketing Act (1957) 7 D.L.R. 2d 257, 264 (Kerwin, C.J.C.), followed in Attorney-General for Manitoba v. Manitoba Egg and Poultry Association (1971) 19 D.L.R. 3d 169, 179 (Martland, J.).

[11] Bingaman v. Golden Eagle Western Lines (1936) 297 US 626, 56 S Ct 624, 80 L Ed 928; Erb v. Morasch (1900) 177 US 584, 20 S Ct 819, 44 L Ed 897, 898.

[12] Samuels v. Readers Digest Association Pty. Ltd. (1969) 120 C.L.R. 1, 16 (dissenting).

[13] "A State cannot . . . impose a prior restraint on trade and commerce." McArthur's Case (1920) 28 C.L.R. 530, 551.

[14] Hughes and Vale Pty. Ltd. v. New South Wales (#1) (1954) 93 C.L.R. 1 (P.C.); Milk Board (NSW) v. Metropolitan Cream Pty. Ltd. (1939) 62 C.L.R. 116, 127 (Latham, C.J.).

[15] Aptly described by Chief Justice Stone of the United States Supreme Court as "little more than using labels to describe a result rather than any trustworthy formula by which it is reached." DiSanto v. Pennsylvania (1927) 273 US 34, 47 S Ct 267, 71 L Ed 524.

§ 3.04

[1] Constitution of India, Part XIII, § 303(1).

[2] Constitution of India, Part XIII, § 304(a).

[3] Fox v. Robbins (1909) 8 C.L.R. 115.

[4] Hughes and Vale Pty. Ltd. v. New South Wales (#2) (1955) 93 C.L.R. 127, 160.

[5] Fox v. Robbins (1909) 8 C.L.R. 115.

[6] Indianapolis Brewing Co. v. Liquor Control Commission (1939) 305 US 391, 59 S Ct 254, 83 L Ed 243; State Board of Equalization v. Young's Market (1936) 299 US 59, 57 S Ct 77, 8 1 L Ed 38; Mahoney v. Joseph Triner Corp. (1938) 304 US 401, 58 S Ct 952, 82 L Ed 1424.

[7] Welton v. Missouri (1876) 91 US 275, 23 L Ed 347.

[8] Guy v. Baltimore (1880) 100 US 434, 25 L Ed 742.

[9] Minnesota v. Barber (1890) 136 US 313, 10 S Ct 862, 34 L Ed 477.

[10] Dean Milk v. Madison (1951) 340 US 349, 71 S Ct 295, 95 L Ed 329.

[11] Attorney-General for Manitoba v. Manitoba Egg & Poultry Association (1971) 19 D.L.R. 3d 169, 179.

§ 3.05

[1] R. v. Smithers; ex parte Benson (1913) 16 C.L.R. 99.
[2] Edwards v. California (1941) 314 US 160, 62 S C6 164, 86 L Ed 119.
[3] Winner v. S.M.T. Ltd. (1951) S.C.R. 887, 918 (Rand, Kerwin Estey and Cartwright, Jj.)
[4] Compagnie Francaise de Navigation a Vapeur v. Louisiana Board of Health (1902) 186 US 380, 22 S Ct 811, 46 L Ed 1209.
[5] Baldwin v. G.A.F. Seelig Inc. (1935) 294 US 511, 527, 55 S Ct 497, 79 L Ed 1032.
[6] Polar Ice Creame Co. v. Andrews (1964) 375 US 361, 84 S Ct 378, 11 L Ed 2d 389.
[7] Philadelphia v. New Jersey (1978) 437 US 617, 98 S Ct 2531, 57 L Ed 2d 475.
[8] Crickard v. Attorney-General for British Columbia (B.C.S.Ct. 1958) 14 D.L.R. 2d 58 (could not prohibit the importation of eggs into the province).
[9] Gold Seal Ltd. v. Dominion Express (1921) 62 D.L.R. 62, 86.
[10] Attorney-General for Manitoba v. Manitoba Egg and Poultry Association (1971) 19 D.L.R. 3d 169, 189-190.
[11] Re Kelly Douglas Co. Ltd. v. British Columbia Broiler Marketing Board (1977) 84 D.L.R. 3d 133, 146-7 (B.C.S.Ct.)
[12] Burns Foods Ltd. v. Attorney-General for Manitoba (1973) 40 D.L.R. 3d 731.
[13] Attorney-General for Ontario v. Attorney-General for Canada (1896) A.C. 348. Note, however, the Importation of Intoxicating Liquor Act, R.S.C. 1970, c. I-4, in which the Dominion Parliament forbade the importation of liquor into a province unless for the government of the province.
[14] MacArthur Ltd. v. Queensland (1920) 28 C.L.R. 530, 555.
[15] Grundgesetz of German Federal Republic, Article 72.
[16] Roasauer v. Mendoza (1937) 179 S.C.N. 69.

§ 3.06

[1] Smith v. Maryland (1855) 18 How. 71, 15 L Ed 269; McCready v. Virginia (1877) 94 US 391, 24 L Ed 248; Manchester v. Massachusetts (1891) 139 US 240, 11 S Ct 559, 35 L Ed 159; Hudson County Water Co. v. McCarter (1908) 209 US 349, 28 S Ct 529, 52 L Ed 828; Champlin Refining Co. v. Corporation Commission of Oklahoma (1932) 286 US 210, 52 S Ct 559, 76 L Ed 1062. Geer v. Connecticut (1896) 161 US 519, 16 S Ct 600, 40 L Ed 793 was over-ruled in Hughes v. Oklahoma (1979) 441 US 332, 99 S Ct 1727, 60 L Ed 2d 250.
[2] Hughes v. Oklahoma (1979) 441 US 332, 99 S Ct 1727, 60 L Ed 2d 250.
[3] Sligh v. Kirkwood (1915) 237 US 52, 35 S Ct 501, 59 L Ed 835.
[4] Hood and Sons v. DuMond (1949) 336 US 525, 531, 69 S Ct 657, 93 L Ed 865.
[5] Ibid., US p. 539.
[6] Hudson County Water Co. v. McCarter (1908) 209 US 349, 28 S Ct 529, 52 L Ed 828.
[7] Pennsylvania v. West Virginia (1923) 262 US 553, 43 S Ct 658, 67 L Ed 1117.
[8] Milk Control Board v. Eisenberg Farm Products (1939) 306 US 346, 59 S Ct 528, 83 L Ed 752.
[9] Parker v. Brown (1943) 317 US 341, 63 S Ct 307, 87 L Ed 315.
[10] Reeves Inc. v. Stake (1980) 447 US 429, 100 S Ct 2271, 65 L Ed 2d 244.
[11] Central Canada Potash Co. Ltd. v. Saskatchewan (1978) 88 D.L.R. 3d 609, 630 (Laskin, J.)
[12] R. v. Boscowitz (B.C. S. Ct. 1895) 4 B.C. 132.
[13] Central Canada Potash Co. Ltd. v. Saskatchewan (1978) 88 D.L.R. 3d 609 (as to potash going into interprovincial and foreign trade, province could not limit production and prorate the same, to raise prices of its local product.)
[14] Canadian Industrial Gas & Oil Ltd. v. Saskatchewan (1977) 80 D.L.R. 3d 449, 464.

[15] Carnation Co. Ltd. v. Ontario Agricultural Marketing Board (1968) 67 D.L.R. 2d 1 (sustaining price controls on milk purchased from a producer in the province by a processor operating there.)

[16] Attorney-General for Manitoba v. Manitoba Egg & Poultry Association (1971) 19 D.L.R. 3d 169, 187-189.

[17] Societe Asbestos Ltee v. Societe Nationale de L'Amiante (Q.Ct.App. 1981) 128 D.L.R. 3d 405, 418 (Bisson, J.A.)

[18] Shannon v. Lower Mainland Dairy Production Board (B.C.) (1938) 4 D.L.R. 81 (A.C.); Prince Edward Island Potato Marketing Board v. Willis (1952) 4 D.L.R. 146, 166.

[19] In re Saskatchewan Grain Marketing Act 1931 (1931) 2 W.W.R. 146 (Ct. App.); British Columbia Marketing Act 1926-7; Lawson v. Interior Fruit and Vegetable Commission (1931) 2 D.L.R. 193 (S.Ct. of Can.); Graham & Strang v. Dominion Express Co. (1920) 48 O.L.R. 83 (liquor); "The right to sell or export cannot be restricted or regulated by provincial legislation" Re Sheep & Swine Marketing Scheme (P.E.I. S.Ct. 1941) (1941) 3 D.L.R. 569, 575 (Saunders, J.).

[20] James v. South Australia (1927) 40 C.L.R. 1.

[21] Peanut Board v. Rockhampton Harbour Board (1933) 48 C.L.R. 266, 275.

[22] Milk Board (NSW) v. Metropolitan Cream Pty. Ltd. (1939) 62 C.L.R. 116, 151.

[23] Compania Azucarera Concepcion v. Tucuman (1935) 173 S.C.N. 429.

§ 3.07

[1] New South Wales v. Commonwealth (The Wheat Case) (1915) 20 C.L.R. 54.

[2] Duncan v. Queensland (1916) 22 C.L.R. 556.

[3] Foggitt, Jones and Co. Ltd. v. New South Wales (1916) 21 C.L.R. 357.

[4] McArthur's Case (1920) 28 C.L.R. 530.

[5] Wilcox Moflin Ltd. v. New South Wales (1952) 85 C.L.R. 488, 519.

[6] Grannal v. Marrickville Pty. Ltd. (1955) 93 C.L.R. 55.

[7] Beal v. Marrickville Margarine Pty. Ltd. (1966) 114 C.L.R. 283.

[8] O'Sullivan v. Miracle Foods (S.A.) Pty. Ltd. (1966) 115 C.L.R. 177, 186.

[9] Bartter's Farms Pty. Ltd. v. Todd and Others (1978) 139 C.L.R. 499.

[10] Central Canada Potash Co. Ltd. v. Saskatchewan (1978) 88 D.L.R. 3d 609, 630.

[11] Carnation Co. Ltd. v. Ontario Agricultural Marketing Board (1968) 67 D.L.R. 2d 1.

[12] Societe Asbestos Ltee. v. Societe Nationale de L'Amiante (Q. Ct. App 1981) 128 D.L.R. 3d 405, 418.

[13] Re The Queen and Cattrell Forwarding Co. (Ont. H. Ct. 1981) 124 D.L.R. 3d 674.

[14] Milk Control Board v. Eisenberg Farm Products (1939) 306 US 346, 59 S Ct 528, 83 L Ed 752.

[15] Dahnke-Walker Milling Co. v. Bondurant (1921) 257 US 282, 291, 42 S Ct 106, 66 L Ed 239.

§ 3.08

[1] O'Sullivan v. Miracle Foods (S.A.) Pty. Ltd. (1966) 115 C.L.R. 177, 186.

[2] Wragg v. New South Wales (1953) 88 C.L.R. 353.

[3] Harper v. Victoria (1966) 114 C.L.R. 361.

[4] Milk Board (NSW) v. Metropolitan Cream Pty. Ltd. (1939) 62 C.L.R. 116. 116.

[5] Grannall v. C. Geo. Kellaway and Sons Pty. Ltd. (1955) 93 C.L.R. 36.

[6] Williams v. Metropolitan and Export Abattoirs Board (1953) 89 C.L.R. 66.

[7] O'Sullivan v. Miracle Foods (S.A.) Pty. Ltd. (1966) 115 C.L.R. 177.

[8] Associated Steamships Pty. v. Western Australia (1969) 120 C.L.R. 92.

[9] Attorney General for Ontario v. Attorney General for Canada (1896) A.C. 348.

[10] R. v. Nat Bell Liquors Ltd. (1922) 65 D.L.R. 1 (P.C.); Regina v. Gautreau (N.B. S.Ct. 1978) 88 D.L.R. 3d 718.

[11] Home Oil Distributors Ltd. v. Attorney General for British Columbia (1940) 2 D.L.R. 609.

[12] Highland Farms Dairy v. Agnew (1937) 300 US 608, 57 S Ct 549, 81 L Ed 835.
[13] Plumley v. Massachusetts (1894) 155 US 461, 15 S Ct 154, 39 L Ed 223.
[14] Vacuum Oil Co. Pty. Ltd. v. Queensland (1934) 51 C.L.R. 108.
[15] Fish Board v. Paradiso (1956) 95 C.L.R. 443.
[16] Milk Board (NSW) v. Metropolitan Cream Pty. Ltd. (1939) 62 C.L.R. 116, 151 (Evatt, J.)
[17] York Manufacturing Co. v. Colley (1918) 247 US 21, 38 S Ct 430, 11 ALR 611.

§ 3.09

[1] Pure Oil Co. v. Minnesota (1918) 248 US 158, 39 S Ct 35, 63 L Ed 180.
[2] Hughes and Vale Pty. Ltd. v. New South Wales (#1) (1954) 93 C.L.R. 1, 25.
[3] Clyde Mallory Lines v. Alabama (1935) 296 US 261, 266, 56 S Ct 194, 80 L Ed 215.
[4] Armstrong v. Victoria (#2) (1957) 99 C.L.R. 28 (holding additionally, however, that registration fees applicable to firms using state highways in purely interstate commerce were unconstitutional).
[5] Aero Mayflower Transit Co. v. Board of Commissioners (1947) 332 US 495, 68 S Ct 167, 92 L Ed 99; Capitol Greyhound Lines v. Brice (1950) 339 US 542, 70 S Ct 806, 94 L Ed 1053, 17 ALR 2d 407.
[6] Sprout v. South Bend (1928) 277 US 163, 48 S Ct 502, 72 L Ed 833, 62 ALR 45.
[7] Evansville-Vanderburgh Airport Authority v. Delta Airlines Inc. (1972) 405 US 707, 92 S Ct 1349, 31 L Ed 2d 620.

§ 3.10

[1] H.P. Hood & Sons v. DuMond (1949) 336 US 525, 69 S Ct 657, 93 L Ed 865.
[2] Compagnie Francaise de Navigation a Vapeur v. Louisiana State Board of Health (1902) 186 US 380, 22 S Ct 811, 46 L Ed 1209.
[3] "A Province cannot prevent a Canadian from entering it except, conceivably, in temporary circumstances, for some local reason as, for example health." Winner v. S.M.T. Ltd. (1951) S.C.R. 887, 918 (Rand, Kerwin, Estey and Cartwright, Jj.)
[4] Smith v. St. Louis and S.W. Rr. (1901) 181 US 248, 255-6, 21 S Ct 603, 45 L Ed 847.
[5] Missouri, K. & T. Rr. v. Haber (1898) 169 US 613, 18 S Ct 488, 42 L Ed 878; Rasmussen v. Idaho (1901) 181 US 198, 21 S Ct 594, 45 L Ed 820.
[6] Ex parte Nelson (1928) 42 C.L.R. 209.
[7] Hughes & Vale Pty. Ltd. v. New South Wales(#1) (1954) 93 C.L.R. 1, 19.
[8] Missouri, K. & T. Rr. v. Haber (1898) 169 US 613, 623, 18 S Ct 488, 42 L Ed 878.
[9] Nigerian Constitution 1979, Second Schedule, Part I (53). British North America Act, § 91(11), but cf. St. Louis du Mile-End v. Montreal (1923) 1 D.L.R. 869.
[10] Sligh v. Kirkwood (1915) 237 US 52, 35 S Ct 501, 59 L Ed 835; New Mexico ex rel. McLean v. Denver and Rio Grande Rr. (1906) 203 US 38, 27 S Ct 1, 51 L Ed 78; Pure Oil Co. V. Minnesota (1918) 248 US 158, 39 S Ct 35, 63 L Ed 180; Patapsco Guano Co. v. Board of Agriculture (1898) 171 US 345, 18 S Ct 862, 43 L Ed 191.
[11] Constitution of Australia, Section 112.
[12] Brimmer v. Rebman (1891) 138 US 78, 11 S Ct 213, 34 L Ed 862; Voight v. Wright (1891) 141 US 62, 11 S Ct 213, 35 L Ed 638; Hale v. Bimco Trading, Inc. (1939) 306 US 375, 59 S Ct 526, 83 L Ed 771.
[13] D.E. Foote & Co. v. Stanley (1914) 232 US 494, 34 S Ct 377, 58 L Ed 698; Askren v. Continental Oil Co. (1920) 252 US 444, 40 S Ct 355, 64 L Ed 654; Standard Oil Co. v. Graves (1919) 249 US 389, 39 S Ct 320, 63 L Ed 662.
[14] Cf. Savage v. Jones (1912) 225 US 501, 32 S Ct 715, 56 L Ed 1182.
[15] Head v. New Mexico Board of Examiners in Optometry (1963) 374 US 424, 83 S Ct 1759, 10 L Ed 2d 983.
[16] Huron Portland Cement Co. v. Detroit (1960) 362 US 440, 80 S Ct 813, 4 L Ed 2d 852.
[17] United States Constitution, Twenty-First Amendment.
[18] Joseph S. Finch & Co. v. McKittrick (1939) 305 US 395, 398, 59 S Ct 256, 83 L Ed 246.

19 Hostetter v. Idlewild Bon Voyage Liquor Corp. (1964) 377 US 324, 84 S Ct 1293, 12 L Ed 2d 350, 356.
20 Attorney General for Ontario v. Attorney General for Canada (1896) A.C. 348.
21 Importation of Intoxicating Liquor Act R.S.C. 1970, c. I-4.
22 Regina v. Bautreau (N.B. S. Ct. 1978) 88 D.L.R. 3d 718.
23 Constitution of India, Union List, Art. 253(42).
24 Constitution of India, State List, Art. 253(8).
25 Constitution of Australia, § 113.
26 Peterswald v. Bartley (1904) 1 C.L.R. 497.
27 Dennis Hotels Pty. Ltd. v. Victoria (1961) 104 C.L.R. 529, 569.
28 O'Sullivan v. Miracle Foods (S.A.) Pty. Ltd. (1966) 115 C.L.R. 177 (unrelated to health was requirement that small amounts of dry starch or arrowroot be added to margarine sold in South Australia).

§ 3.11

1 South Carolina State Highway Dept. v. Barnwell Bros. (1938) 303 US 177, 186 fn. 2, 58 S Ct 510, 82 L Ed 734.
2 Nashville, C. & St. L. Rr. v. Alabama (1888) 128 US 96, 9 S Ct 28, 32 L Ed 352.
3 Erb v. Morasch (1900) 177 US 584, 20 S Ct 819, 44 L Ed 897.
4 Nashville, C. & St. L. Rr. v. White (1929) 278 US 456, 49 S Ct 189, 73 L Ed 452.
5 Atchison, T. & S. F. Rr. v. Public Utilities Commission (1953) 346 US 346, 74 S Ct 92, 98 L Ed 51.
6 Missouri Pacific Rr. v. Norwood (1931) 283 US 249, 51 S Ct 458, 75 L Ed 1010.
7 Sproles v. Binford (1932) 286 US 374, 52 S Ct 581, 76 L Ed 1167.
8 South Carolina State Highway Dept. v. Barnwell Bros. (1938) 303 US 177, 58 S Ct 510, 82 L Ed 734.
9 Railway Express Agency v. New York (1949) 336 US 106, 69 S Ct 463, 466, 93 L Ed 533.
10 Bibb v. Navajo Freight Lines (1959) 359 US 520, 79 S Ct 962, 3 L Ed 2d 1003; Southern Pacific Co. v. Arizona (1945) 325 US 761, 65 S Ct 1515, 89 L Ed 1915.
11 Hughes & Vale Pty. Ltd. v. New South Wales (#1) (1954) 93 C.L.R. 1.
12 Idem.
13 Attorney General for Ontario v . Winner (1954) 4 D.L.R. 657, 674, 676 (Lord Porter).
14 Regina v. Letco Bulk Carriers Inc. (Ont. H. Ct. 1979) 105 D.L.R. 3d 725, 729.
15 Montreal v. Montreal Street Ry. (1912) A.C. 333; British Columbia Electric Ry. v. C.N.R. (1932) S.C.R. 161.
16 Attorney-General for Ontario v. Winner (1954) 4 D.L.R. 657, (1954) A.C. 541 (dictum).
17 Re Tank Truck Transport (1960) O.R. 497 (H Ct), affirmed (Ontario S.Ct.); R. v. Cooksville Magistrate Court; ex parte Liquid Cargo Lines Ltd. (1963) 1 O.R. 272, (1965) 1 O.R. 84 (H Ct).

§ 3.12

1 Constitution of the United States, Twenty-first Amendment; Constitution of Australia, § 113: "All fermented, distilled, or other intoxicating liquids passing into any State or remaining therein for use, consumption, sale, or storage, shall be subject to the laws of the State as if such liquids had been produced in the State."
2 Ziffrin Inc. v. Reeves (1939) 308 US 132, 60 S Ct 163, 84 L Ed 128.
3 Mansell v. Beck (1956) 95 C.L.R. 550.
4 Ibid. p. 568.
5 Ibid. p. 573.
6 Ibid. p. 584.
7 Miller v. California (1973) 413 US 15, 93 S Ct 2607, 37 L Ed 2d 419; Times Film Corp. v. Chicago (1961) 365 US 43, 81 S Ct 391, 5 L Ed 2d 403.
8 California v. LaRue (1972) 409 US 109, 93 S Ct 390, 34 L Ed 2d 342.

§ 3.13

[1] Samuels v. Readers Digest Association Pty. Ltd. (1969) 120 C.L.R. 1, 36.
[2] Ibid. p. 23.
[3] Ibid. p. 19.
[4] California v. Thompson (1941) 313 US 109, 115, 61 S Ct 930, 85 L Ed 1219.
[5] Florida Lime & Avocado Growers, Inc. v. Paul (1963) 373 US 132, 83 S Ct 1210, 10 L Ed 2d 248.
[6] Plumley v. Massachusetts (1894) 155 US 461, 15 S Ct 154, 39 L Ed 223, 227, 229.
[7] Rast v. Van Deman Co. (1916) 240 US 342, 36 S Ct 370, 60 L Ed 679.
[8] Breard v. Alexandria (1951) 341 US 622, 71 S Ct 920, 95 L Ed 1233.
[9] Savage v. Jones (1912) 225 US 501, 32 S Ct 715, 56 L Ed 1182.

§ 3.14

[1] Complete Auto Transit v. Brady (1977) 430 US 274, 97 S Ct 1076, 51 L Ed 2d 326; Colonial Pipeline Co. v. Traigle (1975) 421 US 100, 95 S Ct 1538, 44 L Ed 2d 1.
[2] Associated Steamships Pty. Ltd. v. Western Australia (1969) 120 C.L.R. 92, 113 (Windeyer, J.).
[3] New South Wales v. Commonwealth (The Wheat Case) (1915) 20 C.L.R. 54.
[4] Howard, *Australian Federal Constitutional Law* (2d ed. 1972, Sydney) 288: "A better ground of decision would have been to subject § 92 to the needs of national defense."
[5] Idem.
[6] Breard v. Alexandria (1951) 341 US 622, 71 S Ct 920, 95 L Ed 1233.
[7] Bob-Lo Excursion Co. v. Michigan (1948) 333 US 28, 68 S Ct 358, 92 L Ed 455.

§ 3.15

[1] DiSanto v. Pennsylvania (1927) 273 US 34, 47 S Ct 267, 71 L Ed 524, overruled on other grounds in California v. Thompson (1941) 313 US 109, 61 S Ct 930, 85 L Ed 1219; Bob-Lo Excursion Co. v. Michigan (1948) 333 US 28, 68 S Ct 358, 92 L Ed 455; Ray v. Atlantic Richfield Co. (1978) 435 US 151, 98 S Ct 988, 55 L Ed 2d 179.
[2] Compagnie Francaise de Navigation a Vapeur v. Louisiana State Board of Health (1902) 186 US 380, 22 S Ct 811, 46 L Ed 1209.
[3] Bob-Lo Excursion Co. v. Michigan (1948) 333 US 28, 68 S Ct 358, 92 L Ed 455.
[4] Constitution of the United States, Art. I, § 10, cl. 2. Pure Oil Co. v. Minnesota (1918) 248 US 158, 39 S Ct 35, 63 L Ed 180.
[5] State Board of Equalization v. Young's Market (1936) 299 US 59, 57 S Ct 77, 81 L Ed 38.
[6] Hostetter v. Bon Voyage Liquor Corp. (1964) 377 US 324, 84 S Ct 1293, 12 L Ed 2d 350 (voiding New York regulation of liquor sales at an international airport, where delivery would be abroad).
[7] Cooley v. Board of Wardens of Port of Philadelphia (1851) 12 How. 299, 13 L Ed 996; Ray v. Atlantic Richfield Co. (1978) 435 US 151, 98 S Ct 988, 55 L Ed 2d 179; Olsen v. Smith (1904) 195 US 332, 25 S Ct 52, 49 L Ed 224.
[8] Henderson v . New York (1876) 29 US 259, 274, 23 L Ed 543.
[9] Constitution of Australia, § 51(i).
[10] Howard, *Australian Federal Constitutional Law* (2d ed. 1972, Sydney) 250.
[11] Reference Farm Products Marketing Act of Ontario (1957) 7 D.L.R. 2d 257, 268.
[12] Canada Drugs Ltd. v. Attorney-General for Saskatchewan (1922) 67 D.L.R. 3, 5 (but sustaining that part of the statute restricting export liquor warehouses to certain cities).
[13] Constitution of Canada (British North America Act) § 92(13), emphasis added.
[14] Hogg, *Constitutional Law of Canada* (1977) 319.

CHAPTER FOUR

CHAPTER FOUR

Chapter Four

STATE POWER TO TAX INTERSTATE AND FOREIGN COMMERCE

§ 4.00 Taxation affecting interstate and foreign commerce—generally

In virtually all the federal societies there are constitutional clauses either explicitly or implicitly limiting the powers of the states to tax interstate and foreign commerce. For instance, the Australian Constitution provides that "trade, commerce, and intercourse among the States . . . shall be absolutely free,"[1] and this is a restriction upon the power of the states to tax.[2]

In the United States, the Commerce Clause of the Constitution[3] not only confers power on the federal government, but limits the power of the states to tax interstate and foreign commerce.[4]

States in India are limited in their power to tax interstate commerce by Article 301 of the Constitution—the commerce clause.[5] Additionally, Article 304(a) forbids taxation discriminating against goods or products from other states.[6] From this Article, however, Justice Gajendragadkar of the Supreme Court has inferred that "taxation can be levied by the State Legislatures on goods manufactured or produced within its territory."[7]

The Constitution of Argentina 1853, as amended, provides in Article 10 that "the circulation of goods of national production or manufacture is free from duties in the interior of the Republic, as is also that of goods and merchandise of all kinds dispatched through the national customs houses." Provincial taxes on interprovincial and foreign commerce are generally unconstitutional.[8] When marine insurance contracts were integral parts of interprovincial or foreign commerce, they were immunized from taxation by the provinces.[9]

The Constitution of Brazil provides that states cannot "establish a tax differential between goods of any nature by reason of their provenance or destination."[10]

In Venezuela, the Constitution denies state power to tax in a number of areas affecting commerce. Article 18 provides that states may not "(1) Create custom houses or taxes on imports, export taxes, or taxes on transit of foreign or domestic goods . . . , (2) Tax consumer goods before they enter into circulation within their territory, (3) Prohibit consumption of goods produced outside their territory or tax them differently from those produced within their jurisdiction."

Canada's Constitution (the British North America Act) provides, as to both the provinces and the Dominion, that: "All articles of the growth, produce or manufacture of any one of the provinces shall . . . be admitted free into each of the other provinces."[11] Furthermore, § 92(2) of the Act permits the provinces to impose only "direct" taxes and this limits provincial power to tax interstate and foreign commerce, as by outlawing customs and excise taxes.[12] The ban upon "indirect" provincial taxation is treated in the following chapter.

It has frequently been said in federal societies that state taxes on interstate trade and commerce are generally unconstitutional,[13] but it is fair that interstate commerce, too, must pay its way[14] and following sections indicate many instances where state taxes having some effect upon interstate and foreign commerce are valid.

It can be said generally that all state taxes discriminating against the persons or products of sister states in a federation will be unconstitutional. The United States Supreme Court states: "The Commerce Clause forbids any such discrimination against the free flow of trade over state boundaries."[15]

§ 4.01 State taxation of goods destined for interstate and foreign commerce

Even in the federal societies, states have ordinarily been able to impose property taxes upon goods destined for interstate and foreign commerce, when the tax attaches to the goods before physical movement has actually begun in such commerce. So long as there is a possibility that the goods can still be diverted to local use or consumption, the tax power of the states has continued.[1]

The United States Supreme Court has additionally held that a state could impose a license tax upon an entrepreneur whose goods would shortly move into interstate commerce. Said the Court: "Here the privilege taxed is exercised before interstate commerce begins, hence the burden of the tax upon the commerce is too indirect and remote to transgress constitutional limitations."[2]

Although admittedly Commonwealth legislation was involved, a unanimous High Court of Australia held in 1968 that a tax on hens kept for commercial purposes did not violate the interstate commerce clause (in Australia binding both the Commonwealth and the states), justifying an inference at least that the same tax levied by a state would be valid, even under the particular facts of the case, where the entire egg production moved interstate.[3]

Although the Argentine Supreme Court has allowed a province to impose taxes on hides that would at some undefined later date be exported,[4] it later held that a province could not impose a tax on goods about to be transported to another province.[5]

§ 4.02 State taxation of persons or goods moving through their territories

In federal societies, the component entities are customarily under constitutional bans preventing them from levying taxes upon persons or goods passing through their territories. The ban at times is expressed in specific language. Thus, the Mexican Constitution provides that states may not "levy duty on persons or goods passing their territory,"[1] nor may Mexican states "tax the circulation of domestic or foreign goods by imposts or duties."[2] By the Constitution, states of Venezuela are not to "create . . . taxes on transit of foreign or domestic goods."[3] Under the Constitution of Argentina, "articles of national or foreign production or manufacture, as well as livestock of all kinds, that may pass through the territory of one Province to another, shall be free from so-called transit duties."[4] In Brazil the Constitution forbids the states to "establish limitations on the transit of persons or goods, by means of taxes on interstate or inter-municipal movement."[5] There are to be no internal customs borders, according to the Constitution of Austria.[6]

In the United States, the privileges and immunities clause of Article Four invalidates state taxes upon persons passing through the state,[7] and the Commerce Clause will also result in voiding state taxes upon persons and goods passing through the state.[8] However, if the owner of goods moving in interstate commerce breaks the movement within one state for his economic advantage and for an indefinite pause, the goods are subject to taxes by the state or its political subdivision that provides them protection.[9] Where the break is only to protect the goods from the perils of the journey, such pause does not subject them to state taxation.[10]

The Supreme Court of India has held unconstitutional the State of Assam's tax on goods carried by road and inland waterways, as violative of Article 301 of the Constitution (the commerce clause).[11] Another provision of the Constitution gives to the Union exclusive power to impose terminal taxes on passengers or goods carried by railways, sea or air.[12] However, Entry 56 on the State List in the Constitution gives the states power to impose "taxes on goods and passengers carried by road or on inland waterways," and the Supreme Court has held that such a tax on goods could be measured by their value and such a tax on passengers could be measured by the fares they paid.[13]

In Australia, too, the High Court has indicated that there is to be no state tax on the interstate movement of persons or goods.[14]

§ 4.03 State taxation of goods coming in from interstate commerce

Generally, states cannot tax the entry of persons or goods into their territories from other states of the federation.[1] The High Court of Australia has said: "No tax or impost whatever can be laid upon the entry of goods or people into a State from another State. . . . No part of the operation of Section 92 (the Commerce Clause) is less open to dispute than that."[2]

Occasionally in a federal society the constitution specifically authorizes the states to tax goods that have come in from sister states, so long
as the imposition is nondiscriminatory. Thus, the Indian Constitution
allows a state to impose upon goods imported from another state "any tax
to which similar goods manufactured or produced in that state are
subject, so, however, as not to discriminate between goods so imported
and goods so manufactured or produced."[3]

In most federal societies, even without express constitutional authorizations, the states at some point of time after all interstate or foreign
commerce has ended are generally able to impose nondiscriminatory
property taxes upon the goods which have been brought in and which are
now benefiting from protections and services provided by the states and
their political subdivisions. In the United States, once goods imported
from sister states have come to rest and become part of the common
mass of property within the state, they can be subjected to nondiscriminatory property taxes by the states and their political subdivisions
providing common governmental protections, even if the goods are still in
the original package.[4] The United States Supreme Court has said:

> Things acquired or transported in interstate commerce may be sub-
> jected to a property tax, non-discriminatory in its operation, when they
> have become part of the common mass of property within the state of
> destination. This is so, indeed, though they are still in the original
> package.[5]

Even though goods have come into the state earlier from interstate or
foreign commerce, states can impose nondiscriminatory privilege taxes
upon the utilization or enjoyment of the goods—commonly called "use
taxes"—within the state.[6] States with use taxes can constitutionally
compel out-of-state firms delivering goods to residents of the taxing state
to collect the use tax for the state, so long as the out-of-state firm has
sufficient contacts in the taxing state to make it reasonable and fair that it
collect the tax.[7]

There have been some instances where a state of destination has
been unable to tax goods that have recently arrived from interstate
commerce or the tax would have the effect of prohibiting, or at least
seriously detering, the movement of interstate commerce. To illustrate,
when petrol was brought into South Australia from sister states, the High
Court of Australia in 1926 denied that state the power to impose a tax of
about two cents per gallon upon the first sale of the petrol in South
Australia; the Court concluded this was an impermissible restraint upon
the free movement of goods and violative of section 92.[8]

§ 4.04 State taxation of imports

Imports is used in this section with reference only to goods brought
in from foreign countries, and federal constitutions rather generally ban
the states from imposing customs duties on imports.

By the Constitution of Argentina "goods and merchandise of all kinds dispatched through the national customs houses" are free from duties imposed by the states.[1] Taxes on imports by provinces have been held unconstitutional,[2] and the original package doctrine has been followed, generally immunizing the articles from provincial taxation while in the original container.[3] The first wholesale of imported goods has been protected from provincial taxation,[4] but provinces can tax the goods imported once they become part of the general mass of property in the province, even though they are yet in the original packages.[5] Discriminatory taxes on imported goods are unconstitutional, even though they have become part of the common mass of property in a province.[6] The Supreme Court has held that a province could not impose an inspection tax upon imported meats.[7]

The Australian Constitution as drafted provided: "On the imposition of uniform duties of customs the power of the Parliament to impose duties of customs . . . shall become exclusive."[8] Parliament having long since imposed such duties, there is no power in the Australian states to impose customs duties.

The Constitution of India confers upon the Union Parliament exclusive power to impose "duties of customs."[9]

The Grundgesetz or Basic Law of the German Federal Republic provides that: "The Federation shall have exclusive power to legislate on customs matters."[10]

The Mexican Constitution indicates that the states may not: "Prohibit or levy duty, directly or indirectly, upon the entrance into . . . their territory of any domestic or foreign goods,"[11] and additionally provides that the states may not, without the consent of the federal Congress, "levy imposts or taxes on imports."[12]

States are comparably prohibited from taxing imports by the Constitutions of Venezuela[13] and Nigeria.[14]

The United States Constitution provides: "No State shall, without the consent of Congress, lay any impost or duties on imports or exports, except what may be absolutely necessary for executing its inspection laws."[15] Under this clause, goods are ordinarily protected from state taxation while they are in the original package.[16] However, once sold the goods become taxable even though still in that package.[17] Stated generally, goods imported become subject to state taxation when they "become incorporated and mixed up with the mass of property" within the state.[18] Goods imported for use or manufacture become taxable when use or manufacture has begun.[19] The import clause has been held to protect not only the goods, but importers and auctioneers who handle imported goods.[20] However, a railroad moving imported goods can be subjected to a franchise tax measured by gross receipts, including receipts from moving the imports.[21]

§ 4.05 State taxation of exports

In federal societies, states are frequently subject to specific constitutional clauses forbidding taxation of exports or giving the central government exclusive power to levy export duties.

Under the Constitution of Argentina, the provinces cannot tax exports.[1] The Supreme Court has further ruled that a provincial local government could not impose inspection fees on fruits being exported.[2]

The Australian Constitution provides that the Commonwealth Parliament has exclusive power "to impose duties of customs,"[3] and this has been said to embrace both goods coming into, and leaving, Australia.[4]

The Mexican Constitution indicates that the states may not "prohibit or levy duty, directly or indirectly upon the . . . exit from their territory of any domestic or foreign goods,"[5] and further that states cannot, without the consent of the federal Congress, "levy impost or duties on . . . exports."[6]

Under the Constitution of India, the Union Parliament has exclusive power to levy "duties of customs including export duties."[7]

The Nigerian Constitution gives to the federal government exclusive power to impose export duties.[8]

The states, under the Constitution of Venezuela, are prohibited from imposing "export taxes."[9]

The United States Constitution indicates that: "No State shall, without the consent of Congress, lay any impost or duties on . . . exports, except what may be absolutely necessary for executing its inspection law."[10] Once the goods have been irrevocably committed to the export stream, they cannot be subjected to property taxes by the states.[11] However, until they have been so committed, goods can be taxed, even though the owner intends to export them shortly.[12] Under the export clause, the Supreme Court deems unconstitutional excise taxes closely related to the export process and has voided a state tax on proceeds of goods being exported, when the goods were already on the buyer's vessel in the harbor.[13] The Court has further held that "a stamp tax on a foreign bill of lading is in substance and effect equivalent to a tax on the articles included in the bill of lading and, therefore, a tax or duty on exports, and in conflict with the constitutional prohibition."[14]

The immunity from state taxation is seemingly broader under the Constitution of Brazil 1891, which in Article 9, § 2 denies the states power to tax the products of other states destined for export.

§ 4.06 Taxes on carriers moving interstate and foreign commerce and their power sources

The Constitution of Argentina provides that "the vehicles, ships or beasts" on which domestic or foreign goods are carried through a province shall be free from taxation.[1] Accordingly, the Supreme Court of Argentina has voided a provincial tax on trucks used to deliver within the province goods coming in from other provinces.[2]

The High Court of Australia has indicated that the states are not to impose property taxes upon vehicles used there by interstate haulers.[3] The High Court has also ruled that a state cannot levy a stamp duty on a certificate of registration for a vehicle used there solely in interstate commerce.[4]

In the German Federal Republic, matters involving the federal railroads and air transportation are assigned by the Grundgesetz or Basic Law to the exclusive control of the federation.[5]

In the United States, neither the Commerce Clause nor the Due Process Clause of the Fourteenth Amendment is violated when the state of domicile of a transportation company owning carriers used in interstate commerce is taxed on the total value of all carriers owned by the company, absent proof by the company that some of the carriers may be taxed by other states.[6] However, the Supreme Court has held that a domiciliary state could not tax all the property of a carrier, when it appeared that nondomiciliary states might impose upon the carriers used there properly apportioned taxes.[7]

The Supreme Court recognizes that carriers can acquire a 'tax situs' in nondomiciliary states to support an entire year's tax if they are used there every day of the tax year, as well as a 'tax situs' to support a properly apportioned tax if they are regularly used in the nondomiciliary state on a recurring basis during the year. Railroad cars,[8] buses and trucks,[9] airplanes,[10] and barges[11] have all been subjected to reasonably apportioned taxes by nondomiciliary states.[12]

The United States Supreme Court has denied the states power to tax the use of gasoline and oil to power the movement within their borders of interstate carriers.[13] However, if a state can find a "local" event (such as withdrawal of gasoline from storage), a privilege tax can be imposed upon the occasion, even though the gasoline will shortly thereafter be used to move interstate commerce.[14] In Australia, the High Court has indicated a willingness to uphold state taxes upon petrol used within the state in the movement of interstate commerce.[15]

§ 4.07 State compensatory charges for the use of roads and other facilities

States in federal systems have generally been able to levy charges upon firms, even those engaged solely in interstate or foreign commerce, for the use of their roads, so long as the charges were reasonable compensation and nondiscriminatory.

The High Court of Australia has sustained such charges, when the formula used considered the weight and capacity of the vehicle, as well as the distance driven over the state roads, and the charges collected were used only for road maintenance.[1] On later occasions, however, the High Court has refused vehicle owners the opportunity to prove that the charges, in their particular cases, were unreasonable.[2]

The United States Supreme Court has also sustained reasonable, compensatory and nondiscriminatory highway use taxes or charges, even in application to vehicles used within the state in purely interstate or foreign commerce.[3] In the United States it is not required that the proceeds go into a road maintenance fund; it being sufficient that they are assigned to a general fund.[4] Here individuals subjected to such taxes are given the opportunity to show that, on the particular facts of their case, the amount charged is an unreasonable levy for their use of the roads, or is discriminatory, in which cases the Supreme Court voids the application of the charge under the circumstances.[5]

In the United States, the owners of vessels operating in interstate and foreign commerce can be compelled by the states or their political subdivisions to pay reasonable charges for the use of wharves, elevators and other port facilities.[6] Again, the persons using airports in interstate and foreign commerce can be compelled by the states or their political subdivisions to pay reasonable charges for the use of public airport facilities.[7]

The Supreme Court of India has ruled that "measures imposing compensatory taxes for the use of trading facilities do not come within the purview of the restrictions contemplated by Article 301 (the commerce clause)."[8]

§ 4.08 Bans on tonnage duties and port charges

Constitutions in some of the federal societies specifically prohibit the states from imposing tonnage duties upon vessels entering their harbors, as well as port charges generally.

The Constitution of Argentina 1853, as amended, provides that: "The Provinces may not . . . impose tonnage duties,"[1] and adds: "Ships bound from one Province to another shall not be obliged to . . . pay duties by reason of transit."[2] The Supreme Court of Argentina has ruled tonnage duties are generally unconstitutional.[3]

The Constitution of Mexico indicates that without the consent of the federal Congress the states shall not "establish ship tonnage dues, or any other port charges. . . ."[4]

The United States Constitution provides that: "No state shall, without the consent of Congress lay any duty of tonnage."[5] Fees for entering or leaving ports are forbidden by this clause, even when not measured by tonnage.[6] The Supreme Court has said: "Whatever is in its essence a contribution claimed for the privilege of arriving and departing from a port of the United States, is within the prohibition."[7] However, where special facilities or services are provided to a vessel or its owners, the state or its political subdivision can impose reasonable, nondiscriminatory charges for the facilities or services, even when graduated according to the tonnage of the vessel.[8]

§ 4.09 State privilege taxes on persons engaged in commerce

Without violating the constitutional commerce clauses, states can tax the doing therein of local or intrastate commerce, even by out-of-state firms primarily engaged in interstate or foreign commerce within the taxing state, so long as the tax is nondiscriminatory.[1] Local, intrastate activity sufficient to support state privilege taxes has often been found when firms deal with goods before the interstate commerce in them begins. For instance, a state could tax catching and processing of fish in its waters as local events, even though shortly thereafter all the fish entered interstate commerce.[2] The High Court of Australia has said that the activity of a freight forwarder arranging for the movement of goods into interstate commerce was "local," and sustained imposition upon him—as not violating the commerce clause—of a stamp duty the amount of which was calculated by the total business done in the state, including business in interstate commerce.[3]

Comparably, local or intrastate activity sufficient to support state privilege taxes is found when business firms deal with goods after their interstate or foreign movement has completely ended. Thus, the peddling of goods around a city has been held to be such local or intrastate activity sufficient to support local privilege taxes, even when the goods peddled have only recently arrived from interstate commerce.[4]

In 1928 the United States Supreme Court indicated the conditions under which it would sustain state privilege taxes upon doing local business, imposed upon firms also doing interstate commerce within the state. It said:

> In order that the fee or tax shall be valid, it must appear that it is imposed solely on account of the intrastate business; that the amount is not increased because of the interstate business done; that one engaged in interstate commerce would not be subject to the imposition; and that the person could discontinue the intrastate business without withdrawing also from the interstate business.[5]

Since that time, however, the United States Supreme Court has indicated that states can tax the privilege of doing local, intrastate business by firms also doing interstate commerce therein, and "within reasonable limits, may compute the amount of the charge by applying the tax rate to a fair proportion of the taxpayer's business done within the state, including both interstate and intrastate."[6]

Some activities have been held to affect interstate or foreign commerce only "incidentally" and these can be subjected to privilege taxes by states and their political subdivisions.[7] On the other hand, certain activities done locally are so close to the essence of inter-state/foreign commerce itself, that the courts have felt they should be insulated from state and local privilege taxes. "Local incidents," says the United States Supreme Court, "such as gathering up or putting down interstate commerce are an integral part of their interstate movement and are not adequate grounds for a state license, privilege or occupation tax."[8]

Many state taxes have been held unconstitutional by the United States Supreme Court when the Court characterized them as business, occupation or license taxes imposed for the "privilege" of doing within the state purely interstate commerce. The Court said in 1928: "The privilege of engaging in such commerce is one which a state cannot deny. A state is equally inhibited from conditioning its exercise on the payment of an occupation tax."[9] Since 1977, however, the Court has allowed states to impose privilege taxes upon firms doing therein purely interstate or foreign commerce, so long as there is a substantial nexus between the taxpayer and the taxing state, the tax does not discriminate against those engaged in interstate or foreign commerce, and the charge is reasonable payment for the protection, services, and benefits provided by the state to the taxpayer.[10]

Australian High Court justices have traditionally been unsympathetic to the idea that states might impose privilege taxes upon firms doing purely interstate or foreign commerce within the state,[11] Chief Justice Barwick remarking as recently as 1969: "In its nature therefore a law imposing a tax upon or in respect of an interstate activity is incompatible with the absolute freedom of that activity and of the freedom to do so of the person engaging or to engage in it."[12] However, with his departure from the Court, there is a greater likelihood that the present Justices will appreciate somewhat more the increasing needs of the states for revenue sources of their own, and the equity implicit in the frequent observation that interstate commerce, too, must pay its way for protections, services and benefits received when operating in a particular state. In Australia, the states are unable to impose "excise duties" and this is discussed in the following chapter.

§ 4.10 Taxes on income and receipts from commerce

Canadian provinces have been able to tax the gross receipts from business done within the province.[1]

Australian states have not been able to impose gross receipts taxes on firms doing therein solely interstate business. Justice Kitto said in 1969: "I have no doubt that a law purporting to tax gross receipts from the carriage of goods for reward, would, in its application to receipts from the interstate carriage of goods, collide with section 92 and be inoperative accordingly.[2] However, net income taxes have been sustained even where the income included receipts from interstate trade, the High Court holding that Queensland could tax the profits made by a New South Wales company by a formula that considered the percentage of sales in Queensland to the total sales of the company.[3]

Since 1951, the United States Supreme Court has allowed the states to impose properly apportioned gross receipts taxes upon corporations doing purely interstate or foreign commerce within their borders. The Court said:

> It is settled that a non-discriminatory gross receipts tax on an interstate enterprise may be sustained if fairly apportioned to the business done within the taxing state, and not reaching any activities carried on beyond the borders of the state.[4]

Prior to 1964 the Supreme Court had regularly voided unapportioned gross receipts taxes,[5] but in that year (over four dissents) the Court held that a state could impose an unapportioned gross receipts tax upon a firm doing interstate commerce. The Court indicated the time had come for a broader test of constitutionality. "The validity of the tax," said the Court, "rests upon whether the State is exacting a constitutionally fair demand for that aspect of interstate commerce to which it bears a special relation."[6] For virtually a hundred years, the Supreme Court has sustained gross receipts taxes upon firms doing within a state both intrastate and interstate commerce, so long as the tax reached only the receipts from the former.[7] States can impose net income taxes upon foreign corporations doing interstate commerce in the state, so long as a formula is used that fairly apportions the total income to that derived from business in the taxing state.[8]

§ 4.11 Sales taxes affecting interstate and foreign commerce

In Canada, the provinces can only impose "direct" taxes,[1] and sales taxes have been described as "indirect" levies and held invalid when they were not paid by the ultimate consumer.[2] However, when sales taxes are levied upon the ultimate consumer and cannot be passed along to others, they are deemed "direct" taxes and are constitutional.[3]

In Australia, the states cannot levy "excises" and the High Court held in 1949 that a tax upon those who sold and distributed milk of one-tenth a cent per gallon was an excise tax and invalid, the Court emphasizing that the Milk Board which received the tax performed "no particular service" for the taxpayers.[4] This is to be contrasted with a 1966 decision where the High Court held valid as not an excise, but rather a payment for services provided, a Victoria statute requiring egg distributors to pay fees for eggs sold, when the Egg Marketing Board graded the eggs, marked and stamped them for the market.[5]

Even though the goods have come into a state from interstate or foreign commerce, a state in the United States can impose a sales tax upon the transfer of the goods if they were physically present in the state and transferred there, at least where either title passes in the taxing state[6] or the seller has a sales agency within the state.[7] On one occasion, the Supreme Court ruled that a state sales tax could not be applied where title to the goods passed outside the state and where, by the terms of the sales contract, the delivery to a common carrier outside the taxing state fulfilled the seller's obligations.[8] There were four dissents. The majority seem to have acknowledged that a "use" tax would have been constitutional if applied by the taxing state, into which the goods were delivered, and it is questionable whether the tax powers of states should hinge upon the labels that are appended to various taxes.

In India, the Constitution allows the states to impose sales taxes on the sale or purchase of goods (other than newspapers) within their borders.[9] However, it also gives to the Union government exclusive power to impose "taxes on the sale or purchase of goods other than newspapers where the sale or purchase takes place in the course of inter-State trade or commerce."[10] The Constitution further specifies that: "No law of a State shall impose or authorize the imposition of, a tax on the sale or purchase of goods where such sale or purchase takes place: (a) outside the State, or (b) in the course of the import of the goods into or export of the goods out of, the territory of India."[11] Under the latter subsection it has been held that sales previous to export are only protected when they cause the export.[12] In all instances, state sales taxes discriminating against articles from sister states are unconstitutional.[13]

§ 4.12 Taxation of locally situated property owned by firms doing interstate commerce

Even business firms doing purely interstate or interprovincial business within a state or province can be subjected to property taxes on their real and personal property situated there.[1]

The United States Supreme Court allows such a state to utilize any reasonable formula to arrive at the full value of the property.[2] Where the corporation owning the property is a unitary or organic enterprise, the property "may be taxed according to its value as part of the system, although the other parts be outside the state; in other words, the tax may be made to cover the enhanced value which comes to the property in the state through its organic relation to the system."[3]

In lieu of imposing property taxes upon firms engaged in interstate commerce, the states in the United States have been sustained in imposing other forms of taxes—however denominated—even when measured by gross receipts from interstate commerce, the Court demanding only that the amount of tax be reasonably approximate to what property taxes would have produced.[4]

FOOTNOTES

§ 4.00

1 Constitution of Australia, § 92.
2 Fox v. Robbins (1909) 8 C.L.R. 115; Commonwealth and Commonwealth Oil Refineries v. South Australia (1926) 38 C.L.R. 408; Vacuum Oil Pty. Ltd. v. Queensland (1934) 51 C.L.R. 108; Hughes and Vale Pty. Ltd. v. New South Wales (#1) (1954) 93 C.L.R. 1; Associated Steamships Pty. Ltd. v. Western Australia (1969) 120 C.L.R. 92.
3 Constitution of the United States, Article I, Section 1.
4 West Point Wholesale Grocery Co. v. Opelika (1957) 354 US 390, 77 S Ct 1091, 1 L Ed 2d 1420.
5 Constitution of India, Article 301; Atiabari Tea Co. v. State of Assam A.I.R. 1961 S.C. 232; State of Madras v. Bhailal Bhai, A.I.R. 1964 S.C. 1006.
6 Constitution of India, Article 304(a) permitting a state to impose upon goods imported from another state "any tax to which similar goods manufactured or produced in that State are subject, so, however, as not to discriminate between goods so imported and goods so manufactured or produced." Mentab Majid & Co. v. State of Madras, A.I.R. 1963 S.C. 928.
7 Atiabari Tea Co. v. State of Assam, (1961) 1 S.C.R. 809, 856.
8 Amadeo, *Argentine Constitutional Law* (Columbia U. Press, N.Y. 1943) 155.
9 La Immobilaria S.A. Cia de Seguros v. Corrientes (1937) 179 S.C.N. 42.
10 Constitution of Brazil 1969, as amended, Article 20(III).
11 Constitution Act of Canada (British North America Act) § 121.
12 Attorney-General for British Columbia v. Canadian Pacific Ry. (1927) A.C. 934.
13 Hughes and Vale Pty. Ltd. v. New South Wales (#2) (1955) 93 C.L.R. 127; Zines, *The High Court and the Constitution* (Sydney 1981) 121. Barwick, C.J., dissenting in Associated Steamship Co. v. Western Australia (1969) 120 C.L.R. 92, 102.
14 "We have frequently reiterated that the Commerce Clause does not immunize interstate instrumentalities from all state taxation, but that such commerce may be required to pay a non-discriminatory share of the tax burden." Braniff Airways v. Nebraska State Board of Equalization and Assessment (1954) 347 US 590, 597, 74 S Ct 757, 98 L Ed 967.
15 West Point Wholesale Grocery Co. v. Opelika (1957) 354 US 390, 392, 77 S Ct 1091, 1 L Ed 2d 1420.

§ 4.01

1 Diamond Match Co. v. Ontonagon (1903) 188 US 82, 23 S Ct 266, 47 L Ed 394; Coe v. Errol (1886) 116 US 517, 6 S Ct 475, 29 L Ed 715.
2 Federal Compress & Warehouse Co. v . McLean (1934) 291 US 17, 54 S Ct 267, 78 L Ed 622, 627.
3 Damjanovic & Sons Pty. Ltd. v. Commonwealth (1968) 117 C.L.R. 390.
4 Arias v. Entre Rios (1878) 20 S.C.N. 304.
5 Freitas y Gurgio v. Corrientes (1904) 101 S.C.N. 8.

§ 4.02

1 Mexican Constitution of 1917, Art. 117 (IV).
2 Ibid., Art. 117 (VI).
3 Venezuela Constitution, Art. 18(1).
4 Argentina Constitution of 1853, as amended, Art. 11.
5 Constitution of Brazil 1969, as amended, Art. 19(II).
6 Constitution of Austria 1920/1929, as amended, Art. 4(2).

[7] Crandall v. Nevada (1868) 18 L Ed 745.
[8] Champlain Realty Co. v. Brattleboro (1922) 260 US 366, 43 S Ct 146, 67 L Ed 309.
[9] Susquehanna Coal Co. v. South Amboy (1913) 228 US 665, 33 S Ct 712, 57 L Ed 1015;
Independent Warehouses v. Scheele (1947) 331 US 70, 67 S Ct 1062, 91 L Ed 1346.
[10] Champlain Realty Co. v. Brattleboro (1922) 260 US 366, 43 S Ct 146, 67 L Ed 309.
[11] Atiabara Tea Co. v. State of Assam, A.I.R. 1961 S.C. 232.
[12] Constitution of India, Union List I, Entry 89.
[13] Constitution of India, State List, Entry 56; Sainik Motors v. Rajasthan (1962) 1 S.C.R.
517.
[14] Hughes and Vale Pty. Ltd. v. New South Wales (#2) (1955) 93 C.L.R. 127, 176-7 (Dixon,
C.J.); 213 (Fullagar, J.).

§ 4.03

[1] Edwards v. California (1941) 314 US 160, 62 S Ct 164, 86 L Ed 119; Constitution of
Brazil 1891, Art. 11(1).
[2] Hughes and Vale Pty. Ltd. v. New South Wales (#2) (1955) 93 C.L.R. 127, 176-7.
[3] Constitution of India, Part XIII, Article 304(a).
[4] Cudahy Packing Co. v. Minnesota (1918) 246 US 450, 38 S Ct 373, 62 L Ed 827; Wiloil
Co. v. Pennsylvania (1935) 294 US 169, 55 S Ct 358, 79 L Ed 838; Brown-Forman Co.
v. Kentucky (1910) 217 US 563, 30 S Ct 578, 54 L Ed 883.
[5] Henneford v. Silas Mason Co. (1937) 30 US 577, 582, 57 S Ct 524, 81 L Ed 814.
[6] Southern Pacific Co. v. Gallagher (1939) 306 US 167, 59 S Ct 389, 83 L Ed 586; United
Air Lines Inc. v. Mahin (1973) 410 US 623, 93 S Ct 1186, 35 L Ed 2d 545.
[7] National Geographic Society v. California Board of Equalization (1977) 430 US 551, 97
S Ct 1386, 51 L Ed 2d 631.
[8] Commonwealth and Commonwealth Oil Refineries v. South Australia (1926) 38 C.L.R.
408.

§4.04

[1] Constitution of Argentina 1853, as amended, Article 10.
[2] Tirasso v. Buenos Aires (1935) 174 S.C.N. 192.
[3] Benci v. Medina (1883) 26 S.C.N. 94.
[4] Ovejero Hermanos v. Tiseyro y Pirola (1886) 30 S.C.N. 332.
[5] Justo v. Cordoba (1937) 163 S.C.N. 285; Chiossone v. San Luis (1931) 163 S.C.N. 285.
[6] Antony v. Santa Fe (1917) 125 S.C.N. 333.
[7] Swift de la Plata v. Tucuman (1933) 168 S.C.N. 268.
[8] Constitution of Australia, section 90.
[9] Constitution of India, Seventh Schedule, Union List, Entry 83.
[10] Grundgesetz of German Federal Republic, Article 105(1).
[11] Constitution of Mexico, Article 117(V).
[12] Constitution of Mexico, Article 118(I).
[13] Constitution of Venezuela, Article 18.
[14] Constitution of Nigeria 1979, Second Schedule, Part I(15).
[15] Constitution of the United States, Article I, Section 10, Clause 2.
[16] Brown v. Maryland (1827) 12 Wheat. 419, 6 L Ed 678.
[17] Waring v. Mobile (1869) 8 Wall. 110, 19 L Ed 342.
[18] Brown v. Maryland (1827) 12 Wheat. 419, 6 L Ed 678, 686 (Marshall, C.J.).
[19] Youngstown Sheet & Tube Co. v. Bowers (1959) 358 US 534, 79 S Ct 383, 3 L Ed 2d
490.
[20] Cook v. Pennsylvania (1878) 97 US 566, 24 L Ed 1015.
[21] Canton Rr. v. Rogan (1951) 340 US 511, 71 S Ct 447, 95 L Ed 488.

§ 4.05

[1] Mendoza v. San Juan (1865) 3 S.C.N. 131; Las Palmas Produce Co. v. Buenos Aires
(1904) 100 S.C.N. 364.

2 Cerruti v. Municipalidad de San Nicolas (1920) 132 S.C.N. 205.
3 Constitution of Australia, section 90.
4 Commonwealth and Commonwealth Oil Refineries Ltd. v. South Australia (1926) 38 C.L.R. 408, 438.
5 Constitution of Mexico 1917, Article 117(V).
6 Constitution of Mexico 1917, Article 118(I).
7 Constitution of India, Seventh Schedule, Union List, Entry 83.
8 Constitution of Nigeria 1979, Second Schedule, Part I (22).
9 Constitution of Venezuela, Article 18(1).
10 Constitution of the United States, Article I, Section 10, Clause 2.
11 A.G. Spalding & Bros. v. Edwards (1923) 262 US 66, 69-70, 43 S Ct 485, 67 L Ed 865.
12 Empresa Siderurgica v. County of Merced (1949) 337 US 154, 69 S Ct 995, 93 L Ed 1276; Kosydar v. National Cash Register Co. (1974) 417 US 62, 94 S Ct 2108, 40 L Ed 2d 62.
13 Richfield Oil Co. v. State Board of Equalization (1946) 329 US 69, 67 S Ct 156, 91 L Ed 80.
14 Fairbank v. United States (1901) 181 US 283, 21 S Ct 648, 45 L Ed 862.

§ 4.06

1 Constitution of Argentina 1853, as amended, Article 11.
2 South American Stores v. Buenos Aires (1927) 149 S.C.N. 137.
3 Hughes and Vale Pty. Ltd. v. New South Wales (#2) (1955) 93 C.L.R. 127, 213 (Fullagar, J.).
4 Finemores Transport v. New South Wales (1978) 52 A.L.J.R. 465 (but note dissent of Murphy, J.).
5 Grundgesetz of German Federal Republic, Article 73(6).
6 Central Railroad of Pennsylvania v. Pennsylvania (1962) 370 US 607, 82 S Ct 1297, 8 L Ed 2d 720.
7 Standard Oil v. Peck (1952) 342 US 382, 385, 72 S Ct 309, 96 L Ed 427.
8 Pullman Palace Car Co. v. Pennsylvania (1891) 141 US 18, 11 S Ct 876, 35 L Ed 613.
9 Capitol Greyhound Lines v. Brice (1950) 339 US 542, 70 S Ct 806, 94 L Ed 1053.
10 Braniff Airways v. Nebraska (1954) 347 US 590, 74 S Ct 757, 98 L Ed 967.
11 Ott v. Mississippi Valley Barge Lines (1949) 336 US 169, 69 S Ct 432, 93 L Ed 585.
12 Use of an unfair formula by a state voids the tax. Norfolk & Western Railway v. Missouri (1968) 390 US 317, 88 S Ct 995, 19 L Ed 2d 1201.
13 Helson v. Kentucky (1929) 279 US 245, 49 S Ct 279, 73 L Ed 683; Bingaman v. Boeing Air Transport (1933) 289 US 249, 53 S Ct 591, 77 L Ed 1155.
14 Edelman v. Boeing Air Transport (1933) 289 US 249, 53 S Ct 591, 77 L Ed 1155.
15 Hughes and Vale Pty. Ltd. v. New South Wales (#2) (1955) 93 C.L.R. 127.

§ 4.07

1 Hughes & Vale Pty. Ltd. v. New South Wales (#2) (1955) 93 C.L.R. 127; Armstrong v. Victoria (No. 2) 99 C.L.R. 28; Commonwealth Freighters v. Sneddon; Boland v. Sneddon (1959) 102 C.L.R. 280.
2 Breen v. Sneddon (1961) 106 C.L.R. 406; Allwright's Transport Ltd. v. Ashley (1962) 107 C.L.R. 662.
3 Interstate Transit v. Lindsey (1931) 283 US 183, 51 S Ct 380, 75 L Ed 953; Bode v. Barrett (1953) 344 US 583, 73 S Ct 468, 97 L Ed 567; Aero Mayflower Transit Co. v. Board of Commissioners (1947) 332 US 495, 68 S Ct 167, 92 L Ed 99; Hicklin v. Coney (1933) 290 US 169, 54 S Ct 142, 78 L Ed 247; Morf v. Bingaman (1936) 298 US 407, 56 S Ct 756, 80 L Ed 1245; Capitol Greyhound Lines v. Brice (1950) 339 US 542, 70 S Ct 806, 94 L Ed 1053.
4 Aero Mayflower Transit Co. v. Board of Commissioners (1947) 332 US 495, 68 S Ct 167, 92 L Ed 99.

5 Sprout v. South Bend (1928) 277 US 163, 48 S Ct 502, 72 L Ed 833.
6 Clyde Mallory Lines v. Alabama (1935) 296 US 261, 56 S Ct 194, 80 L Ed 215.
7 Evansville-Vanderburgh Airport Authority District v. Delta Airlines Inc. (1972) 405 US 707, 92 S Ct 1349, 31 L Ed 2d 620.
8 Automobile Transport v. State of Rajasthan, A.I.R. 1962 S.C. 1406, 1424.

§ 4.08

1 Constitution of Argentina 1853, as amended, Article 108.
2 Constitution of Argentina 1853, as amended, Article 12.
3 Casares v. Sivori (1872) 11 S.C.N. 257.
4 Constitution of Mexico, Article 118.
5 Constitution of the United States, Article I, Section 10.
6 Southern Steamship Co. v. Port Wardens (1867) 6 Wall. 31, 18 L Ed 749.
7 Cannon v. New Orleans (1874) 20 Wall. 577, 22 L Ed 417, 419.
8 Clyde Mallory Lines v. Alabama (1935) 296 US 261, 56 S Ct 194, 80 L Ed 215.

§ 4.09

1 American Manufacturing Co. v. St. Louis (1919) 250 US 459, 39 S Ct 522, 63 L Ed 1084; Dunbar-Stanley Studios v. Alabama (1969) 393 US 537, 89 S Ct 757, 21 L Ed 2d 759.
2 Alaska v. Arctic Maid (1961) 366 US 199, 81 S Ct 929, 6 L Ed 2d 227.
3 Associated Steamship Co. v. Western Australia (1969) 120 C.L.R. 92.
4 Wagner v. Covington (1919) 251 US 95, 40 S Ct 93, 64 L Ed 157.
5 Sprout v. South Bend (1928) 277 US 163, 171, 48 S Ct 502, 72 L Ed 833.
6 Spector Motor Service v. O'Connor (1951) 340 US 602, 71 S Ct 508, 95 L Ed 573, overruled on another point in Complete Auto Transit v. Brady (1977) 430 US 274, 97 S Ct 1076, 51 L Ed 2d 326.
7 Ficklen v. Taxing District (1892) 145 US 1, 12 S Ct 810, 36 L Ed 601.
8 Railway Express Agency v. Virginia (1954) 347 US 359, 74 S Ct 558, 98 L Ed 757.
9 Sprout v. South Bend (1928) 277 US 163, 171, 48 S Ct 502, 72 L Ed 833.
10 Complete Auto Transit v. Brady (1977) 430 US 274, 97 S Ct 1076, 51 L Ed 2d 326; Department of Revenue v. Association of Washington Stevedoring Companies (1978) US 435 US 734, 98 S Ct 1388, 55 L Ed 2d 682.
11 Hughes and Vale Pty. Ltd. v. New South Wales (#2) 93 C.L.R. 127.
12 Associated Steamship Co. v. Western Australia (1969) 120 C.L.R. 92, 102 (Barwick, C.J., dissenting).

§ 4.10

1 Ontario v. Canadian Life Assurance Co. (1915) 33 O.L.R. 433.
2 Associated Steamship Co. v. Western Australia (1969) 120 C.L.R. 92, 111.
3 Australasian Scale Co. v. Commissioner of Taxation (Q) (1935) 53 C.L.R. 534, 556 (Starke, J.).
4 Canton Rr. v. Rogan (1951) 340 US 511, 515, 71 S Ct 447, 95 L Ed 488.
5 Joseph v. Carter & Weekes Stevedoring Co. (1947) 330 US 422, 67 S Ct 815, 91 L Ed 993.
6 General Motors Corp. v. Washington (1964) 377 US 436, 84 S Ct 1564, 12 L Ed 2d 430, 435.
7 Ficklen v. Taxing District (1892) 145 US 1, 12 S Ct 810, 36 L Ed 601.
8 Northwestern States Portland Cement Co. v. Minnesota (1959) 358 US 450, 79 S Ct 357, 3 L Ed 2d 421; Moorman Manufacturing Co. v. Bair (1978) 437 US 267, 98 S Ct 2340, 57 L Ed 2d 197 (percentage of gross sales in the state to the total of the company).

§ 4.11

1 British North America Act, § 92(2).
2 Attorney-General for British Columbia v. Canadian Pacific Ry. (1927) A.C. 934.

3   Attorney-General for British Columbia v. Kingscombe Navigation Co. (1934) A.C. 45;
    Atlantic Smoke Shops v. Conlon (1943) A.C. 550.
4   Parton v. Milk Board (Vic.) (1949) 80 C.L.R. 229.
5   Harper v. Victoria (1966) 114 C.L.R. 361.
6   McGoldrick v. Berwind-White Coal Mining Co. (1940) 309 US 33, 60 S Ct 388, 84 L Ed
    565; State Tax Commission v. Pacific States Cast Iron Pipe Co..(1963) 372 US 605, 83 S
    Ct 925, 10 L Ed 2d 8: "A State may levy and collect a sales tax, since the passage of title
    and delivery to the purchaser took place within the State."
7   McGoldrick v. Felt and Tarrant Mfg. Co. (1940) 309 US 70, 60 S Ct 404, 84 L Ed 584;
    McGoldrick v. Compagnie Generale Transatlantique (1940) 309 US 430, 60 S Ct 670,
    84 L Ed 849.
8   McLeod v. Dilworth (1944) 322 US 327, 64 S Ct 1023, 88 L Ed 1304.
9   Sixth Constitutional Amendment Act 1956, § 2; Tata Iron & Steel Co. v. State of Bihar
    (1958) S.C.R. 1355.
10 Constitution of India, Union List, Entry 92A.
11 Constitution of India, Article 286(1).
12 State of Mysore v. Mysore Shipping and Manufacturing Co. (1958) A.S.C. 1002.
13 Mehtab Majid & Co. v. State of Madras, A.I.R. 1963 S.C. 928.

§ 4.12

1   United River Plate Telephone Co. v. Buenos Aires (1929) 154 S.C.N. 104; Hughes &
    Vale v. New South Wales (#2) (1955) 93 C.L.R. 127; Commonwealth Freighters v.
    Sneddon; Boland v. Sneddon (1959) 102 C.L.R. 280; Pullman Co. v. Richardson (1923)
    261 US 330, 43 S Ct 366, 67 L Ed 682; Railway Express Agency Inc. v. Virginia (1959)
    358 US 434, 79 S Ct 411, 3 L Ed 2d 450.
2   Adams Express Co. v. Ohio State Auditor (1897) 166 US 185, 17 S Ct 604, 41 L Ed 965.
3   Pullman Co. v. Richardson (1929) 261 US 330, 339, 43 S Ct 366, 67 L Ed 682.
4   Railway Express Agency Inc. v. Virginia (1959) 358 US 434, 79 S Ct 411, 3 L Ed 2d 450;
    United States Express Co. v. Minnesota (1912) 223 USD 335, 32 S Ct 211, 56 L Ed 459.

CHAPTER FIVE

Chapter Five

STATE POWER TO TAX

§ 5.00 State power to tax—generally

As noted earlier, many federal societies recognize that the states possess the residuum of power, which gives them full power to tax, except as denied by provisions in the federal constitution. Under Section 107 of the Australian Constitution, continuing every power of the Parliament of a state at federation unless vested by the Constitution in the Commonwealth or withdrawn from the states, the states have, in the language of Chief Justice Griffith, "unlimited powers of taxation of all property within the limits of the States, and of all persons who come within the State by its permission." "Such a power," said the Chief Justice, "is an attribute of sovereignty."[1]

The constitutions of virtually all federal societies contain either general or specific limitations upon the tax powers of the states. For instance, the tax power of the Australian States is severely limited by Section 90 of the Constitution which provides: "On the imposition of uniform duties of customs the power of the Parliament to impose duties of customs and of excise, and to grant bounties on the production or export of goods, shall become exclusive." Section 114 of the Constitution additionally provides: "A State shall not, without the consent of the Parliament of the Commonwealth . . . impose any tax on property of any kind belonging to the Commonwealth. . . ." Furthermore, the power of the states to levy income taxes is extremely limited, since, under Section 96 of the Constitution, the Commonwealth Parliament can make grants to the states and condition such grants as it desires.[2]

The Nigerian Constitution of 1979 is patterned after the Australian Constitution in giving to the federal government exclusive power to levy customs and excise duties.[3]

The states of the United States have plenary power to tax, subject only to restrictions or limitations imposed by the federal Constitution. Article One, Section 10 of the Constitution provides: "No State shall, without the Consent of the Congress, lay any Imposts or Duties on Imports or Exports, except what may be absolutely necessary for executing its inspection laws. . . ." As noted at length in the previous chapter, the Commerce Clause (Article One, Section 8) of the Constitution limits in many ways the taxing powers of the states. Additionally, the Equal Protection Clause of the Fourteenth Amendment results in the invalidation of tax laws with invidious or unreasonable discrimination, and the Due Process Clause of the same Amendment has at times voided state taxes on the ground that they were unreasonable or confiscatory, or that they were not for public purposes. These limitations are discussed in the sections that follow.

The provinces of Argentina have tax powers roughly comparable to those of the states in the United States.[4] The Supreme Court of Argentina has held that the provincial "power of taxation extends to persons, property, possessions, franchises, professions, or any other rights which may be subject to taxation."[5]

In federal societies, where the component entities are not the residuaries of power, they must look to grants in the federal constitution as sources of their power to tax. In Canada, the provinces have constitutional power to impose direct taxes,[6] but no power to impose indirect taxes,[7] which include, *inter alia,* taxes on "customs and excise."[8] Canadian provinces also have under the Constitution power to impose "shop, saloon, tavern, auctioneer, and other licenses in order to the raising of a revenue for provincial, local, or municipal purposes."[9]

As in Canada, in Switzerland direct taxes are primarily for the cantons.[10]

There is no clause in the Indian Constitution specifically assigning the tax power either to the Union or to the states, although a number of taxes, including the "corporation tax," are assigned exclusively to the Union.[11] The State List in the Seventh Schedule empowers Indian states to levy:

   (a) "Taxes on goods and passengers carried by road or on inland waterways,"[12]
   (b) "Taxes on vehicles . . . suitable for use on roads,"[13]
   (c) "Taxes on animals and boats,"[14]
   (d) "Taxes on professions, trades, callings and employments,"[15]
   (e) "Capitation taxes,"[16] and
   (f) "Taxes on luxuries, including taxes on entertainments, amusements, betting and gambling."[17]

Additionally, the Constitution Sixth Amendment Act 1956, section 2 confers upon the states power to impose "taxes on the sale or purchase of goods other than newspapers."

In the German Federal Republic, the Laender "are left with no more than a minimum of original taxation."[18] Where the Federal Government occupies a particular field of taxation, there is no power in the Laender to tax in the area.[19] So, too, in both Brazil and Mexico, most of the tax powers belong to the federal government, the central government in Mexico receiving all but 14% of the taxes collected.[20]

In a number of federal societies there are specific constitutional bans made applicable to the states. For instance, in Brazil, the states cannot impose taxes upon "places of worship of any sect,"[21] nor upon "books, newspapers, or periodicals, or the paper intended for printing them."[22]

§ 5.01 Constitutional clauses forbidding indirect taxation

At times the constitutions of federal societies forbid the component entities to impose indirect taxes. For example, the British North America Act authorizes the provinces to levy "direct taxation within the province for raising revenue for provincial purposes,"[1] and this prohibits indirect taxation by the provinces. Canadian jurists have said that the line between direct and indirect taxes is "to be gathered from the common understanding of these words among the economists" at the time the Act was enacted.[2] There has been considerable respect for the opinion of John Stuart Mill who wrote:

> A direct tax is one which is demanded from the very person who it is intended or desired should pay it. Indirect taxes are those which are demanded from one person in the expectation and intention that he shall indemnify himself at the expense of another; such as the excise or customs.[3]

A tax will be a direct tax and within provincial power, said the Privy Council in 1943, when "the person who pays the tax is the person who actually bears it."[4]

Taxes on land have always been accepted as direct taxes;[5] so, too, taxes on minerals in situ.[6] Taxes on personal property located within the province are acceptable direct taxes.[7]

Income taxes have long been accepted as direct taxes, within provincial authority.[8] Taxes on persons and corporations doing business within a province are deemed direct taxes.[9] The Privy Council stated in 1887 that "any person found within the province" was taxable and so also was any corporation (domestic or foreign) "carrying on business" there.[10] A tax on consumers of tobacco has been held valid, even though it was collected for the province by the retailer. It is "direct," said the Privy Council, because "the person who pays the tax is the person who actually bears it."[11] Inheritance taxes are treated as direct taxes.[12]

Customs duties are indirect taxes forbidden to the provinces.[13] Transaction taxes are ordinarily indirect taxes.[14] Chief Justice Rinfret wrote: "Customs or excise duties were the classical type of indirect taxes."[15] A tax upon the gross revenue from the sale of coal has been held a forbidden indirect tax,[16] as has an export tax on timber cut within the province.[17] A tax on the first purchase of fuel oil within a province has been held to be an impermissible indirect tax.[18] Canadian courts generally call a tax "indirect" if it probably will be passed on to someone else. When not paid by the ultimate consumer, sales taxes are "indirect" and invalid when levied by the provinces,[19] but where paid by the ultimate consumer who cannot pass along the charge, a sales tax is "direct" and constitutional.[20]

Under Section 92(2) of the British North America Act, property must be "within the Province" to be taxable, and the Supreme Court of

Canada has held Manitoba could not impose a misnamed "sales tax" upon Air Canada for overflights above the province, or even for occasions when its planes landed temporarily in the province.[21]

§ 5.02 Constitutional clauses forbidding duties of excise

In some of the federal societies, the states are forbidden to levy duties of excise. The Australian Constitution, for example, denies the states power to impose "duties of customs or of excise."[1] The 1979 Constitution of Nigeria follows that of Australia and assigns to the federal government exclusive power to levy customs and excise duties.[2] In India, the Constitution confers upon the Union Government exclusive power to levy "duties of excise on tobacco or other goods manufactured or produced in India" except alcohol and narcotics,[3] and with these exceptions the states cannot impose excises.

Varying definitions have been given to the term "excise duties" by the justices of the Australian High Court. Early dictum spoke of an excise as limited to a tax "imposed upon goods either in relation to quantity or value when produced or manufactured,"[4] but the High Court soon moved to broaden the term to events beyond manufacturing. In 1963 the High Court said: "It is now established that for constitutional purposes duties of excise are taxes directly related to goods imposed at some step in their production or distribution before they reach the hands of consumers."[5] The following year Justice Kitto stated:

> A tax . . . is not a duty of excise unless the criterion of the person's liability is the fact that some act of his possesses the quality of a contribution either to the physical character of goods as subjects of commerce or to the sequence of events which result in their being available, as in the hands of a consumer, to be put to their ultimate purpose.[6]

Chief Justice Barwick, writing in 1974, defined an excise duty as follows:

> A duty of excise for the purposes of the Australian Constitution . . . is a tax upon the taking of a step in a process of bringing goods into existence or to a consumable state or of passing them down the line which reaches from the earliest stage in production to the point of receipt by the consumer, including the step which puts the goods into consumption.

However, as the High Court then sustained a tax of $7\frac{1}{2}\%$ of the value of tobacco consumed as not being an excise, the Chief Justice added: "A tax upon the act of consuming goods, completely divorced from the manner or time of their acquisition by purchase, must now be regarded as outside the scope of Section 90 and within the competence of a State legislature."[7]

Under the Australian constitutional clause referred to, a number of state programs to raise revenue have been invalidated. When New South Wales took title to all wheat at what was said to be a "fair and reasonable price" and then sold it back to the grower at a higher price, the High Court voided the arrangement as a forbidden excise.[8] Sales taxes have been said to be forbidden excises.[9] Taxes upon distributors have been invalidated as excises, at least when calculated by the amount of goods distributed.[10]

Since the High Court states that it will find a tax to be an excise only when it is "directly related to goods," the Court is willing to sustain state taxes only "indirectly" related to goods, as for their transportation to market.[11] Licensing fees for selling goods have been held not to be excises, even when the fee was calculated by reference to the amount of sales.[12] The Court has also, on occasion, sustained stamp taxes or duties upon the receipt of monies from goods.[13]

Where a state levy has been a reasonable charge for state services provided by the state to the person responsible for the fee, the High Court has ruled an excise was not present and sustained the charge.[14] Sometimes, when the charge was deducted from proceeds owed a producer or grower from a state marketing board, the Court has indicated that such a deduction was not an excise or tax of any kind.[15]

§ 5.03 Constitutional clauses banning discrimination in state taxation

States in federal societies are at times bound by equality or equal protection clauses which to some extent limit their tax powers.

Article 16 of the Argentine Constitution provides: "All its inhabitants are equal before the law." The Supreme Court holds that unreasonable classifications are unconstitutional,[1] but that reasonable classifications in provincial tax statutes are valid.[2]

Canadian provinces have traditionally been able to discriminate freely in tax legislation,[3] but the Constitution Act, 1981 in Part I, Schedule B, section 15 (1) now has an equal protection clause which will limit discrimination, unless the legislature of the province declares its tax act is not subject to this section of the Constitution, as authorized in Section 33(1) of the Constitution Act, 1981.

The Equal Protection Clause of the Fourteenth Amendment to the United States Constitution requires states in their tax laws to avoid invidious arbitrary, or unreasonable discriminations and classifications.[4] However, reasonable distinctions and classifications are constitutional and the United States Supreme Court allows great leeway to the states and their local governments in deciding properties and activities that are to be taxed or exempted.[5] There is, in effect, a presumption that classifications used in tax statutes are reasonable and constitutional.[6]

Article Four, Section Two of the United States Constitution Provides:

"The citizens of each State shall be entitled to all Privileges and Immunities of Citizens in the several States." In 1871 the Supreme Court stated: "The clause plainly and unmistakably secures and protects the rights of a citizen of one State . . . to be exempt from any higher taxes or excises than are imposed by the State upon its own citizens."[7] Business taxes and fees will be voided when there is no reasonable basis for treating citizens of other states differently from a state's own citizens. In voiding a state statute imposing license fees of $2500 upon nonresidents, while taxing local citizens only $25, the Supreme Court indicated some differentiated treatment may be permissible under the Article if "substantial reasons" exist and if they "bear a reasonable relationship" to the degree of discrimination practiced.[8]

In Australia, the Constitution forbids discrimination by a state against residents of other states,[9] and this seemingly forbids unreasonable discrimination in tax laws.

The Constitution of India allows a state to impose upon goods imported from another state "any tax to which similar goods manufactured or produced in that State are subject, so, however, as not to discriminate between goods so imported and goods so manufactured or produced."[10] State taxes discriminatory against goods from other states are unconstitutional.[11]

The Austrian Constitution provides that every federal citizen has in every Land the equal rights and duties as the citizen of the Land itself.[12] By the Grundgesetz or Basic Law of the German Federal Republic it is provided that: "Every German shall have in every Land the same political rights and duties."[13] The States of Brazil are forbidden to create distinctions between Brazilians.[14] Discrimination because of one's place of origin is forbidden by the Constitution of Nigeria.[15] The Constitution of Malaysia bans discrimination against residents of other parts of the federation.[16]

§ 5.04 State power to tax under substantive due process clauses

State power to tax in the United States is confined by the Due Process Clause of the Fourteenth Amendment, but the Supreme Court indicates that state taxes will not be voided as violative of this Clause unless they are "palpably unreasonable."[1] In general terms, the test of whether a particular state tax violates the Due Process Clause is whether it bears some reasonable fiscal relation to the protection, opportunities and benefits given by the state, or whether the state has provided something for which in fairness it can ask such a return.[2]

Although the Supreme Court has hinted at times that "confiscatory" taxation would be impermissible, the Court has sustained state taxes severely reducing the profit margins of private businesses. Thus, in 1934 the Court allowed a tax of fifteen cents per pound on all butter substitutes, which eliminated all profit from this business by the taxpayer.[3] In 1974 the Court sustained a tax of twenty percent of the gross receipts of private parking lot operators, who could not then likely compete with public parking lots, remarking that it would not ordinarily question the size of taxes, except in those few instances where they might amount to unconstitutional "taking" without compensation.[4]

Traditionally, the United States Supreme Court has allowed states to tax only for "public purposes." It once said: "To lay with one hand the power of the government on the property of the citizen, and with the other to bestow it upon favored individuals to aid private fortunes, is none the less a robbery because it is done under the forms of law and is called taxation."[5] However, currently the Supreme Court defers greatly to the judgment of state legislatures that the purpose of a particular tax is sufficiently "public" to satisfy the Due Process Clause of the Fourteenth Amendment.[6]

Ordinarily, the United States Supreme Court has been reluctant to allow "double taxation" of tangible properties by two or more states or political subdivisions providing protection,[7] but the Supreme Court adds: "There is no constitutional rule of immunity from taxation of intangibles by more than one State."[8]

Although no substantive due process clause binds the States of India, Indian constitutional law requires that there be a satisfactory nexus between a taxpayer who is being taxed and the state imposing the tax.[9] Chief Justice Sinha of the Supreme Court said in 1961 of the power to tax: "The judicial department of the State is not expected to deal with such matters, because it is not for the courts to determine the policy and incidence of taxation."[10] In India, state taxes do not become unconstitutional solely because they are retrospective.[11]

Although no substantive due process clause restricts Canadian provinces in imposing taxes, something like the "public purpose" limitation in the United States appears in the clause of the British North America Act giving tax powers to the provinces "for provincial purposes."[12] However, the language has provided virtually no limitation upon the taxing power of the provinces.[13] Chief Justice Duff of the Supreme Court of Canada has said: "The words 'for provincial purposes' mean neither more nor less than this: the taxing power is given to them for raising money for the exclusive disposition of the legislature."[14]

§ 5.05 State power to tax real property and tangible chattels

In the federal societies, the component entities such as Laender, provinces and states customarily have plenary power to tax land and tangible chattels situated within their borders. The High Court of Australia has said: "The property in New South Wales of any person can be taxed in such manner as the Parliament of New South Wales determines."[1]

The Constitution of India confers upon the states power to impose taxes on "land and buildings."[2] The Provinces of Canada have full power to tax land situated within their borders.[3] The Laender of the German Federal Republic have acknowledged power to tax tangible chattels in their midst.[4]

The power of the Argentine Provinces to tax real and personal property situated within their borders has long been recognized, even when owned by nonresidents.[5] However, the Supreme Court has indicated it will not hold constitutional unreasonable or confiscatory taxation of property by the provinces.[6]

In the United States, under the Due Process Clause of the Fourteenth Amendment, the states have jurisdiction to tax not only land and real property within their borders, but also tangible personal property which has acquired a situs there.[7] Where tangible personal property owned by a nonresident or a foreign corporation is within a state for only part of a year, the Supreme Court has sustained taxes that are fairly apportioned to the time the article was present in the state,[8] but has rejected efforts of such a state to impose a full year's property tax.[9]

§ 5.06 State power to tax intangible personalty

Courts in the British Commonwealth countries,[1] as well as in the United States,[2] have been inclined to apply common law principles in determining whether a component entity in a federal society has power to tax intangible personalty. Such rulings are to be made under common law principles, said the Privy Council in 1942.[3] However, the constitutionalizing of common law principles in this area has at times been called into question by scholars in Commonwealth countries.[4]

Under the maxim, mobilia sequuntur personam, the state of domicile of the owner has often been accorded power to tax his intangible personal interests.[5] In sustaining the power of Queensland to impose a gift duty upon a domiciliary, even though the share certificates were outside the state at the time, Chief Justice Latham for the High Court of Australia said: "The cases cited all relate to death duties of one kind or another. But the principle that domicile in a territory constitutes sufficient connection with that territory to enable its legislature to tax persons so domiciled is not limited to the case of death duties."[6]

Where under the proper law, as defined by principles of private international law or conflicts of laws, intangible interests are represented by documents capable of acquiring situs, the state of situs can then impose property taxes upon them.[7] Since 1942, the United States Supreme Court has held there is no constitutional ban upon double taxation of intangible interests, and the Court allows property taxation by any state which provides protection to the document, the owner or the relationship, so long as the charge is reasonable for the protection provided.[8] Although there is no constitutional ban upon double taxation in Canada,[9] the constitutional language, "in the province" in Section 92(3) of the British North America Act, conferring tax power on the provinces, prevents a province from imposing property taxes upon intangibles that have acquired a situs outside the province.[10]

As set forth in the earlier Section 1.03, in Australia there are territorial limitations upon the power of the states to tax. As a matter of constitutional law, there must be a sufficient connection between the state and the intangible property to justify a particular tax upon the owner or those dealing with it.[11] What is a sufficient connection has never been fully defined and undoubtedly varies with the kind of tax involved. Justice Dixon indicated considerable judicial deference to legislative judgments was appropriate. "If a connection exists," he wrote, "it is for the legislature to decide how far it should go in the exercise of its powers."[12]

Where, under the proper law governing the intangible interest, all right and title have been fused into a document or certificate, its transfer can be taxed by the state of transfer, even though it is issued by a foreign corporation and owned by a nonresident.[13] So, too, the transfer of a stock certificate (into which all title has been fused) can be taxed by the state where the transfer occurred.[14]

§ 5.07　State taxation of income

In the states having, under federal constitutions, the residuum of power, they can generally impose income taxes. In Australia, however, under a Commonwealth scheme, the Commonwealth Parliament imposed an income tax "not only to collect revenue and to make grants to the States, but to prevent the States imposing taxation upon incomes" (with the grants going to the states that agreed not to exercise their taxing power in this form), and the High Court sustained the arrangement. The Court remarked:

> The Act does not purport to deprive the State Parliament of the power to impose an income tax. The Commonwealth Parliament cannot deprive any State of that power . . . . Notwithstanding the Grants Act a State Parliament could at any time impose an income tax. The State would then not benefit by a grant under the Act, but there is nothing in the Grants Act which could make the State income-tax legislation invalid.

The Court added generally that the Commonwealth may constitutionally induce a state by money grants "to abstain from exercising its powers."[1] The Commonwealth States Grant Act, which replaced the earlier grant provision, did not contain the earlier requirement that states refrain from taxing income as a condition to grants, and Australian States can in theory resume their original powers to tax income, although there seems to be a political understanding between the states and Commonwealth that the states will only impose a surcharge on top of the Commonwealth tax.[2]

In 1937, before enactment of the First Uniform Tax Act, the Australian High Court had sustained New South Wales in taxing the income earned there by a Victoria corporation carrying on business in the former state, and permitted New South Wales to include in the income taxed, interest on a loan made outside New South Wales, when the loan was secured by property in that state. The Court said: "There is no doubt that the Legislature of New South Wales can impose such conditions as it thinks proper by way of taxation or otherwise upon persons who carry on business in New South Wales and therefore bring themselves within the legislative authority of the State." It added by way of dictum that: "A resident of New South Wales can be taxed in New South Wales in respect of his income wherever derived."[3]

In the United States, a state can tax the income earned by its residents, wherever the income is earned.[4] States can also tax the income earned within the state by nonresidents and foreign corporations.[5]

In Canada, income taxes are deemed direct taxes and with provincial power.[6] Provinces can tax income earned therein,[7] even by nonresidents.[8] The tax on income of residents can include income earned outside his province.[9] A Dominion company has been held liable to a provincial income tax.[10]

Under the Constitution of India, the Union Government has the exclusive jurisdiction to tax income other than agricultural income.[11] Comparably, under the Constitution of Nigeria, the "taxation of incomes, profits and capital gains, except as otherwise prescribed by this Constitution" is an exclusive federal power.[12]

§ 5.08 State taxation of the transmission of property at death

States of federal societies in which real property or tangible property is situated can generally tax their transmission or inheritance at death.[1] A Canadian court has said: "When personal property is situated within the Province, the Province has the power to levy estate tax against such property," adding: "The Province has such power to tax property situated within the Province even if the deceased was domiciled in another Province."[2] In this situation, the maxim mobilia sequuntur personam does not apply.

State jurisdiction to tax in the United States is confined by the Due Process Clause of the Fourteenth Amendment,[3] and the power of Canadian provinces to tax property is somewhat correspondingly limited by the language "within the Province" in the section of the British North America Act conferring the tax power on the provinces.[4] It has been held that a succession tax on a person resident in a Canadian province regarding personal property situated outside the province passing from a deceased who resided outside the province was *ultra vires.*[5] In the United States, the states cannot tax the inheritance of land located outside the state, nor the inheritance of tangible personal property owned by a domiciliary where the property has acquired a situs outside the state.[6]

The High Court of Australia has placed territorial limitations upon the taxing power of the states, voiding attempted death duties when the connection of the state to the property involved was too remote. In 1932 a New South Wales statute demanding a death duty from a person domiciled in Victoria holding shares in a Victoria company, on the ground the company was engaged in mining in New South Wales, was held unconstitutional on application to the facts. The connection was "too remote," said the Court.[7] Again, in 1956 the Privy Council held New South Wales could not impose a tax on a Victoria resident to reach Victoria property passing to him as a remainderman under a will of a New South Wales domiciliary.[8]

Where personal property, under the proper law, has not acquired a situs apart from the domicile of the owner, that domicile can generally impose inheritance taxes upon the passage of the property at death, mobilia sequuntur personam applying here.[9] Thus, the Privy Council has held that where a deceased was domiciled in a particular Canadian province, it could levy a tax on the transmission of his personalty, and include personalty outside the province.[10] The Privy Council also held that a beneficiary could be taxed by his province of domicile on transmission to him of personal property outside his province so long as it had not acquired a situs outside, but that the province could not impose a tax on such property that had acquired a situs outside.[11] Chief Justice Latham of the High Court of Australia has said: "It is well settled that in the case of death duties the domicile of a deceased person may be adopted as affording a sufficient connection with a territory to justify taxation by the legislature of that territory with respect to the personal property of the deceased person wherever that property may be situated."[12]

Inheritance taxes can be imposed as to intangibles by the state of domicile of the decedent.[13] Furthermore, any state that has provided protection or benefits to intangible personal property, the owner or the documents of title can tax its succession. The United States Supreme Court has said: "In the case of shares of stock, 'jurisdiction to tax,' is not restricted to the domiciliary state. Another state which has extended benefits or protection, or which can demonstrate 'the practical fact of its power' or sovereignty as respects the shares . . . may likewise constitutionally make its exaction."[14] On another occasion, the Court had said: "We perceive no better reason for denying the right of New York to impose a succession tax on debts owed by its citizens than upon tangible chattels found within the State at the time of the death."[15]

The law of India allows the states to impose "duties in respect of succession to agricultural land,"[16] but the Constitution adds that the Union has exclusive jurisdiction to impose "estate duty in respect of property other than agricultural land,"[17] and "duties in respect of succession to property other than agricultural land."[18]

The provinces of Argentina have power to impose inheritance taxes.[19]

§ 5.09 State power to tax occupations and activities

States in federal societies generally have adequate power to tax occupations, businesses, and activities carried on within their borders.

When the United States Supreme Court sustained a Wisconsin tax on foreign corporations permitted to do business there, it remarked: "A state is free to pursue its own fiscal policies, unembarrassed by the Constitution, if by the practical operation of a tax a state has exerted its power in relation to opportunities which it has given, to protection which it has afforded, to benefits which it has conferred. . . . The simple but controlling question is whether the state has given anything for which it can ask a return."[1]

In sustaining a tax of 20% of gross receipts by private parking lot operators, the United States Supreme Court indicated it will not ordinarily under due process question the size of a tax, but in rare cases might void a tax when it became an unconstitutional taking without compensation.[2]

The Supreme Court of India has sustained the State of Bombay in taxing gambling within the state.[3]

The Argentine Supreme Court has sustained the power of the Province of Buenos Aires to tax the manufacture of sugar.[4]

Canadian provinces have been sustained in imposing corporation[5] and other business[6] taxes upon firms doing business within the province.

Where a person or corporation is doing business within an Australian state, the state can, so far as the Australian constitution is concerned, impose business taxes upon the enterprise in amounts deemed proper by the legislature of the state, so long as there is not violation of the Commerce Clause, as discussed in the previous chapter.[7]

§ 5.10 State transfer and sales taxes

For a long time, states in federal societies have been able to tax the transfer or sale of goods occurring within their jurisdiction. In 1869 the United States Supreme Court held that a political subdivision of a state could tax the sale of merchandise within its borders, even though the goods had been brought in from out-of-state and were still in the original packages.[1] In 1907 the Court held that the transfer of a stock certificate could constitutionally be taxed by the state of transfer, even though it had been issued by a foreign corporation and owned by a nonresident.[2]

Under Canadian constitutional law, sales taxes are "direct" taxes and valid if levied upon the ultimate consumer of the goods so that they will not be passed on to others.[3] However, a sales tax that can be passed on to others is called "indirect" and *ultra vires* the provinces.[4]

In Australia, sales taxes falling on sellers or distributors have been held to be "excises" and beyond state power.[5] The High Court in 1926 invalidated a state law imposing a tax on the first sale of petrol within the state, deeming it to be an excise.[6] The following year, the Court again voided a state tax imposed on publishers for the first sale of newspapers published within the state.[7]

In 1958 an Indian State sales tax was sustained on a transfer within the state,[8] but a discriminatory sales tax adversely affecting goods brought in from other states was held unconstitutional under Article 304(a) of the Constitution.[9] The Sixth Constitutional Amendment Act 1956 in Section 2 allows the states to impose "taxes on the sale or purchase of goods other than newspapers." However, the Constitution gives to the Union Government exclusive power to impose "taxes on the sale or purchase of goods other than newspapers where the sale or purchase takes place in the course of inter-State trade or commerce."[10] Article 286(1) of the Constitution provides that: "No law of a State shall impose or authorize the imposition of, a tax on the sale or purchase of goods where such sale or purchase takes place: (a) outside the State, or (b) in the course of the import of the goods into or export of the goods out of, the territory of India." Under Article 286(1) (b) it has been held that sales previous to export are only protected under this subsection when they cause the export.[11]

Beginning in 1940, the United States Supreme Court in a series of decisions sustained the power of the states and their political subdivisions to impose sales taxes, even upon goods coming in from out-of-state, where the seller by the terms of the contract was obligated to deliver the goods into the taxing jurisdiction, and did so deliver the goods.[12] In some of the cases, the presence of a sales agent in the taxing jurisdiction was commented upon by the Court.[13] Four years later, the Supreme Court ruled that a state sales tax could not be applied where title to the goods passed outside the state and where, by the terms of the sales contract, delivery to a common carrier outside the taxing state fulfilled the seller's obligations.[14] There were four dissents, and they represent the better view. Power of a state to tax sales should not hinge, even in part, on where the parties arrange for title to pass, and so long as the sale is consummated by delivery into the taxing state by an organization assigned the task by the vendor, the state of delivery of the goods should have power to impose a sales tax on the transaction.

§ 5.11 State taxation of the federal government—generally

By the constitutions in all the federal societies, the states are under explicit or implicit restraints upon taxing the operations and the properties of the federal government.

In Australia, the Constitution specifically forbids the states to "impose any tax on property of any kind belonging to the Commonwealth."[1] Furthermore, the High Court of Australia seems willing to recognize an implied immunity of the Commonwealth from all state taxation upon operations of the Commonwealth within the sphere of its constitutional powers.[2] In 1947 the High Court held that a city could not impose a property tax on the Commonwealth for its use of private property during World War II. Justice Dixon stated generally: "To my mind the incapacity of the States directly to tax the Commonwealth in respect of something done in the exercise of its powers or functions is a necessary consequence of the system of government established by the Constitution."[3] Any discriminatory taxation by a state against the Commonwealth would clearly be unconstitutional.[4]

In Brazil, the Constitution explicitly forbids the states to impose taxes on "the property, revenue or services" of the federal government.[5]

In Canada, under the Constitution (the British North America Act), the provinces cannot generally tax property belonging to the Dominion. Section 125 of the Act provides: "No lands or property belonging to Canada or any province shall be liable to taxation." However, a province can tax the beneficial interests of private parties in using Dominion lands.[6]

In India, the Constitution immunizes the property of the Union from all state taxes, unless the Union Parliament provides otherwise.[7]

Although the United States Constitution has no specific clause exempting the property or operations of the federal government from taxation by the states, it has been settled from an early date that the states cannot, without the consent of the Congress, tax the operations of the central government,[8] or its real or personal property.[9] Without Congressional consent, states cannot impose personal property taxes upon federal government bonds held by their citizens,[10] nor can they impose taxes upon the income earned by their citizens from such securities.[11]

Federal governments generally have power to create an immunity from state tax laws.[12]

§ 5.12 State taxation of the interest of private parties in federal properties

States in federal societies have often been sustained in taxing the interests of private persons and corporations in federally owned properties.

The Supreme Court of Canada has ruled that the provinces can tax the interest of private persons in Dominion lands.[1] Occupants of Crown lands can be taxed by the provinces and their local governments.[2]

In the United States, purchasers of federal lands can be taxed by the states on their interests, even though legal title is still in the federal government for security.[3] The Supreme Court has also held that a state can impose an inheritance tax on a legacy of personal property to the federal government.[4] The Court has also sustained state and local taxes upon private businesses for the privilege of using within the community federally owned properties, even though the economic burden of the tax, by contract or otherwise, is ultimately borne by the federal government.[5]

§ 5.13 State taxation of federal corporations and instrumentalities

The Privy Council had held that a province can tax the property of the Canadian Pacific Railroad located in the province, this being a direct tax authorized by the British North America Act.[1]

In the United States, the states cannot tax the operation of federal instrumentalities, without the consent of the federal Congress.[2] The Supreme Court has also said that "lands owned by the United States of America or its instrumentalities are immune from state and local taxation."[3] Many of the federal instrumentalities, such as the national banks, are privately owned. Congress has exempted such national banks from state and local sales taxes as purchasers, and the Supreme Court has sustained the exemption.[4] It is suggested it is highly undesirable to reduce state tax powers in instances such as this when it is not necessary to protect the functioning of the federal government.

In Australia the Commonwealth Parliament can exempt from state taxation corporations set up by it, even though they do not qualify as federal "instrumentalities."[5]

§ 5.14 State taxation of income received by federal government personnel

In the United States, persons citizens (or residents) of a state can be subjected to state income taxes on the incomes earned there from the federal government.[1] In Australia, the Commonwealth Salaries Act of 1907 allows states to impose nondiscriminatory taxes upon compensation received therein by employees of the Commonwealth.[2]

However, the United States Congress has been held to have power to immunize the income of members of the armed forces from taxation by nondomiciliary states to which they have been sent.[3]

In 1937 the High Court of Australia held that New South Wales could impose its income tax upon a pension received by a former employee of the Commonwealth government, the Court indicating that the Commonwealth Parliament had power to exempt such sums from state taxation. Any discriminatory taxation against the Commonwealth and its employees would clearly be unconstitutional, said Chief Justice Latham.[4]

§ 5.15 State taxes on firms doing business with the federal government

In sustaining a state tax on the privilege of storing gasoline, as imposed upon a corporation doing business with the federal government which held technical title to the fuel, the United States Supreme Court stated: "Federal ownership of the fuel will not immunize such a private contractor from the tax on storage. . . . The Constitution does not extend sovereign exemption from state taxation to corporations or individuals, contracting with the United States, merely because their activities are useful to the Government."[1] Such privilege taxes are not rendered unconstitutional because the business has a "cost-plus-fixed-fee" contract with the federal government.[2]

Where contractors operate within a state, that state can impose a gross receipts tax upon them for the privilege of doing business, and include within the tax base moneys received from the federal government.[3]

The United States Supreme Court holds that states can impose sales taxes upon private contractors having cost-plus contracts with the United States Government,[4] but the Court has been reluctant to allow sales taxes when it believes "the real purchaser" is the federal government[5] States have been unable to collect sales taxes on transactions occuring on federal enclaves.[6]

§ 5.16 State power to raise revenue by license and other fees

At times, the component entities in federal societies are given express constitutional power to impose license and other fees. Thus, under the British North America Act, the provinces are specifically authorized to impose license fees.[1] By the Constitution of India, the states have specific authority to charge "fees in respect of any of the matters" on the State List of legislative powers.[2] The Constitution of Malaysia confers upon the states power to levy entertainment duties, fees, and receipts from government services, as well as revenue from licenses on things other than vehicles, electrical installations and registration of businesses.[3]

Even without specific constitutional authorizations to levy fees for revenue, states in federal societies customarily have power to charge fees reasonably adequate to cover the cost of their authorized policing activities.[4] The High Court of Australia has, on a number of occasions, sustained state license fees for a citizen's "franchise to carry on a business," without requiring proof by the state that the fees are necessary for policing the activity.[5]

FOOTNOTES

§ 5.00

1. Deakin v. Webb (1904) 1 C.L.R. 585, 617.
2. First Uniform Tax Case (1942) 65 C.L.R. 373; Second Uniform Tax Case (1957) 99 C.L.R. 575.
3. Constitution of Nigeria, Second Schedule, Part I (15).
4. Amadeo, *Argentine Constitutional Law* (Columbia U. Press, N.Y. 1943) 154.
5. Iglesias v. Buenos Aires (1906) 105 S.C.N. 273 (agricultural products).
6. British North America Act, § 92(2).
7. King v. Caledonian Collieries (1928) 3 D.L.R. 657, (1928) A.C. 358.
8. Charlottetown v. Foundation Maritime Ltd. (1932) 3 D.L.R. 353, 357 (Rinfret, C.J.C.).
9. British North America Act, § 92(9).
10. Hughes, *The Federal Constitution of Switzerland* (Westport, Conn. 1970) 12.
11. Constitution of India, List I, Entry 85.
12. Constitution of India, List II, Entry 56.
13. List II, Entry 57.
14. List II, Entry 58.
15. List II, Entry 60.
16. List II, Entry 62.
17. List II, Entry 66.
18. Blair, *Federalism and Judicial Review in West Germany* (Oxford 1981) 5.
19. BVerfGE 7, 244 (Baden Wine Tax).
20. Lewis, *The Governments of Argentina, Brazil and Mexico* (New York 1975) 97, 105.
21. Constitution of Brazil 1969, as amended, Art. 19(b).
22. Constitution of Brazil 1969, as amended, Art. 19(d).

§ 5.01

1. British North America Act, § 92(2).
2. Charlottetown v. Foundation Maritime Ltd. (1932) 3 D.L.R.   353, 357-8 (Rinfret, C.J.C.).
3. *Mill on Political Economy* (1886 ed.) vol. II, p. 367; followed in Bank of Toronto v. Lambe (1887) 12 A.C. 575.
4. Atlantic Smoke Shops Ltd. v. Attorney-General for Canada (1943) A.C. 550, 566.
5. Regina v. Churchill (1972) 29 D.L.R. 3d 368 (tax on operators of mobile home park).
6. Utah Company v. Attorney-General for British Columbia (B.C. Ct. App. 1959) 19 D.L.R. 2d 705.
7. Untermyer v. Attorney-General for British Columbia (1929) 1 D.L.R. 315 (tax on shares); Colpitts Ranches v. Attorney-General for Alberta (S Ct Alb. 1954) 3 D.L.R. 121 (stock in goods); Cairns Construction Co. v. Saskatchewan (1960) S.C.R. 619 (building materials).
8. Halifax v. Fairbanks Estate (1928) A.C. 117; "Taxes on property or income are commonly regarded as direct taxes." Charlottetown v. Foundation Maritime Ltd. (1932) 3 D.L.R. 353, 357 (Rinfret, C.J.C.).
9. Brewers and Maltsters Association v. Attorney-General for Ontario (1897) A.C. 231.
10. Bank of Toronto v. Lambe (1887) 12 A.C. 575.
11. Atlantic Smoke Shops v. Attorney-General for Canada (1943) A.C. 550, 566.
12. Alleyn v. Barthe (1922) 1 A.C. 215.
13. Attorney-General for British Columbia v. Attorney-General for Canada (1923) 1 D.L.R. 223.
14. Attorney-General for British Columbia v. Canadian Pacific Ry. (1927) A.C. 934.
15. Charlottetown v. Foundation Maritime Ltd. (1932) 3 D.L.R. 353, 357 (Rinfret, C.J.C.).
16. King v. Caledonian Collieries (1928) 3 D.L.R. 657, (1928) A.C. 358.

17 Attorney-General for British Columbia v. Macdonald Murphy Lumber Co. (1930) 2 D.L.R. 721, (1930) A.C. 357.
18 Attorney-General for British Columbia v. C.P.R. (1927) A.C. 934.
19 Attorney-General for British Columbia v. C.P.R. (1927) A.C. 934.
20 Attorney-General for British Columbia v. Kingscombe Navigation Co. (1934) A.C. 45; Atlantic Smoke Shops v. Conlon (1943) A.C. 550.
21 Queen in Right of Manitoba v. Air Canada (S Ct 1980) 111 D.L.R. 3d 513.

§ 5.02

1 Constitution of Australia, Section 90.
2 Constitution of Nigeria 1979, Second Schedule, Part I (15).
3 Constitution of India, Seventh Schedule, Union List, entry 84.
4 Peterswald v. Bartley (1904) 1 C.L.R. 497, 509. The classic treatment of Section 90 of the Australian Constitution is that of Michael Coper, Senior Lecturer, the Law School of the University of New South Wales, in: "The High Court and Section 90 of the Constitution," 7 *Fed. L. Rev.* 1 (1976).
5 Bolton v. Madsen (1963) 110 C.L.R. 265, 271.
6 Anderson Pty. Ltd. v. Victoria (1964) 111 C.L.R. 353, 374.
7 Dickenson's Arcade v. Tasmania (1974) 130 C.L.R. 177, 185-6.
8 Attorney-General for New South Wales v. Homebuch Flour Mills Ltd. (1937) 56 C.L.R. 390.
9 Commonwealth and Commonwealth Oil Refineries Ltd. v. South Australia (1926) 38 C.L.R. 408; John Fairfax and Sons Ltd. v. New South Wales (1927) 38 C.L.R. 408.
10 Parton v. Milk Board (Vic.) (1949) 80 C.L.R. 229.
11 Bolton v. Madsen (1963) 110 C.L.R 265 (not an excise was a state fee for a permit to employ a vehicle for the carriage of goods).
12 Dennis Hotels Pty. v. Victoria (1960) 104 C.L.R. 529, followed in Sleigh Ltd. v. South Australia (1977) 136 C.L.R. 475, 495. But compare M.G. Kailis v. Western Australia (1974) 130 C.L.R. 245 (license fee for processing fish measured by value of fish processed, held excise).
13 Anderson's Pty. Ltd. v. Victoria (1964) 111 C.L.R. 353. But compare Western Australia v. Hammersely Iron Pty. Ltd. (#1) (1969) 120 C.L.R. 42 and Western Australia v. Chamberlain Industries Pty. Ltd. (1970) 121 C.L.R. 1 (where the High Court held taxes on receipts were forbidden excise duties when the tax was in effect a levy on the sale of goods measured by the value or price).
14 Harper v. Victoria (1966) 114 C.L.R. 361.
15 Crothers v. Sheil (1933) 49 C.L.R. 399; Hartley v. Walsh (1937) 57 C.L.R. 372.

§ 5.03

1 Cruz v. Santiago del Estero (1938) 179 S.C.N. 98.
2 Moran v. Entre Rios (1934) 171 S.C.N. 390.
3 R. v. Marchioness of Donegal (1924) 2 D.L.R. 1191.
4 Wheeling Steel Corp. v. Glander (1949) 337 US 562, 69 S Ct 1291, 93 L Ed 1544.
5 Bell's Gap Railroad v. Pennsylvania (1890) 134 US 232, 237, 10 S Ct 533, 33 L Ed 892; Walters v. St. Louis (1954) 347 US 231, 74 S Ct 505, 98 L Ed 660; Allied Stores v. Bowers (1959) 358 US 522, 79 S Ct 437, 3 L Ed 2d 480.
6 Madden v. Kentucky (1940) 309 US 83, 88, 60 S Ct 406, 84 L Ed 590.
7 Ward v. Maryland (1871) 12 Wall. 418, 20 L Ed 449, 452. Semble: Travis v. Yale & Towne Manufacturing Co. (1920) 252 US 60, 40 S Ct 228, 64 L Ed 460.
8 Toomer v. Witsell (1948) 334 US 385, 68 S Ct 1156, 1162, 92 L Ed 1460.
9 "A subject of the Queen, resident in any State, shall not be subject in any other State to any disability or discrimination which would not be equally applicable to him if he were a subject of the Queen resident in such other State." Constitution of Australia, § 117.
10 Constitution of India, Art. 304(a).

11 Mehtab Majid & Co. v. State of Madras, A.I.R. 1963 S.C. 928; State of Madras v. Bhailal Bhai, A.I.R. 1964 S.C. 1006.
12 Austrian Constitution of 1920/1929 as amended, Art. 6(3).
13 Grundgesetz of German Federal Republic, Article 33.
14 Constitution of Brazil 1969, as amended, Art. 9(1).
15 Constitution of Nigeria 1979, Chapter IV, § 39.
16 Constitution of Malaysia 1968, as amended, Art. 8(4).

§ 5.04

1 Railway Express Agency v. Virginia (1959) 358 US 434, 79 S Ct 411, 3 L Ed 2d 450; Mobil Oil Corp.v. Commissioner of Taxes (1980) 445 US 425, 100 S Ct 1223, 63 L Ed 2d 510.
2 Wisconsin v. J.C. Penney Co. (1940) 311 US 435, 445, 61 S Ct 246, 85 L Ed 267; Ott v. Mississippi Valley Barge Lines (1949) 336 US 169, 174, 69 S Ct 432, 93 L Ed 585.
3 A. Magnano v. Hamilton (1934) 292 US 40, 44, 54 S Ct 599, 78 L Ed 1109. (State taxes valid unless they constitute "in substance and effect, the direct exertion of a different and forbidden power, as, for example, the confiscation of property . . . . ")
4 Pittsburgh v. Alco Parking Corp. (1974) 417 US 369, 94 S Ct 2291, 41 L Ed 2d 132.
5 Citizens Savings and Loan Association v. Topeka (1875) 20 Wall. 655, 664, 22 L Ed 455.
6 Jones v. Portland (1917) 245 US 217, 38 S Ct 112, 62 L Ed 252; Green v. Frazier (1920) 253 US 233, 40 S Ct 499, 64 L Ed 878.
7 Frick v. Pennsylvania (1925) 268 US 473, 45 S Ct 603, 69 L Ed 1058.
8 State Tax Commission of Utah v. Aldrich (1942) 316 US 174, 181, 62 S Ct 1008, 86 L Ed 1358.
9 State of Bombay v. R. M. D. Chanarbaugwala, A.I.R. (1957) S.C. 699; Tata Iron & Steel Co. v. State of Bihar (1958) S.C.R. 1355.
10 Atiabari Tea Co. v. State of Assam A.I.R. 1961 S.C. 232, 238-9 (dissenting).
11 Tata Iron & Steel Co. v. State of Bihar (1958) S.C.R. 1355.
12 British North America Act, § 92(2).
13 LaForest, *The Allocation of Taxing Power under the Canadian Constitution* (Toronto 1981) 75.
14 Reference re Employment and Social Insurance Act (1936) S.C.R. 427, 434 (dissenting).

§ 5.05

1 Broken Hill South Ltd. v. Commissioner of Taxation (NSW) (1937) 56 C.L.R. 337, 356 (Latham, C.J.).
2 Constitution of India, List II, Entry 49.
3 Untermeyer v. British Columbia (1929) S.C.R. 84; Hogg, *Constitutional Law of Canada* (Toronto 1977) 410.
4 BVerfGE 14, 76; 31, 8; 31, 119; 40, 52; 40, 56; 42, 38.
5 Griet Hermanos v. Tucuman (1922) 137 S.C.N. 212; Badenia v. Salta (1937) 179 S.C.N. 86; Iglesias v. Buenos Aires (1937) 179 S.C.N. 273.
6 Barrera v. San Juan (1930) 168 S.C.N. 305.
7 City Bank Farmers Trust Co. v. Schrader (1934) 293 US 112, 55 S Ct 29, 79 L Ed 228; Central Railroad v. Jersey City (1908) 209 US 473, 28 S Ct 592, 52 L Ed 896.
8 Braniff Airways v. Nebraska (1954) 347 US 590, 74 S Ct 757, 98 L Ed 967.
9 Hays v. Pacific Mail Steamship Co. (1855) 17 How. 596, 15 L Ed 254; Morgan v. Parham (1873) 16 Wall. 471, 21 L Ed 303.

§ 5.06

1 Hogg, *Constitutional Law of Canada* (Toronto 1977) 410-411.
2 Buck v. Beach (1907) 206 US 392, 401, 27 S Ct 712, 51 L Ed 1106.
3 R. v. Williams (1942) A.C. 541, 559.
4 Hogg, *Constitutional Law of Canada* (Toronto 1977) 411; LaForest, *The Allocation of Taxing Power under the Canadian Constitution* (Toronto 1981) 115.

[5] Buck v. Beach (1907) 206 US 392, 27 S Ct 712, 51 L Ed 1106; Barthe v. Alleyn-Sharples (1919) 60 S.C.R. 1; R. v. Sharp, ex parte Turnbull (1901) 35 N.B.R. 477.
[6] Commissioner of Stamps (Q.) v. Counsell (1937) 57 C.L.R. 248, 256 (Latham, C.J.).
[7] Scottish Union v. Bowland (1905) 196 US 611, 25 S Ct 345, 49 L Ed 619.
[8] State Tax Commission of Utah v. Aldrich (1942) 316 US 174, 62 S Ct 1008, 86 L Ed 1358.
[9] Charlottetown v. Heartz (1882) 2 P.E.I. 444; Hogg, *Constitutional Law of Canada* (Toronto 1977) 56.
[10] R. v. National Trust Co. (1933) S.C.R. 670.
[11] Johnson v. Commissioner for Stamp Duties (NSW) (1956) A.C. 331.
[12] Broken Hill South Ltd. v. Commissioner of Taxation (NSW) (1937) 56 C.L.R. 337, 375.
[13] Hatch v. Reardon (1907) 204 US 152, 27 S Ct 188, 51 L Ed 415.
[14] State Tax Commission of Utah v. Aldrich (1942) 316 US 174, 62 S Ct 1008, 86 L Ed 1358.

§ 5.07

[1] South Australia v. The Commonwealth (First Uniform Tax Case) (1942) 65 C.L.R. 373, (Latham, C.J.) followed in Victoria v. The Commonwealth (Second Uniform Tax Case) (1957) 99 C.L.R. 575.
[2] Lane, *The Australian Federal System* (2d ed. 1979 Sydney) 118-9.
[3] Broken Hill South Ltd. v. Commissioner of Taxation (NSW) (1937) 56 C.L.R. 337, 355-6 (Latham, C.J.).
[4] New York ex rel Cohn v. Graves (1937) 300 US 308, 57 S Ct 466, 81 L Ed 666.
[5] Shaffer v. Carter (1920) 252 US 37, 40 S Ct 221, 64 L Ed 445; Hans Rees Sons v. North Carolina ex rel. Maxwell (1931) 283 US 123, 51 S Ct 385, 75 L Ed 879. A state can include dividends from affiliated companies outside the state if it is a unitary business, so long as a fair apportionment formula is used. Mobil Oil Corp. v. Commissioner of Taxes (1980) 445 US 425, 100 S Ct 1223, 63 L Ed 2d 510.
[6] Halifax v. Fairbanks Estate (1928) A.C. 117; Charlottetown v. Foundation Maritime Ltd. (1932) 3 D.L.R. 353, 357 (Rinfret, C.J.C.).
[7] Forbes v. Attorney-General for Manitoba (1937) A.C. 260.
[8] International Harvester v. Provincial Tax Commission (1949) A.C. 36.
[9] Kerr v. Alberta (1942) S.C.R. 435.
[10] Re Income Tax Act 1932 (Sask. 1937) 3 W.W.R. 680.
[11] Constitution of India, Union List I, Entry 82.
[12] Constitution of Nigeria 1979, Second Schedule, Part I (58).

§ 5.08

[1] Untermeyer v. British Columbia (1929) S.C.R. 84.
[2] Canada Trust v. Attorney-General for British Columbia (B.C. S.Ct 1978) 86 D.L.R. 3d 267, 269.
[3] City Bank v. Schrader (1934) 293 US 112, 120-121, 55 S Ct 29, 79 L Ed 228.
[4] British North America Act, § 92(2).
[5] Canada Trust v. Attorney-General for British Columbia (B.C. S.Ct. 1978) 86 D.L.R. 3d 267.
[6] Frick v. Pennsylvania (1925) 268 US 473, 45 S Ct 603, 69 L Ed 1058; Treichler v. Wisconsin (1949) 338 US 251, 70 S Ct 1, 94 L Ed 37.
[7] Millar v. Commissioner for Stamp Duties (1932) 48 C.L.R. 618, 632.
[8] Johnson v. Commissioner for Stamp Duties (NSW) (1956) A.C. 331.
[9] Blodgett v. Silberman (1928) 277 US 1, 48 S Ct 410, 72 L Ed 749.
[10] Burland v. The King; Alleyn-Sharples v. Barthe (1921) 62 D.L.R. 515; (1922) 1 A.C. 215.
[11] Alberta v. Kerr (1933) A.C. 710 (P.C.).
[12] Commissioner of Stamps (Q) v. Counsell (1937) 57 C.L.R. 248, 255.
[13] Blodgett v. Silberman (1928) 277 US 1, 48 S Ct 410, 72 L Ed 749.
[14] State Tax Commission of Utah v. Aldrich (1942) 316 US 174, 182, 62 S Ct 1008, 86 L Ed 1358.

15 Blackstone v. Miller (1903) 188 US 189, 206, 23 S Ct 277, 47 L Ed 439.
16 Constitution of India, List II, Entry 47.
17 Constitution of India, List I, Entry 87.
18 Constitution of India, List I, Entry 88.
19 Migoni v. Mendoza (1904) 100 S.C.N. 157.

§ 5.09

1 Wisconsin v. J.C. Penney Co. (1940) 311 US 435, 445, 61 S Ct 246, 85 L Ed 267.
2 Pittsburgh v. Alco Parking Corp. (1974) 417, US 369, 94 S Ct 2291, 41 L Ed 2d 132.
3 State of Bombay v. R.M.D. Chanarbaugwala, A.I.R. (1957) S.C. 699.
4 Griet Hermanos v. Tucuman (1922) 137 S.C.N. 212.
5 Industrial Acceptance Corp. v. Treasurer of Ontario (Ont. 1961) 30 D.L.R. 2d 497.
6 Re Mowat & Lorne Murphy Foods Ltd. (Ont. 1972) 23 D.L.R. 3d 543.
7 Bolton v. Madsen (1963) 110 C.L.R. 265; Dennis Hotels Pty. v. Victoria (1960) 104 C.L.R. 529; Sleigh Ltd. v. South Australia (1977) 136 C.L.R. 475; Anderson's Pty. Ltd. v. Victoria (1964) 111 C.L.R. 353.

§ 5.10

1 Woodruff v. Parham (1869) 8 Wall. 123, 19 L Ed 382.
2 Hatch v. Reardon (1907) 204 US 152, 27 S Ct 188, 51 L Ed 415.
3 Attorney-General for British Columbia v. Kingscombe Navigation Co. (1934) A.C. 45; Atlantic Smoke Shops v. Conlon (1943) A.C. 550.
4 Attorney-General for British Columbia v. C.P.R. (1927) A.C. 934.
5 Parton v. Milk Board (Vic.) (1949) 80 C.L.R. 229.
6 Commonwealth and Commonwealth Oil Refineries Ltd. v. South Australia (1926) 38 C.L.R. 408 (called an "income tax").
7 John Fairfax and Sons Ltd. v. New South Wales (1927) 39 C.L.R. 139.
8 Tata Iron and Steel Co. v. State of Bihar (1958) S.C.R. 1355.
9 Mehtab Majid & Co. v. State of Madras, A.I.R. 1963 S.C. 928.
10 Constitution of India, Union List, Entry 92A.
11 State of Mysore v. Mysore Shipping and Manufacturing Co. (1958) A.S.C. 1002.
12 McGoldrick v. Berwind White Coal Mining Co. (1940) 309 US 33, 60 S Ct 388, 84 L Ed 565 (title also passing within the taxing jurisdiction); McGoldrick v. Felt & Tarrant Manufacturing Co. (1940) 309 US 70, 60 S Ct 404, 84 L Ed 584; McGoldrick v. Compagnie Generale Transatlantique (1940) 309 US 430, 60 S Ct 670, 84 L Ed 849.
13 McGoldrick v. DuGrenier (1940) 309 US 70, 60 S Ct 404, 84 L Ed 584.
14 McLeod v. Dilworth (1944) 322 US 327, 64 S Ct 1023, 88 L Ed 1304.

§ 5.11

1 Constitution of Australia, § 114.
2 Australian Coastal Shipping Commission v. O'Reilly (1962) 107 C.L.R. 46, 62 (Menzies J.); Howard, *Australian Federal Constitutional Law* (2d ed. 1972, Sydney) 104.
3 Essendon Corp. v. Commonwealth (1947) 74 C.L.R. 1, 18-19.
4 West v. Commissioner of Taxation (NSW) (1937) 56 C.L.R. 657 (Latham, C.J.).
5 Constitution of Brazil 1969, as amended, Art. 19(III).
6 Calgary and Edmonton Land Co. v. Attorney-General for Alberta (1911) 45 S.C.R. 170 Spooner Oils v. Turner Valley Gas Conserv. 'ion Board (1933) 4 D.L.R. 545.
7 Constitution of India, Article 285.
8 McCulloch v. Maryland (1819) 4 Wheat. 316, 4 L Ed 579.
9 Van Brocklin v. Tennessee (1886) 117 US 151, 6 S Ct 670, 29 L Ed 845; United States v Allegheny County (1944) 322 US 174, 64 S Ct 908, 88 L Ed 1209.
10 Weston v. Charleston (1829) 2 Pet. 449, 7 L Ed 481.
11 Macallen Co. v. Massachusetts (1929) 279 US 620, 49 S Ct 432, 73 L Ed 874, 878.
12 West v. Commissioner of Taxation (NSW) (1937) 56 C.L.R. 657; Commonwealth v

Queensland (1920) 29 C.L.R. 1; Australian Coastal Shipping Commission v. O'Reilly (1962) 107 C.L.R. 46; Cleveland v. United States (1945) 323 US 329, 65 S Ct 280, 89 L Ed 274.

§ 5.12

1 Southern Alberta Land Co. v. McLean (1916) 53 S.C.R. 151.
2 Spooner Oils Ltd. v. Turner Valley Gas Conservation Bd. (1933) S.C.R. 629, (1933) 4 D.L.R. 545; Fraser v. Montreal (1914) 23 Q.K.B. 242.
3 S.R.A. v. Minnesota (1946) 327 US 558, 66 S Ct 749, 90 L Ed 851.
4 United States v. Perkins (1896) 163 US 625, 16 S Ct 1073, 41 L Ed 287, 289 ("imposed upon the legacy before it reaches the hands of the government").
5 United States v. Detroit (1958) 355 US 466, 78 S Ct 474, 2 L Ed 2d 424; United States v. Boyd (1964) 378 US 39, 84 S Ct 1518, 12 L Ed 2d 713, 718.

§ 5.13

1 C.P.R. v. Notre Dame de Bonsecours (1899) A.C. 367 (P.C.).
2 McCulloch v. Maryland (1819) 4 Wheat. 316, 4 L Ed 579.
3 Rohr Aircraft Corp. v. County of San Diego (1960) 362 US 628, 80 S Ct 1050, 4 L Ed 2d 1002, 1006.
4 First Agricultural National Bank v. State Tax Commission (1968) 392 US 339, 88 S Ct 2173, 20 L Ed 2d 1138 (but note dissent of Marshall, Harlan and Stewart, Jj).
5 Australian Coastal Shipping Commission v. O'Reilly (1962) 107 C.L.R. 46.

§ 5.14

1 Graves v. New York (1939) 306 US 466, 59 S Ct 595, 83 L Ed 927.
2 Chaplin v. Commissioner of Taxes (1911) 12 C.L.R. 375; West v. Commissioner of Taxation (1937) 56 C.L.R. 657 (Commonwealth pensions subject to state taxation).
3 Dameron v. Broadhead (1953) 345 US 322, 73 S Ct 721, 97 L Ed 1041.
4 West v. Commissioner of Taxation (NSW) (1937) 56 C.L.R. 657.

§ 5.15

1 Esso Standard Oil Co. v. Evans (1953) 345 US 495, 73 S Ct 800, 97 L Ed 1174.
2 United States v. Boyd (1964) 378 US 39, 84 S Ct 1518, 12 L Ed 2d 713, 721.
3 Alward v. Johnson (1931) 282 US 509, 51 S Ct 273, 75 L Ed 496; Crowder v. Commonwealth (Va. 1955) 87 SE 2d 745, appeal dismissed 350 US 957.
4 Alabama v. King & Boozer (1941) 314 US 1, 62 S Ct 43, 86 L Ed 3; Washington v. United States (1983) 103 S Ct 1344.
5 Kern-Limerick Inc. v. Scurlock (1954) 347 US 110, 74 S Ct 403, 98 L Ed 546.
6 Standard Oil Co. v. California (1934) 291 US 242, 54 S Ct 381, 78 L Ed 775.

§ 5.16

1 British North America Act, § 92(9); Reference re Prov. Co. Legislation (1913) 48 S.C.R. 331.
2 Constitution of India, Seventh Schedule, State List, Entry 66.
3 Constitution of Malaysia 1968, as amended, Tenth Schedule, Part III.
4 Pure Oil Co. v. Minnesota (1918) 248 US 158, 39 S Ct 35, 63 L Ed 180; Hughes and Vale Pty. Ltd. v. New South Wales (#1) (1953) 87 C.L.R. 49, 75; Brown's Transport Pty. Ltd. v. Kropp (1958) 100 C.L.R. 117, 130.
5 Dennis Hotels Pty. Ltd. v. Victoria (1961) 104 C.L.R. 529, 591; Peterswald v. Bartley (1904) 1 C.L.R. 497; Dickenson's Arcade v. Tasmania (1974) 130 C.L.R. 177.

CHAPTER SIX

Chapter Six

STATE PROPRIETARY POWERS

§ 6.00 Generally

Where states have the residuum of power, as in Argentina, Australia, Brazil, the German Federal Republic, Malaysia, Mexico, Pakistan, Switzerland, the United States of America, and Venezuela, the states have ample power to undertake proprietary ventures, unless forbidden to them by express clauses in the federal constitution, or by the language of their own constitutions. In states where the residuum of power is in the central government, as in Austria, Canada, India, Nigeria and the U.S.S.R., the component political entities must find a grant of power in the federal constitution as the basis for their proprietary undertakings.

In the majority of federal societies, the component entities can embark upon any proprietary venture approved by the state legislative authorities. Sometimes, state constitutions specifically authorize the state and local governments to embark upon proprietary undertakings.[1] Thus, the Arizona Constitution provides: "The State of Arizona and each municipal corporation within the State of Arizona shall have the right to engage in industrial pursuits."[2]

§ 6.01 Public purpose and provincial purpose limitations

Since 1875, the United States Supreme Court has held that in the states and their political subdivisions "there can be no lawful tax which is not laid for a public purpose."[1] By 1917 the Court could say that: "It is well settled that moneys for other than public purposes cannot be raised by taxation, and that exertion of the taxing power for merely private purposes is beyond the authority of the State."[2] There has been no case where the Court imposed a "public purpose" limitation upon the states or their political subdivisions where nontax funds were involved.

However, since about 1917, the Supreme Court has deferred greatly to the judgment of state legislatures that a variety of projects satisfied the public purpose test.[3] The specific projects are indicated in succeeding sections.

Outside the United States, the states are not subject to a public purpose limitation when embarking upon ventures that might be described as "proprietary," as distinguished from "governmental."

The section of the British North America Act conferring the tax power upon the provinces limits the power to "the raising of revenue for provincial purposes."[4] However, this has not been the equivalent of the public purpose limitation and is virtually no restraint upon a Canadian province desiring to spend for proprietary projects. Chief Justice Duff said in 1936 that the clause means only "for the exclusive disposition of the legislature,"[5] and the leading authority on the clause, Professor LaForest, writes that the "provincial purposes" clause "does not really impose any limitation on the provincial taxing power."[6]

§ 6.02 Power to operate financial institutions

In both Australia and Canada, the states and provinces operate banking institutions, and their constitutionality can be accepted.[1]

The United States Supreme Court ruled in 1920 that North Dakota could, if it desired, operate banking facilities without violating the public purpose limitation.[2]

Elsewhere, in federal systems wherein the states have the residuum of power, there would seemingly be no constitutional barrier to the creation of state financial institutions, subject to federal controls.

§ 6.03 Transportation facilities

Some Australian states operate railways, and this is accepted as constitutional, subject to Commonwealth control in their interstate operations.[1]

The Privy Council in 1875 sustained provincial power to operate trains in Canada,[2] and this provincial activity has continued,[3] subject to Dominion control of interprovincial operations.

In the United States, Cincinnati, Ohio[4] and New York City[5] have operated trains under state authorization and this is now accepted as constitutional. So long as the governmental entity has power under the proper law, operation of transportation facilities will always satisfy the public purpose limitation.[6]

Pacific Western Airlines is owned by the Province of Alberta, and operates in a number of provinces and abroad. Its operation is seemingly constitutional,[7] though subject to Dominion control in its interprovincial and foreign operations. In Australia and the other federal societies, states can constitutionally establish and operate air lines.[8]

§ 6.04 Operation of industrial establishments

State courts have held constitutional establishment of a number of industrial plants by the states and their political subdivisions.[1] Conceivably, the United States Supreme Court could hold the "public purpose" doctrine does not permit such activity by the public sector, but its latest rulings indicate such holding is unlikely, given the traditional deference of that Court to judgments of state legislatures and courts in this area.[2]

Elsewhere there appears to be no constitutional objection to the component governments in federations establishing industrial plants.

§ 6.05 Merchandising establishments

The United States Supreme Court ruled in 1920 that North Dakota could, under the public purpose doctrine, establish grain elevators to aid in the orderly marketing of wheat grown there.[1] In 1927 in a *per curiam* ruling without a written opinion the Supreme Court affirmed[2] an earlier Nebraska holding that the state could authorize its municipalities to engage in the distribution of gasoline.[3]

There was no violation of the Fourteenth Amendment, ruled the Supreme Court, when Maine authorized the City of Portland to establish and operate yards for the sale of coal, wood and other fuels.[4]

Courts have held that the public purpose doctrine was not violated when municipalities, under state authorization, engaged in the sale of ice.[5]

§ 6.06 Other proprietary activities

The United States Supreme Court has held that a state could embark upon a program of building homes for its people without violating the public purpose limitation.[1]

State court authority supports the view that the public purpose test is satisfied by governmental operation of a health spring,[2] public baths,[3] a cotton warehouse,[4] a slaughterhouse[5] a stone quarry,[6] and markets.[7]

Where there is no public purpose limitation, states and their political subdivisions with power under national and state law are seemingly freed from federal restraints upon the kind of proprietary activities they desire to undertake.

FOOTNOTES

§ 6.00

[1] E.g. Louisiana Constitution, Art. 14, § 18; Oklahoma Constitution, Art. 18, § 6.
[2] Arizona Constitution, Art. 2, § 34.

§ 6.01

[1] Citizens Savings and Loan Ass'n v. Topeka (1875) 87 US 655, 22 L Ed 455.
[2] Jones v. City of Portland (1917) 245 US 217, 221, 38 S Ct 112, 62 L Ed 252. "The authority of the State to tax does not include the right to impose taxes for merely private purposes." Green v. Frazier (1920) 253 US 233, 238, 40 S Ct 499, 64 L Ed 878.
[3] Jones v. City of Portland (1917) 245 US 217, 38 S Ct 112, 62 L Ed 252; Standard Oil v. City of Lincoln (1927) 275 US 504, 48 S Ct 155, 72 L Ed 395; Green v. Frazier (1920) 253 US 233, 40 S Ct 499, 64 L Ed 878.
[4] British North America Act, § 92(2).
[5] Unemployment Insurance Reference (1936) S.C.R. 427, 434 (dissenting).
[6] LaForest, *The Allocation of Taxing Power under the Canadian Constitution* (2d ed. 1981, Toronto) 75.

§ 6.02

[1] Bank of New South Wales v. Commonwealth (1948) 76 C.L.R. 1; Melbourne Corp. v. Commonwealth (1947) 74 C.L.R. 31.
[2] Green v. Frazier (1920) 253 US 233, 40 S Ct 499, 64 L Ed 878.

§ 6.03

[1] Cf. Brennan v. Victorian Railway Commissioner (1902) 27 Vic. L. Rep. 728; Commissioner of Railways (NSW) v. O'Donnell (1938) 60 C.L.R. 681.
[2] Dow v. Black (1874-5) 6 A.C. 272.
[3] The Queen v. Board of Transport Commissioners (1968) S.C.R. 118.
[4] Cincinnati v. Kentucky (1943) 292 Ky 597, 167 SW 2d 709; State v. LeBlond (1923) 108 Ohio St 41, 140 NE 491; Walker v. Cincinnati (1871) 21 Ohio St 14.
[5] Sun Printing & Publishing Co. v. Mayor of New York (1897) 152 NY 257, 46 NE 499.
[6] City of Mill Valley v. Saxton (1940) 41 Cal App 2d 290, 106 P 2d 455; Attorney-General v. Boston (1877) 123 Mass 565.
[7] Re Pacific Western Airlines (1977) 2 Alta L R (2d) 72.
[8] Cf. Australian National Airways Pty. v. Commonwealth (1945) 71 C.L.R. 29.

§ 6.04

[1] Albritton v. Winona (1938) 181 Miss 75, 178 So 799, 115 ALR 1436; Newberry v. Andalusia (1952) 257 Ala 49, 57 So 2d 629; City of Denton v. Denton Home Ice Co. (Tex Comm App 1930) 27 SW 2d 119, noted in 9 Tex L Rev 456 (1931).
[2] Green v. Frazier (1920) 253 US 233, 40 S Ct 499, 64 L Ed 828 (sustaining power of state to operate bank, warehouse, grain elevator, flour mill and home building project).

§ 6.05

[1] Green v. Frazier (1920) 253 US 233, 40 S Ct 499, 64 L Ed 878.
[2] Standard Oil v. Lincoln (1927) 275 US 504, 48 S Ct 155, 72 L Ed 395.
[3] Standard Oil v. Lincoln (1926) 114 Neb 243, 207 NW 172.
[4] Jones v. Portland (1917) 245 US 217, 38 S Ct 112, 62 L Ed 252.
[5] City of Denton v. Denton Home Ice Co. (Tex Comm App 1930) 27 SW 2d 119, noted in 9 Tex L Rev 456 (1931).

§ 6.06

[1] Green v. Frazier (1920) 253 US 233, 40 S Ct 499, 64 L Ed 828.
[2] State v. Smith (1935) 336 Mo 1104, 82 SW 2d 37.
[3] Bolster v. Lawrence (1917) 225 Mass 387, 114 NE 722.
[4] State ex rel. Lyon v. McCown (1912) 92 SC 81, 75 SE 392.
[5] Moore v. Greensboro (1926) 191 NC 592, 132 SE 565.
[6] Schneider v. Menasha (1903) 118 Wis 298, 95 NW 94.
[7] Bank v. Bell (1923) 62 Cal App 320, 217 Pac 538.

CHAPTER SEVEN

Chapter Seven

STATES' RIGHTS AGAINST THE FEDERATION

§ 7.00 States' rights to be free from federal taxation

In the United States, the states have a limited freedom from taxation by the federal government. States and their political subdivisions are subject to federal excise taxes when, in common with all other entrepreneurs, they operate recreational beaches[1] or stadia for athletic events,[2] or sell alcohol[3] or mineral waters.[4]

In 1869 the Supreme Court indicated by way of dictum that the federal government would not be constitutionally able to tax certain basic governmental powers of the states, such as the power to tax.[5] This broadly stated concept has been recognized in later dictum.[6] The most recent ruling in point is the 1978 case of *Massachusetts v. United States*[7] where the Court sustained a federal registration tax on aircraft, as applied to planes used exclusively for police work. Such a tax will be constitutional, said the Court, "where it is inconceivable that such a revenue measure could ever operate to preclude traditional state activities," and so long as there is "no substantial basis for a claim that the National Government will be using its taxing powers to control, unduly interfere with, or destroy a State's ability to perform essential services."

In Australia, generally the states are subject to Commonwealth taxes, if statutes so provide. In 1971 the High Court ruled that states had to pay the Commonwealth federal payroll tax, Chief Justice Barwick stating generally: "A valid law made by Parliament may bind the Crown in right of a State according to its terms." There is dictum that a tax law aimed at States would be invalid because not among the Commonwealth powers. In dissent, Justices Menzies, Windeyer, Walsh, and Gibbs indicated their belief that a Commonwealth tax law should be invalid if it interferes with the constitutional functions of the states.[8] In 1947 Chief Justice Dixon had said: "The Federal power of taxation will not support a law which places a special burden upon the States."[9]

In Canada, § 125 of the British North America Act provides that: "No lands or Property belonging to Canada or any Province shall be liable to Taxation." Beyond that it cannot be clearly stated at this writing what additional immunity the provinces have from Dominion taxation. The leading Canadian authority on tax powers writes of Dominion tax power under § 91(3) of the Act: "No limitations should be imposed on the power except such as are clearly spelled out or inhere in the federal structure of the Constitution."[10]

States are at times given further protection from federal taxation by constitutional clauses denying to the central government power to tax goods exported from the states.[11]

§ 7.01 States' rights to be free from federal regulation

In a poorly reasoned five-to-four decision in 1976, the United States Supreme Court ruled that the federal government could not impose wage and hour controls upon the states or their political subdivisions when engaged in "integral governmental functions."[1] Justice Blackmun, whose vote was necessary for the majority, made it clear that the Tenth Amendment would not invalidate all federal controls of the states and their political subdivisions, noting that environmental protective legislation would be constitutional in such application.

Two years later, the Supreme Court held federal anti-trust laws could be applied to cities, except in the situation where the state had clearly authorized a monopolistic policy as part of state law.[2] In 1982 the Court ruled operation of a railroad by a local government, under State authority, was subject to the National Railway Labor Act, reasoning that this was "not an integral part of traditional state activities."[3]

The Supreme Court holds that, whatever immunity is mandated by a theory of federalism or the Tenth Amendment, states and their political subdivisions can waive such immunity by conduct knowingly and voluntarily bringing themselves within the terms of valid federal regulations applicable to society generally.[4]

If the only basis for state immunity from federal regulation is the Tenth Amendment, orthodox constitutional reasoning makes subject to federal laws states and their political subdivisions, when the Act of Congress was validly enacted pursuant to authority conferred by constitutional amendments later in time than the Tenth.[5]

In Australia, the states are generally subject to Commonwealth regulatory laws, if the statutes clearly so provide. The disappearance of immunities dates to 1920 when Justice Isaacs of the High Court in the *Engineers* case said: "States, and persons natural or artificial representing States, when parties to industrial disputes in fact, are subject to Commonwealth legislation under placitum xxxv of § 51 of the Constitution, if such legislation on its true construction applies to them."[6] Ten years later the Court held that an award of the Commonwealth Arbitration Court could bind state railways, although there is language that there could be no execution on such an award against state treasuries.[7] In 1947 Chief Justice Dixon, speaking for the High Court in the State Banking Case, said that Commonwealth laws cannot discriminate against the states, or "place a special burden upon the States." The Commonwealth Act was bad since states could not use private banks unless the Commonwealth Treasurer consented, the High Court stating that the Commonwealth cannot "deny to the States banking facilities open to others." There is a constitutional objection to the exercise of all Commonwealth powers, said Dixon, "if under them the States are made the objects of special burdens or disabilities." He added: "The Federal system itself is the foundation of the restraint upon the use of the power to control the States."[8]

In 1971, while suggesting that Commonwealth legislation aimed at or discriminating against states should be invalid because not among Commonwealth powers, Chief Justice Barwick stated: "A valid law made by Parliament may bind the Crown in right of a State according to its terms." The dissent of four justices leaves it still possible that Commonwealth regulation affecting states may be unconstitutional if it unduly prevents them from discharging essential governmental functions.[9]

In Canada, the extent to which the Dominion Parliament can impose its regulatory laws upon the provinces is not yet clear.[10] In 1977 by way of dictum, the Supreme Court of Canada indicated that the Dominion Parliament could if it chose to, but went on to hold as a matter of statutory construction that Alberta, in taking over Pacific Western Airlines, was not subject to controls claimed by the federal transport commission.[11] Professor Katherine Swinton of Osgoode Hall has recently written that "one needs to balance federal and provincial interests in each situation that arises."[12] Probably the provinces will be subject to Dominion regulation when the legislation is very clear, except in that most unusual instance when the Supreme Court concludes that the very essence of provincial governing would be impossible under the statute.

§ 7.02 States' rights to sue the federal government

The United States Supreme Court has refused to recognize a general power of the states to sue the federal government or its officials in attacking the constitutionality or legality of federal actions.[1] The Court does not acknowledge that the states are *parens patriae* to speak for their citizens in opposition to federal legislation. In denying Florida standing to sue the Treasury Secretary in an attack upon the federal inheritance tax law, the Court said:

> Nor can the suit be maintained by the State because of any injury to its citizens. They are also citizens of the United States and subject to its laws. In respect of their relations with the federal government, it is the United States, and not the State, which represents them as parens patriae, when such representation becomes appropriate; and to the former, and not the latter, they must look for such protective measures as flow from that status.[2]

States, like individuals, have standing to sue the federal government when their property or other legal rights are directly and prejudicially affected by federal legislation or other action.[3]

In Australia, an Attorney General for a state can bring suit against the Commonwealth whenever the public in his state is affected by *ultra vires* activity of the Commonwealth,[4] whenever, in the language of the High Court, a federal statute "extends to, and operates within, the State whose interests he represents."[5]

In Italy, the Constitutional Court has accorded a broad power to the regional governments to protect before the Court actions of the national government.[6]

In Canada, the Supreme Court readily accepts references initiated by the Attorneys-General of the provinces when they believe action of the Dominion government is *ultra vires* and affects the public in their provinces.[7] However, Strayer, writing in 1968, said it had not yet been decided whether the Attorney-General of a province could challenge a Dominion statute.[8]

In the German Federal Government, any land or state has standing before the Constitutional Court to question the constitutionality of an act of the federal parliament.[9] In Austria, too, the Laender have standing to attack legislation of the federal government.[10] Likewise in the Federation of Malaysia, the component states have standing to attack the legislation of the Federation as unconstitutional.[11]

In 1964, under a previous constitution, it had been held in Nigeria that attorneys-general of the former Regions had no general standing to contest the constitutionality of actions of the federal government.[12] It is likely that under the present Constitution attorneys-general of the states will be accorded standing on terms roughly comparable to those prevailing in Australia and Canada.

In India, the Constitution gives the Supreme Court original jurisdiction in suits between the states and the Government of India,[13] and the leading authority on the Constitution indicates that the states can sue the central government on "legal rights."[14]

§ 7.03 State immunity from suit in federal courts

In the United States, which has a dual system of state and federal courts throughout the nation, the states were originally subject to suit in the federal courts;[1] but in 1798 the Eleventh Amendment to the Constitution was adopted, providing that "the Judicial power of the United States shall not be construed to extend to any suit in law or in equity, commenced or prosecuted against one of the United States by Citizens of another State, or by Citizens or Subjects of any Foreign State." Although the Amendment is silent on point, the Supreme Court has held that it bars suits in federal courts against a state by a citizen of that state.[2]

The Eleventh Amendment does not immunize a state when sued in federal courts either by the United States or by another state.[3]

§ 7.04 States' freedom from discrimination by the federal government

Constitutions in federal societies are replete with a variety of provisions that guarantee equality of the states or prohibit discrimination against the member states.

For instance, the United States Constitution provides that "no State without its consent shall be deprived of its equal suffrage in the Senate."[1]

Frequently there are provisions barring the central government from giving preferences to one state over another or others in matters of trade and commerce.[2] Federal actions "which incidentally result to the disadvantage" of ports in other states is not forbidden by the clauses, according to the United States Supreme Court.[3]

Only "uniform duties of customs" can be imposed by the Australian Commonwealth Parliament,[4] and the United States Constitution comparably provides: "All duties, imports and excises shall be uniform throughout the United States."[5] This, says the Supreme Court, requires "that what Congress has properly selected for taxation must be identically taxed in every State where it is found."[6]

It is commonly understood that federal governments in exercising their powers over interstate trade and commerce cannot discriminate between the states,[7] and at times the federal tax power is expressed "so as not to discriminate between States or parts of States."[8]

In the United States, the power of the federal Congress to establish bankruptcy laws is limited to "uniform laws on the subject of bankruptcies throughout the United States."[9] The uniformity requirement is a geographical one. The Supreme Court has held that the uniformity requirement is not violated by federal legislation empowering bankruptcy courts to apply varying state laws.[10]

§ 7.05 States' rights to fixed boundaries

— In federal societies the states customarily have some explicit constitutional guaranty that their boundaries will not be changed without their consent. To illustrate, the Australian Constitution allows the Commonwealth Parliament of that state, and the majority of the electors of the state to vote thereon.[1] Another provision allows the Commonwealth Parliament to form new states from the territory of old states "but only with the Consent of the Parliament thereof," adding that a new state may be formed by union of two or more states or parts of states, "but only with the consent of the Parliaments of the States affected."[2] The United States Constitution is quite comparable.[3]

The Constitutions of Argentina, Malaysia, Switzerland, and the U.S.S.R. also give the component province, cantons, and republics assurance that their boundaries will not be changed without their consent.[4]

Under the Mexican Constitution, the Federal Congress can create new states out of existing states if approved by a two-thirds majority of each house of Congress, with ratification by a majority of the state legislatures.[5]

The least protection to the states is found in the constitution of India which allows the Union Parliament to establish new states "on such terms and conditions as it thinks fit."[6]

In federal societies boundary disputes between states can customarily be resolved by the high court of the federation[7] and/or by the legislature of the federation.[8]

§ 7.06 States' rights to protection by the federal government

In a number of federal societies, the government of the federation by the constitution guarantees to every state in the federation a republican form of government.[1] The United States Supreme Court refuses to adjudicate issues arising under the clause on the ground they are "political questions."[2] It has provided dictum, however, that "a republican form of government" is one which acknowledges it exists to safeguard fundamental rights of the citizens.[3]

In even more of the federal societies, the government of the federation is under a constitutional obligation to protect the constituent states from external aggression and internal violence.[4] The Constitution of Australia is representative. It provides: "The Commonwealth shall protect every State against invasion and, on the application of the Executive Government of the State, against domestic violence."[5] As a source of obligation, these clauses have become sources of power to federal governments interfering in state affairs.[6]

§ 7.07 States' immunity from federal creation of new states with greater powers

At federation, the formative states often desire constitutional protection against action of the central government in admitting into the federation new states with greater powers. Article IV, Section Three of the United States Constitution, which provides that: "New States may be admitted by the Congress into this Union," gives power to the Congress "to admit new States . . . only . . . as are equal to each other in power, dignity and authority. . . ."[1] The United States Supreme Court honors "the constitutional principle of the equality of States,"[2] and on a number of occasions has held that any enabling act of Congress must respect the equality doctrine.[3]

While the Australian Constitution authorizes the Commonwealth Parliament to admit new states on "such terms and conditions . . . as it thinks fit,"[4] the orthodox view of constitutional scholars is that upon admission, new states are entitled to complete equality with the earlier states.[5]

At federation, the Imperial Parliament possessed plenary power to admit new provinces to the Dominion of Canada, and it should be recognized that the Dominion Parliament today has like power.[6]

In India, the power of the Union Parliament to establish new states is given in the Constitution "on such terms and conditions as it seems fit,"[7] and the power of a state to prevent a new state from being created in its territory is limited to its participation in the political process.[8]

§ 7.08 States' rights to participate in amending the constitution

In federal societies the states customarily have a significant role in determining whether the constitution is to be amended. In Australia, for example, and amendment to the constitution must be approved by a majority of the voters in a majority of the states, as well as by a majority of all those voting in the Commonwealth.[1] In the United States, constitutional amendment requires ratification by the legislatures of three-fourths of the several states, or by convention in three-fourths of the states, whichever method of ratification is provided for by Congress for the specific amendment.[2] It should be deemed undecided as yet whether a state can reject an amendment and later ratify it,[3] as well as whether a state, after ratifying, can rescind its ratification.[4]

The British North America Act—the original constitutional document for Canada—made no provision for its amendment, apparently assuming the Imperial Parliament could and would amend it when necessary.

In India, the constitution can generally be amended by vote of both Houses of the Union Parliament, without state participation; only in limited instances must an amendment be ratified by the legislatures of one-half of the states.[5]

The High Court of the Federation of Malaysia held in 1963 that the name of the Federation could be changed (from Malaya) and new states admitted without the consent of a plaintiff state.[6]

§ 7.09 States' guaranties of representation in national legislature

States in federal societies are protected at times by constitutional clauses denying the power of the national legislature to reduce their representation in one or both houses of that legislature.

The United States Constitution provides that "no State without its consent shall be deprived of its equal suffrage in the Senate."[1]

The Australian Constitution provides that no amendment to that constitution diminishing the proportional representation of any state in either House or the minimum number of representatives of a state in the House of Representatives, or altering state limits, or in any manner affecting the provisions of the constitution in relation thereto shall become law without the approval of the majority of electors voting in that State.[2] There has been the suggestion that this provision of the Constitution can itself be amended, so as to provide other bases for state political representation.[3]

§ 7.10 States' rights to secede from the federation

Singapore left the Federation of Malaysia on August 9, 1965 and it will likely be possible for other states in the Federation lawfully to secede.[1]

An outstanding Australian scholar has written that a state could in effect secede by authorization of the Imperial Parliament,[2] and wherever the constitution of a member of British Commonwealth is an Act of the Imperial Parliament in theory secession could be effectuated in that way, although the likelihood of such action by the United Kingdom Parliament is very meager.

In Canada, the legality of secession by Quebec or any other province is still an unsettled issue.

In the United States it has been settled both by Civil War and decision of the Supreme Court that a state has no constitutional authority to secede from the Union.[3] The same position can be expected to prevail in Nigeria.

FOOTNOTES

§ 7.00

1 Wilmette Park District v. Campbell (1949) 338 US 411, 70 S Ct 195, 94 L Ed 205.
2 Allen v. Regents of University System of Georgia (1938) 304 US 439, 58 S Ct 980, 82 L Ed 1448.
3 South Carolina v. United States.
4 New York v. United States (1946) 326 US 572, 66 S Ct 310, 90 L Ed 326.
5 Veazie Bank v. Fenno (1869) 8 Wall. 533, 19 L Ed 482.
6 New York v. United States (1946) 326 US 572, 66 S Ct 310, 90 L Ed 326.
7 Massachusetts v. United States (1978) 435 US 444, 98 S Ct 1153, 55 L Ed 2d 403.
8 Victoria v. Commonwealth (1971) 45 A.L.J.R. 251.
9 Melbourne Corp. v. Commonwealth (1947) 74 C.L.R. 31 (the State Banking Case).
10 Strayer, *The Allocation of Tax Power under the Canadian Constitution* (Toronto 1967) 32.
11 Constitution of the United States, Art. I, § 9.

§ 7.01

1 National League of Cities v. Usery (1976) 426 US 833, 96 S Ct 2465, 49 L Ed 2d 245.
2 Lafayette v. Louisiana Power & Light Co. (1978) 435 US 389, 98 S Ct 1123, 55 L Ed 2d 364.
3 Underwriters National Assurance Co. v. North Carolina Life & Accident & Health Insurance Guaranty Ass'n (1982) 455 US 691, 102 S Ct 1357, 71 L Ed 2d 558.
4 United States v. California (1936) 297 US 175, 56 S Ct 421, 80 L Ed 567; Parden v. Terminal Railroad of Alabama State Docks Dept. (1964) 377 184, 84 S Ct 1207, 12 L Ed 2d 233.
5 Cf. Fitzpatrick v. Bitzer (1976) 427 US 445, 96 S Ct 2666, 49 L Ed 2d 614; Christensen v. Iowa (ND Iowa 1976) 417 F Supp 423, affirmed (8th Cir. 1977) 563 F 2d 353; Woods v. Homes & Structures Inc. (D Kan 1980) 489 F Supp 1270.
6 Amalgamated Society of Engineers v. Adelaide Steamship Co. Ltd. (1920) 28 C.L.R. 129 (The Engineers Case).
7 Australian Railways Union v. Victoria Railways Commissioners (1930) 44 C.L.R. 319.
8 Melbourne Corp. v. Commonwealth (1947) 74 C.L.R. 31 (State Banking Case).
9 Victoria v. Commonwealth (1971) 45 A.L.J.R. 251.
10 McNairn, *Governmental and Intergovernmental Immunities in Australia and Canada* (Toronto 1977).
11 Queen in Right of Alberta v. Canadian Transport Commissioners (1977) 75 D.L.R. (3d) 257.
12 Swinton, "Federalism and Provincial Government Immunity," 29 *U Tor L J* 1, 50 (1979).

§ 7.02

1 Massachusetts v. Mellon (1923) 262 US 447, 48 S Ct 597; 67 L Ed 1078; Massachusetts v. Laird (1970) 400 US 886, 91 S Ct 138, 27 L Ed 2d 130.
2 Florida v. Mellon (1927) 273 US 12, 18, 47 S Ct 265, 71 L Ed 511.
3 New York v. United States (1946) 326 US 572, 66 S Ct 310, 90 L Ed 326.
4 Attorney-General for Victoria v. Commonwealth (1945) 71 C.L.R. 237; Western Australia v. Commonwealth; Queensland v. Commonwealth (1975) 134 C.L.R. 201. Lane, *The Australian Federal System* (2d ed. 1979 Sydney) 1155.
5 Attorney-General for Victoria v. Commonwealth (1935) 52 C.L.R. 533, 556.
6 Adams and Barile "The Italian Constitutional Court in its First Two Years of Activity," 7 *Buffalo L. Rev.* 250, 253 (1958).

[7] Rubin, "The Nature, Use and Effect of Reference Cases in Canadian Constitutional Law," 6 *McGill L. Rev.* 168 (1960).

[8] Strayer, *Judicial Review of Legislation in Canada* (Toronto 1968) 104.

[9] Rupp, "Judicial Review in the Federal Republic of Germany," 9 *Am. J. Comp. L.* 29, 36 (1960); Geck, "Judicial Review of Statutes: A Comparative Survey of Present Institutions and Practices," 51 *Cornell L.Q.* 250, 288.

[10] Constitution of Austria 1929, as amended, Art. 140.

[11] Constitution of Malaysia, Art. 4(3); Sheridan and Groves, *The Constitution of Malaysia* (Dobbs Ferry 1967) 30; State of Kelantan v. Federation of Malaya (H Ct 1963) M.L.J. 355.

[12] Attorney-General of Eastern Nigeria v. Attorney-General of the Federation (1964) 1 All N.L.R. 224. But cf. Nwabueze, *Constitutional Law of the Nigerian Republic* (London 1964) 310.

[13] Constitution of India, Art. 131.

[14] Basu, *Commentaries on the Constitution of India* (5th ed. 1967 Calcutta) Vol. III, pp. 99-100.

§ 7.03

[1] Chisholm v. Georgia (1793) 2 Dall. 419, 1 L Ed 440.

[2] Hans v. Louisiana (1890) 134 US 1, 10 S Ct 504, 33 L Ed 842.

[3] United States v. Texas (1892) 143 US 621, 12 S Ct 488, 36 L Ed 285; Wyoming v. Colorado (1922) 259 US 419, 42 S Ct 552, 66 L Ed 999; Arkansas v. Mississippi (1919) 250 US 39, 39 S Ct 422, 63 L Ed 832.

§ 7.04

[1] Constitution of the United States, Art. V.

[2] Constitution of Australia § 99: "The Commonwealth shall not, by any law or regulation of trade, commerce, or revenue, give preference to one State or any part thereof over another State, or any part thereof." Constitution of the United States, Art. I, § 9, clause 6: "No preference shall be given by any regulation of commerce or revenue to the ports of one State over those of another."

[3] Louisiana Public Service Comn. v. Texas & New Orleans Rr. (1931) 284 US 125, 52 S Ct 74, 76 L Ed 201, 205.

[4] Constitution of Australia § 88.

[5] Constitution of the United States, Art. I, § 8.

[6] Fernandez v. Wiener (1945) 326 US 340, 66 S Ct 178, 90 L Ed 116, 134.

[7] Charles Steward Machine Co. v. Davis (1937) 301 US 548, 57 S Ct 883, 81 L Ed 1279, 1290.

[8] Constitution of Australia § 51(ii).

[9] Constitution of the United States, Art. I, § 8, clause 4.

[10] Stellwagen v. Clum (1918) 245 US 605, 38 S Ct 215, 62 L Ed 507.

§ 7.05

[1] Constitution of Australia § 123; 128.

[2] Constitution of Australia § 124.

[3] Constitution of the United States, Art. IV, § 3: "No new State shall be formed or erected within the jurisdiction of any other State; nor any State be formed by the junction of two or more States, or parts of States, without the consent of the Legislatures of the States concerned as well as of the Congress."

[4] Constitution of Malaysia, Article 2; Sen, *Indian Constitutional Law* (New Delhi 1967) Vol. I, p. 111.

[5] Constitution of Mexico, Articles 45 & 73.

[6] Constitution of India, Art. 2. The language in the Australian Constitution (§ 121) authorizing the Commonwealth Parliament to admit new states "on such terms and

conditions . . . as it thinks fit" must be read together with the earlier noted §§ 123 & 124.

7 Arkansas v. Mississippi (1919) 250 US 39, 39 S Ct 422, 63 L Ed 832.

8 "There is no question of Congress' power to fix state land and water boundaries as a domestic matter." United States v. Louisiana (1960) 363 US 1, 80 S Ct 961, 4 L Ed 2d 1025, 1048-9.

§ 7.06

1 Constitution of the United States, Art. IV, § 4; Constitution of Argentina, Art. 6.

2 Pacific States Telephone & Telegraph Co. v. Oregon (1912) 233 US 118, 32 S Ct 224, 56 L Ed 377.

3 Calder v. Bull (1798) 3 Dall. 386, 387-8, 1 L Ed 648; United States v. Cruikshank (1876) 92 US 542, 552, 23 L Ed 588.

4 Constitution of the United States, Art. IV, § 4: "The United States . . . . shall protect each of them against invasion; and on application of the Legislature, or of the Executive (when the Legislature cannot be convened) against domestic violence"; Constitution of Argentina, Art. 6; Constitution of Switzerland, Art. 16; Constitution of India, Art. 355. Mexico Constitution, Art. 122: "The authorities of the Union have the obligation to protect the States against every invasion or external violence."

5 Constitution of Australia § 119.

6 Texas v. White (1869) 7 Wall. 700, 729, 19 L Ed 227, over-ruled on other grounds, Morgan v. United States 113 US 476, 5 S Ct 588, 28 L Ed 1044. Bronfield, "The Guaranty Clause of Article IV," Section 4, 46 *Minn L Rev* 513, 557 (1962).

§ 7.07

1 Skiriotes v. Florida (1941) 313 US 69, 61 S Ct 924, 85 L Ed 1193, 1200.

2 United States v. Oregon (1935) 295 US 1, 14, 55 S Ct 610, 79 L Ed 1267.

3 Ward v. Race Horse (1896) 163 US 504, 507, 16 S Ct 1076, 41 L Ed 244.

4 Constitution of Australia § 121.

5 Wynes, *Legislative, Executive and Judicial Powers in Australia* (5th ed. 1976 Sydney) 111.

6 Attorney-General for Saskatchewan v. Canadian Pacific Rt. (1953) A.C. 594.

7 Constitution of India, Art. 2.

8 Sen, *Indian Constitutional Law* (New Delhi 1967) Vol. I, p. 112.

§ 7.08

1 Constitution of Australia § 128.

2 Constitution of the United States, Art. V.

3 Compare Wise v. Chandler (1937) 270 Ky 1, 108 SW 2d 1024 certiorari dismissed 307 US 474, 59 S Ct 992, 83 L Ed 1407, with Coleman v. Miller (1939) 307 US 433, 59 S Ct 972, 83 L Ed 1385.

4 When Ohio and New Jersey endeavored to rescind their ratification of the Fourteenth Amendment, United States Secretary of State Seward said such action was probably "irregular, invalid and therefore ineffectual."

5 Constitution of India, Art. 368.

6 State of Kelantan v. Federation of Malaya (1963) M.L.J. 355 (H Ct Malaysia) reported in Jayakumar, Constitutional Law Cases from Malaysia and Singapore (Singapore 1971) 195.

§ 7.09

1 Constitution of the United States, Art. V.

2 Constitution of Australia § 128.

3 Wynes, *Legislative, Executive and Judicial Powers in Australia* (5th ed. 1976 Sydney) 540-1.

§ 7.10

[1] Lee, "Constitutional Amendments in Malaysia," 18 *Mal. L. R.* 59 (1976).

[2] Wynes, *Legislative, Executive and Judicial Powers in Australia* (5th ed. 1976 Sydney) 123.

[3] Texas v. White (1869) 7 Wall. 729, 19 L Ed 227.

BIBLIOGRAPHY

BIBLIOGRAPHY

General Works

Friedrich, Carl J. *Trends of Federalism in Theory & Practice.* New York 1968.
Nwabueze, B.O. *Judicialism in Commonwealth Africa.* New York 1971.
McWhinney, Edward. *Comparative Federalism.* 2d ed. Toronto 1962.
Sawer, Geoffrey. *Modern Federalism.* London 1969.
Bowie, Robert, and Friedrich, Carl J., Eds. *Studies in Federalism.* Boston 1954.

Argentina

Lewis, Paul. *The Governments of Argentina, Brazil & Mexico.* New York 1975.
Rosenn, Keith. "Expropriation in Argentina & Brazil." 15 *Va. J. Intl. L.* 277 (1974).

Australia

Fajgenbaum, Jacob, and Hanks, Peter. *Australian Constitutional Law.* Melbourne 1972.
Howard, Colin. *Australian Federal Constitutional Law.* 2d ed. Sydney 1972.
Lane, P. H. *The Australian Federal System.* 2d ed. Sydney 1979.
Sawer, Geoffrey. *Australian Federalism in the Courts.* Melbourne 1967.
Sawer, Geoffrey. *Cases on the Constitution of the Commonwealth of Australia.* 3d ed. Sydney 1964.
Wynes, W. A. *Legislative, Executive and Judicial Power in the Commonwealth.* 4th ed. Sydney 1970.
Zines, Leslie. *The High Court and the Constitution.* Sydney 1981.

Austria

Marcic, Rene. *Verfassung und Verfassungsgericht.* Vienna 1963.

Brazil

James, Herman. *The Constitutional System of Brazil.* Washington 1925.
Lewis, Paul. *The Governments of Argentina, Brazil and Mexico.* New York 1975.
Pedrosa, Bernadette. "Perspectivas do Federalism brasileiro." *Revista brasileira do Estudos politics* 52 (1981): 105-128.

Cameroon Republic

Enonchong, Henry. *Cameroon Constitutional Law.* Yaounde 1967.

Canada

Hogg, Peter. *Constitutional Law of Canada*. Toronto 1977.
La Forest, G. V. *Allocation of Taxing Power under the Canadian Constitution*. Toronto 1981.
Laskin, Bora. *Canadian Constitutional Law*. 4th ed. Abel. Toronto 1975.
Smith, A. *The Commerce Power in Canada & the United States*. Toronto 1963.

German Federal Republic

Blair, Philip. *Federalism and Judicial Review in the Federal Republic of Germany*. Oxford 1981.
Braunthal, Gerard. "Federalism in Germany: The Broadcasting Controversy." 24 *J. of Politics* 545 (1972).
Cole, R. Taylor. "West German Federalism Revisited." 23 *Am. J. Comp. L.* 325 (1975).
Johnson, Neville. *Federalism and Decentralisation in the Federal Republic of Germany*. London: H.M.S.O. 1973.
McWhinney, Edward. *Constitutionalism in Germany and the Federal Constitutional Court*. Leyden 1962.
Sawer, Geoffrey. "Federalism in West Germany." *Public Law* (1961): 126-44.
Wells, Roger. *The States in West German Federalism*. New York 1961.

India

Basu, Durga Das. *Commentary on the Constitution of India*. 6th ed. Calcutta 1973.
Gupta, Bharatbhusan. *Comparative Study of Six Living Constitutions*. New Delhi 1974.
Jain, M. P. *Indian Constitutional Law*. Bombay 1962.
Seervai, H. M. *Constitutional Law of India: A Critical Commentary*. Bombay 1967.
Sen, S.D.K. *A Comparative Study of the Indian Constitution*. Bombay 1960-1966.

Malaysia

Sheridan, L.A. and Groves, Harry. *The Constitution of Malaysia*. Dobbs Ferry 1967.

Mexico

Lewis, Paul. *The Governments of Argentina, Brazil and Mexico*. New York 1975.

Nigeria

Aihe, D.O., and Aloyede, P.A. *Cases and Materials on Constitutiona Law in Nigeria*. Oxford 1979.

Elias, T.O. *Nigeria: The Development of its Law and Constitution.* London 1967.
Kasunmu, A.B. *The Supreme Court of Nigeria 1956-1970.* Ibadan 1977.
Nwabueze, B.O. *Constitutional Law of the Nigerian Republic.* London 1964.
Nwabueze, B.O. *Federalism in Nigeria under the Presidential Constitution.* London 1983.

Pakistan

Jennings, Sir Ivor. *Constitutional Problems in Pakistan.* Cambridge 1957.

Switzerland

Gupta, Bharatbhusan. *Comparative Study of Six Living Constitutions.* New Delhi 1974.
Hughes, M. Christopher. *The Federal Constitution of Switzerland.* Oxford 1954.

United States of America

Antieau, C.J. *Modern Constitutional Law.* 2 vols. Rochester 1969.

U.S.S.R.

Hazard, John. *The Soviet Legal System.* 3d ed. New York 1977.
Hodge, William. "Federalism and the Soviet Constitution of 1977, Commonwealth Perspectives." 55 *Wash. U. L. Rev.* 505 (1980).
Ozakwe, Chris. "The Theories and Realities of Modern Soviet Constitutional Law: An Analysis of the 1977 Soviet Constitution." 127 *U. Pa. L. Rev.* 1350 (1979).

Venezuela

Butte, Woodfin. "Development of Laws and Jurisprudence in Venezuela in 1940." *A.B.A. Section on Intl. & Comp. L.* 86 (1940-1941).

Yugoslavia

Peselj, Bronko. "Socialist Law and the New Yugoslav Constitution." 51 *Geo. L.J.* 651 (1963).

INDEX

INDEX